MW00713077

By the
Grace
of God

Dear Ruby, Faye and James
with appreciation for your
friendship and shared
Ministries and experiences in
our Pelgrimage in life — I
share your gratitude to the
Lord Jesus who sustains us
through the Year — The two
of you were to precious to Same
we miss her — I hope you
enjoy the reading — Remember you are
special to my family —

Grace & Peace
2 Corinthians 13:9
Earl Potter

Christmas 1997

By the Grace of God

Memoirs and Recollections of an Alabama Baptist

A. EARL POTTS

PROVIDENCE HOUSE PUBLISHERS
Franklin, Tennessee

Printed in the United States of America

01   00   99   98   97   5   4   3   2   1

Library of Congress Catalog Card Number: 97–69180

ISBN: 1–57736–059–1

Photographs provided courtesy of Alabama Baptist Historical Commission and A. Earl Potts; illustrations by Marilyn Friedlander.

Cover by Bozeman Design

Scripture is based on: (1) Holy Bible, New International Version. Copyright © 1973, 1978, 1984 International Bible Society. Used by permission of Zondervan Bible Publishers; (2) King James Version. Copyright © 1976 by Thomas Nelson, Inc., Nashville, Tennessee; and (3) New American Standard Bible. © The Lockman Foundation 1960, 1962, 1963, 1968, 1971, 1972, 1973, 1975, 1977 La Habra, California. Used by permission.

PROVIDENCE HOUSE PUBLISHERS
238 Seaboard Lane • Franklin, Tennessee 37067
800-321-5692

To that multitude of Baptists who have gone before us and are gathered about us as "a great cloud of witnesses" (Heb. 12:1),

To those of us whose sacrifices and labors of love fill our churches and communities with life, and

To those of us who continue in the journey until the time we join that great heavenly host.

Contents

Forewords

THE VIEW FROM THE OFFICE OF EXECUTIVE SECRETARY-treasurer of the Alabama Baptist State Convention is indeed a singular one. Imagine a panorama that encompasses more than three thousand Alabama Baptist congregations. Try to envisage all of the convention ministries dedicated to fulfilling spiritual, emotional, physical, and intellectual needs of tens of thousands of Alabama Baptists and others. This is the prospect facing the convention's chief executive.

In order to preserve this special perspective on our denominational history, the Alabama Baptist Historical Commission began, in 1990, to publish memoirs of the convention's executive secretary-treasurers. The inaugural edition was Dr. George Bagley's *My Four Decades with Alabama Baptists: An Oral History Memoir.* The Commission is pleased to continue this series with Dr. A. Earl Potts's work.

The Historical Commission asked Dr. Potts to write a memoir, not an institutional history, but the story of his life among Alabama Baptists as pastor and administrator.

In reading Dr. Potts's manuscript, three things especially impressed me: the love of family that shines through his memoirs, gratitude for his call to the ministry, and devotion to the people in the pews. The Historical Commission is grateful to Dr. Potts for sharing with us his progress from the pew to the pulpit to the executive office, from boyhood to retirement and beyond, always faithful to his call to reach people for Christ.

Frances D. Hamilton
Executive Director
Alabama Baptist Historical Commission

9

EVERY PERSON IS A COMPOSITE OF HIS HERITAGE, INDIVIDUAL life experiences, personal relationships, and the grace of God. In this volume Earl Potts expresses all of these dimensions of his life in absorbing narratives. God's constant guidance can often be seen most clearly in a retrospective of life. His hand and his claim upon the life of Alton Earl Potts are evidenced in the mosaic presented here for the reader's enjoyment and enrichment.

Someone has said, "The future is safe only in the hands of those to whom the past is sacred." The past is held sacred as this Baptist statesman recalls events from Convention history. His unique perspective strengthens our Alabama Baptist heritage.

It is noteworthy that Earl Potts gives gratitude and credit to those who encouraged and mentored him. Countless pastors and staff members as well as church and denominational leaders can join me in saying that the encouragement Earl Potts received was simply mirrored from his life and reinvested in our lives. His genteel nature, his sound judgment, his perceptive wisdom, his unswerving dedication to the task, and his exceptional abilities have served well the churches he pastored and our Alabama Baptist family.

Personally, I am grateful that our life paths intersected. Thirty-five-plus years ago, I met Earl Potts when he was pastor of McElwain Baptist Church and I was pastor of Hillview Baptist Church, both in Birmingham. Years later (in 1988–1990), I would have the distinct opportunity to serve alongside him while he was executive secretary-treasurer and I was president of the Alabama Baptist State Convention. It was during my tenure that we marked the redirection of his ministry with a fitting tribute to a choice servant of God.

To know Earl Potts is to love him. So many in his family, in his churches, and in his beloved denomination were influenced for good and for God by his noble spirit. Providentially and thankfully, I was one of those.

Charles T. Carter
Senior Pastor
Shades Mountain Baptist Church
Birmingham, Alabama

Preface

THE FOLLOWING STORY IS IN PART THE STORY OF A SPECIAL people, the people of God called Alabama Baptists. It is not my story! My life has been shaped by God and his people. The biblical account of the prophet Jeremiah at the potter's house has been a favorite of mine from boyhood. I discovered it during a Sunday morning worship service at Shawmut Baptist Church when I was twelve years old. As my pastor, Earle Trent, read the story, lights came on in my mind and I was fascinated. Later, I was consumed by this story from the Holy Scriptures. Over my lifetime, I have come to realize that the experience of the prophet Jeremiah at the potter's house is a telling story of my life and ministry.

My story is the story of clay molded in the hands of the potter. The potter was reshaping the marred clay: "So the Potter formed it into another pot, shaping it as seemed best to him" (Jer. 18:4). My life has required a lot of reshaping and remaking by the Master Potter, Jesus.

The formation of my faith and practices began with my family. Although we were not wealthy, our house and furnishings satisfied our basic needs with an occasional bit of extravagance, but only a bit.

I often reflect on the disposition of my mother and dad. They were survivors. Mother was more extroverted than Dad, but never ostentatious. She was not a gossiper, but was very good at sharing her inner thoughts and feelings. Her openness aided me in being able to reveal my feelings. Dad was more introverted. He was also strong-willed. In fact, both of my parents possessed strong wills; this helped me learn to stand up for what I believe.

I grew to manhood with a family and challenging responsibilities before I realized how blessed I was to have a beautiful mother and a strong, gentle father, though Dad was not a devout Christian man. However, he never met a stranger, and I never knew him to say no to a person in need. He demonstrated his love in his kindness and actions to others. Mother was a practicing Christian. Her faith was tested in her later years by poor health.

Now, at age seventy-six, I realize my parental blessings as never before in life. I wish my parents were living so I could tell them what remarkable human beings they were. Do you sense some nostalgia in my reflections? If you do, you are right. If your parents are living, don't delay to express your appreciation and love.

I am indebted to both my biological family and my extended families, especially the parents of my late wife, Louise. And I cannot say enough for my faith families—they are as the sand by the sea! All have been so nurturing, encouraging, and supportive.

As I look back over my life, I see the hand of the Master Potter shaping me through the love and care of my parents, Louise's parents, and also my Christian family called Alabama Baptists. Thank you, Lord, for using these special people to mold me according to your will. To you be all the glory!

Acknowledgments

FAR FROM A SOLITARY ENDEAVOR, THE PUBLICATION OF
BY THE GRACE OF GOD was made possible by the ingenuity and creativity
of countless friends and family. The task would be too great to recognize
each person for his or her contribution to this work; however, certain
individuals cannot remain nameless.

I would like to thank my children, David and Libby, for their constant
love and faithful support that continues beyond the bounds of this text.

I owe a special debt of gratitude to the following people for making
contributions to this book: Dr. Troy Morrison, Dr. Thomas E. Corts,
Dr. Timothy George, Dr. Wayne Flynt, Dr. Charles Carter, Walter Belt
White, Dr. Harriet E. Amos Doss, Elizabeth Wells, Shirley Hutchens,
Hortense Barnes, Mary Speed, and Bill Nunnelley.

I would also like to recognize Charles Deweese and Providence
House Publishers for their tireless dedication to the success of my manuscript.

I am particularly indebted to the Alabama Baptist Historical
Commission for offering me the opportunity to express my deep love for
Alabama Baptists. I greatly appreciate the assistance of Dr. Frances D.
Hamilton, executive director of the ABHC, whose encouragements and
suggestions sustained my enthusiasm for completing my memoirs. I wish
to commend Lynn Sillavan, administrative assistant, for her indefatigable efforts in reading and typing my written manuscript. I also want to
thank Jennifer Blair and Jeffrey Anderson for technical assistance in
concluding this work.

CHAPTER 1

Small-Town Alabama Roots

THE THOUGHT OF THIS DAY DURING THE WEEK OF Christmas 1969 being my last day of quality time with Dad never entered my mind. I was enraptured just thinking about a day with him, for such a day was rare. We needed to live it to the fullest.

On this particular day in 1969, Dad and I drove from Roanoke to Dickert, Alabama, crossing High Pine Creek. Our destination was our old homesite, located one mile from Dickert, the hometown of the Potts clan.

To my family, Dickert symbolizes the best of times and the worst of times. One of the lesser-known communities in Randolph County, it was so small you could stand on the front steps of my grandparents' house and see everything that was happening. A railroad ran through the town, but the sparsity of incoming and outgoing mail did not justify a train stop. Our postmaster, Mr. Gray, would put outgoing mail in a mailbag. Adequately secured, the postmaster would hang the mailbags on a "mail pole" of special design to be taken by the attendant in the mail car. The mail attendant would toss the mailbag containing incoming mail to be picked up by Mr. Gray.

Dickert had a sawmill and a brick kiln owned and operated by my grandfather and his five sons. My dad, as I remember, was the chief operator of the sawmill. In fact, he sawed the timbers for the house in which I was born, timbers so solid that the house still stands today. Having

never been painted, the house shows its age, but it stands secure on its foundation after seventy-six years of use in my lifetime. It had four rooms and a breezeway (or dogtrot) separating the main living quarters from the guest room. There was a large front porch and a back porch which sheltered a never-run-dry well and a wash area with a pan, soap, towel, and a bucket of water.

Here on this day in 1969, Dad and I reminisced and looked around for a couple of hours, realizing there could be no turning back to the good times or bad times of this old home place. Dad pointed out the lot, mule/cow barn, corn crib, garage, blacksmith shop, smokehouse, outhouse, garden plot, large fruit orchard, and syrup mill.

Dad and Mother maintained a well-kept yard, building, and fences. The livestock were well fed, sheltered, and pastured. We kids were expected to keep the yard spotless, free of wild grass and weeds. The front yard was adorned by two huge gardenias, the Cape Province variety. When they bloomed, a breathtaking fragrance permeated the air. Alas, the yard we used to tend so carefully is now covered with unkempt and unattended growth. The rock wall that ran the length of the yard is gone. The huge live oak trees have been removed. Unfortunately, there are so many scenes like this scattered all over Alabama.

I was born in that house October 7, 1920. It was also the birthplace of my sisters, Bessie Mae (December 19, 1915) and Fannie Lee (March 3, 1923), and my brother, James Robert (September 13, 1925).

I remember the chores—bringing in the wood, keeping the yard clean, tending to the animals, working in the fields and garden, helping with housework. There was always plenty of work to do for us children, Dad, and Mother. I remember the home-cured hams, the fresh vegetables and fruits, and the fresh milk cooled by being lowered into the well. My mother was a great cook. She was known far and wide for her delicious coconut cakes, fried chicken, and biscuits made from scratch.

Nor shall I forget wash day, laundering our clothes and bed linens. If there were washing machines and dryers in the 1920s, we never heard of them. My mother did have a rub board (a woman with a rub board was considered well off). The laundry was done in the backyard. We began by filling the pot with water and building a fire around it to "boil the clothes" with homemade lye soap. The clothes were taken from the pot of boiling water with a batting board and placed on the batting block. The batting board was then used to remove any stubborn dirt or stain. Next the clothes were put in a tub of water for rinsing and starching, wrung out, and hung on the clothesline to be dried by the sunshine, which made them smell so good and fresh.

I have often wondered how Mother survived wash day for her family of six—Dad, herself, two girls, and two boys—but she did! In fact, my mother believed that "cleanliness is next to godliness." She said, "Your clothes may have patches, but they will be clean for school and church." We kids were taught to take care of our clothes and always changed into our work or play clothes when we got home from school.

My parents were committed to the work ethic and believed the children must work. And we did! Laziness was considered an unforgivable sin in our household. Perhaps many problems arise today in our communities because our children and youth have too much time for idleness and television. My parents believed "an idle mind was the devil's workshop." As the Holy Scripture so wisely says, "He who tills his land will be satisfied with bread, but he who follows frivolity is devoid of understanding" (Prov. 12:11).

Still, we had time for fun. My dad and I often went skinny dipping in High Pine Creek's swimming hole (we didn't have swimming suits in the country in those days). The water was pure, clear, refreshingly cool, and free of pesticides and pollution.

Another pleasure was syrup-making time. My dad had the only syrup mill in the area, and we always grew sugar cane and sorghum. At harvest time, we cut and stripped the canes in the field, loaded them on the wagon, and hauled them to the mill. The mill site was ideal, a beautiful shaded hill with a creek branch flowing past the cooking site located several hundred feet downhill. The mill was mule drawn. The cane was fed into the mill, squeezing the juice from the stalks. The juice ran into a conduit, flowing into a holding vat at the foot of the hill. My dad carefully orchestrated the entire operation. He built a large open fire pit out of clay bricks, over which he placed a large copper cooking pan approximately twelve feet long by three feet wide with eight sections. The cooking process was very exact, requiring constant attention until the finished syrup flowed into the container which was sealed for delivery and consumption. For the kids, syrup making was a work time, but also a time to play and drink sugar-cane juice. Marvelously refreshing, the sugar-cane juice quenched our thirst and satisfied our hunger. Syrup making was an incomparable time for life on our farm.

When I think of the old home place, I can visualize Dr. Clack, my mama's attending physician at my birth. When it came to most things that happened to our family, he took care of it. Dr. Clack was blind. When he began losing his sight in medical school, his wife, "Dr. Miss Ressa" Clack, from Abanda, became his reader. She read the medical books to him; therefore, according to our friend and first-grade school teacher, John Tom Green, she was about as good a doctor as he was. Miss Ressa always went with him on house calls, driving their horse and buggy, and later a Model T Ford, so we had the benefit of a "second opinion." Dr. Clack finally retired at New Hope. He built a home there near the church, and he and Miss Ressa lived there several years before he died.

Living in the country without telephone service made it difficult to reach a doctor quickly, particularly during the night. I had a lot of trouble with earaches when I was a child, especially at night. So my mother treated me, with my sister Bessie helping a little. Mama must have had fifty home remedies, and she tried them all to give me relief. This included heating salt. (Salt was a basic to life in those days. A good supply was always kept available, especially in wintertime for the meat-curing process.) My mother poured the heated salt into a five-pound sugar sack. The heat from the salt felt good to my aching ear.

Today, I have a hearing impairment largely because of scar tissue from childhood earaches. I have been under the care of an otolaryngologist most of my life. But Mama was doctor and nurse in a time when vaccinations for childhood diseases were not available. It was not a matter of whether we would contract childhood illnesses; it was a matter of when. We kids survived them because Mama nursed us back to health.

My dad was a progressive and industrious farmer, as progressive as you could be with mules, plows, and hoes. Basically, there were six major divisions in his agricultural plan: the family garden, the watermelon/muskmelon patch, the fruit orchard, the new ground, the creek bottoms, and the large plateau for growing cotton which we picked by hand. As we children grew, we took on adult-size chores. My dad really needed an additional plowhand; therefore, I became his plowboy at the age of eight.

I shall never forget his training strategy for me. Dad believed his apprentice plowboy could prepare a piece of new ground for cotton. He made the first round, laying out the boundaries; my job was to "break" the new ground thoroughly. I thought the size of the new field was half of the land in Randolph County! I became frightened of being left alone. My imagination took charge, and I began to see wild animals coming toward me and strange people in the distant cotton house. I was amazed at what I conjured up in my mind. Because of my fears, my plowing was carelessly done. I thought everything was okay as long as I covered all the ground with freshly plowed dirt. If you know anything about the process, you know a turning plow will do beautiful work if used properly. But I wanted to get through and back to the security of home and Mama, so I forgot about doing it right. That sure didn't work! I learned a valuable lesson that has stayed with me for seventy-odd years: If a job is worth doing, it is worth doing right, and, I might add, the first time. Yes, my dad reprimanded me by having me return to the task and do it right.

My brother, two sisters, and I learned many valuable lessons with lifetime implications from days on the farm. Dad and Mama were the epitome of good work and were always planning and working with their four children in mind. Each day was filled with repetitious chores, basic to the happiness and survival of the family.

Mama's work was never finished: preparing three meals each day for her family; maintaining a clean, orderly house; working in the fields; planting and working a large garden; canning vegetables and fruits for winter; and directing the activities of four children. She worked incessantly, and, in fact, I cannot remember her ever taking an afternoon nap.

Occasionally, she would find respite in her rocking chair on the front porch, but even then her hands were never still. She would sew new patches on our clothes, make quilts, and crochet. Plus, she was always aware of the whereabouts of the children. Her extrasensory perception always baffled me, and I would often wonder, "How did she know that?" In fact, we kids were often exasperated with her sensitivity and awareness of all our activities. However, it was only when we disobeyed or "sneaked" in forbidden activities that we got in trouble. Mama was the disciplinarian in our house. She disciplined with firmness, yet with love and tenderness. The awful thing about her whipping was that the child had to cut the switch. We knew her expectation for a switch—long, pliable, and large enough to leave an impression.

One of the summertime chores we kids helped with was gathering and preparing fruit. In those days, we dried apples for cobblers to be enjoyed in the winter months. We peeled and sliced the fruit, then laid the slices on the metal roof to dry. A hot tin roof and sunshine were ideal—until the fruit had to be turned. Have you ever turned fruit on a hot tin roof barefooted?

Our nearest neighbor was an African-American family, the Fears, a single mother and two sons. It was a joy not only to be neighbors, but friends and colaborers. I am so glad Mother and Dad demonstrated good neighborliness to them. When Mrs. Nancy Fears needed help, my mother responded to the need. If Dad needed help, Mrs. Fears's sons responded.

My dad was a friend and helper to anybody in need. I am personally indebted to him and my mother for demonstrating good race relations. "Son," Dad would say, "treat everybody as a human being and you will get along with people." In fact, I began to realize the bigness of the planet Earth as I realized there had to be other kinds of people out there. The chorus we sang in Sunday School developed meaning to me:

> Jesus loves the little children,
> All the children of the world.
> Red and yellow, black and white,
> They are precious in His sight,
> Jesus loves the little children of the world.

Good race relations has been a lifetime acceptance and practice for me. Because I was taught in Sunday School that Jesus loves the little children, all the children, and because my nearest neighbors were African-Americans, I was equipped for roles of service as a pastor and as a denominational worker.

One man who inspired me was George Washington Carver, to whom I was introduced through the George Washington Carver Museum at Tuskegee University, Tuskegee, Alabama. Mr. Carver was born a slave in 1861, but was freed at the end of the Civil War. Through dedication to hard work, he overcame the difficulties of attaining an education. In 1896, he received a master's degree from Iowa State Agricultural College. Shortly thereafter he accepted a position at Tuskegee Institute in Alabama, where he dedicated the remainder of his life to helping African Americans and improving the economy of the South. His life is truly a lesson to us all that God is no respecter of persons. My Savior, Jesus Christ, died, was buried, and arose that all people might be saved, becoming brothers and sisters in Christ.

There was no news coming into our little community (at least through technology) in the 1920s. Our country home didn't have a telephone, radio, television, or daily newspaper. I find this hard to imagine now in this age of information and instantaneous transmissions. The introduction of the radio into our home was a big event. We were living in Shawmut Valley. Neighbors and family members gathered around the Stewart-Warner radio, which my dad operated. I remember how strange and bold the music came through the box (radio) from the Grand Ole Opry in Nashville, Tennessee. Our home would never be the same after that night.

HIGH PINE BAPTIST CHURCH

I was introduced to the church pew very early in life when I was old enough to sit alongside my mother at High Pine Baptist Church, seven miles from Roanoke in Randolph County. A church nursery was not provided for infants and children. Mothers held their small children through Sunday School and worship services. Sometimes the preacher had to speak over the cries of tired, restless, and hungry babies.

From my perspective as a beginner in church, I wondered why, this being God's house, God made the pew so uncomfortable for little boys and girls. Hardwood, straight-up backs, and uncushioned pews provided the seating for me and my childhood friends, and it obviously had been built with adults in mind. Incidentally, I began to notice the adults, especially

the men, had problems sitting through Sunday School and preaching services.

The preacher was special and a welcomed guest in our home. Mother often invited him to have Sunday dinner with us. Although we children enjoyed his company, we had been admonished by Mama about our manners; she didn't want us to fuss about having to wait to eat after the grown-ups (we kids had leftovers and always got the bony pieces of chicken). However, in retrospect, I am glad the preacher was always a welcomed guest in our house of humble means. This was back in the 1920s, when the preacher was a very influential person in the church and the community.

The first preacher in my memory is Rev. E. E. Laney. I was a beginner in church, age three or four. I remember Brother Laney's appearance in the pulpit with his healthy, reddish-looking complexion and bushy mass of blondish hair. He was always neatly dressed—suit, shirt, tie, and a pocket watch with a gold chain. There were times in his preaching when I wondered why he never looked at his watch, but I remember the clarity and power of his sermons. He was convincing to a small country boy sitting on a hard pew, legs dangling and unable to reach the church floor.

The church played a dominant role in my young life. I was introduced to God, the church, and his people at High Pine Baptist Church. The church building was a one-room, wood-frame church house built on the high point adjacent to the cemetery. There were two approaches to the red clay, cobblestone churchyard and adequate parking space as I recall. Much of the area was shaded by oak trees. Pine trees edged the outer perimeter of the church grounds. There was outdoor plumbing: two outhouses an adequate distance from each other.

I recall the formations, structures, and furnishings of the interior. The pulpit was centrally located with the lectern in front center of the platform. There were two large chairs on the platform for the preacher and the song leader. If we had a visiting preacher, the song leader would sit on the front pew near the piano. Our singing was congregational; seldom did we have a choir.

"In remembrance of me" was carved into the wooden Lord's Supper table. There were two offering plates and, usually, a fresh bouquet of flowers prepared by one of the ladies in the church. Pews were located on either side of the aisle. The building was cooled with open windows and heated with a pot-bellied stove.

Sunday School, primarily for the children and the ladies, was held weekly. We studied stories from the Bible and had a memory verse to learn each Sunday. Classes were held in the church auditorium, with curtains drawn for privacy. Frequently, the men would remain outside.

High Pine Baptist Church was on quarter-time in the early twenties. Preaching services were held once each month, with long revivals held in the summer months at times most convenient for working the crops or gathering the harvest. Revivals were times of powerful preaching for the saving of souls. My oldest sister was converted in a summer revival and baptized in High Pine Creek at Pooles' Mill.

Outside the church building, there was a long wooden table that had been constructed for "dinner-on-the-ground" meals and fellowship. These occasions provided for the time to partake of delectable foods. Weight-watching and dietary foods were not priorities in those days. I remember the waist-high tables, built especially for the adults and laden with choice foods prepared from the favorite recipes of the ladies. We children could not see the food, which wasn't so bad because our mothers prepared our plates anyway. Tablecloths were placed on the table by each family, and the lady would spread out her food. Of course, everyone was free to move up and down the table to choose food prepared by other ladies. Food was prohibited in the church house and in the automobiles, however.

These events were anticipated by all ages and all families, and the children were uninhibited in their playful activities on the big church grounds. There was quality time for the mothers to discuss concerns of common interest—child raising, childhood diseases, family problems, the latest quilt design, patterns and designs used in children's and girls' clothes and, of course, the perennial topics, recipes and home remedies.

In the 1920s, churches were centers of information as well as centers for preaching the gospel. Alcoholism was a curse to family life. Divorce, abortion, and abuse were not major public concerns.

The world of my dad and mother revolved around their four children: Bessie Mae, Alton Earl, Fannie Lee, and James Robert. My parents and, I believe, we children identify with the large poor Alabama population because we were poor. Poor, but proud! And we children were fortunate with our parentage. Papa and Mama were parents who had unfeigned love and devotion for their four children. All dreams, plans, and activities were focused on us. Papa spent his adult life working to provide for his wife and four children. He believed in the work ethic by precept and example and taught his children to work by working alongside them. Our beautifully tilled land showed his pride in his work. His farming was an expression of faith in God and his desire to provide for his family. He believed in preparing the soil, sowing the seed, and knowing it was God who gave the water and the increase. He believed in soil conservation and preservation—all were expressions of thanksgiving to God for the land.

Papa applied those work principles when he made a job change from farming to dairying, and later in life to the service-station business, which he enjoyed because of the contact and communication with people. He was a person-centered man, always with an extended hand. I

wished quite often that I had the love and compassion my dad had for people. He was always ready to help others.

Both Dad and Mama wanted their children to excel in life. I recall a particular dinner-table conversation. The table setting was simple. A tablecloth covered the table. The silver was stainless flatware. The plates were white with a few chipped places, and the tumblers were real glass. I don't remember the menu, but all of our meals were prepared from homegrown vegetables, meats, and fruits. My dad's table conversation was unusually mellifluous. He engaged Mother in conversation about the children. It was an affirming conversation, somewhat rare with Papa. He made a statement definitive of his hopes and desires for each of the four children. "I want to make something good out of you," he said, talking to us. I have never forgotten that affirming statement. It has been a source of encouragement and enablement through the years. There is no substitute for parental affirmations in the lives of their children. We kids wanted our parents to be proud of their children. They were!

Mama spent her life caring for the family. Her travels were restricted to a radius of 200 miles from home. She did little traveling but, oh, how she cared for her family. I can remember her taking us to the field so she could work there (our day care was a pallet of quilts under the shade of a tree). She never worked for pay outside the home. In our rural Alabama community, there was little outside work available for a woman, nor was it fashionable or even acceptable for the mother to work outside the home. But Mama had plenty of unpaid work in the home setting. In fact, she never caught up!

Dad was the bread provider. He worked from daybreak until dark. However, our family life was interdependently communal—each family member had responsibility for the other members. Life in the country was both good and hard.

PLAY TIME

But, life was not "all work and no play," and we had our fun. We kids could play while we worked, if we were working outside. Toys and games were largely dependent on the creative ingenuity of family members, especially the children, and the open spaces provided us with play areas and opportunities. There were no children living near us (Mrs. Fears's children were older), but we had each other. Our favorite games were very physical:

Hopscotch—Players tossed a small object into numbered spaces of a pattern of rectangles drawn on the ground. They took turns hopping or jumping through the spaces to retrieve the object.

Marbles—This game took on many different formations. We played "for keeps." One formation was to dig a hole in the ground as a pocket. Each player tried to hit another player's marble into the hole, and thus claim the marble.

Hand-Me-Over (Handy-Over)—This game was played with two teams. Team one was on one side of the house and team two on the opposite side. The team with the ball called out "hand-me-over." The player who caught the ball tried to hit a player on the other team with the ball so that player would have to drop out or join the other team.

Drop the Handkerchief—The players, the more the merrier, formed a circle. A player was selected to drop the handkerchief behind another player and run around the circle to where the handkerchief was dropped before being caught.

Stick Horse—The players ran around on their "horses," and, of course, any old stick long enough to be ridden would do. Our imaginations ran wild. Many years later, stick horse became one of my son's favorite "play likes." He ran many miles on his horse, always corralling it overnight.

Town Ball—Town ball was baseball for families who didn't have the money to buy a baseball. To make a town ball, we unraveled an old sock, put a wad of cotton in the center of the unraveled threads, then wrapped the thread around the cotton until the "ball" was big enough to play with. It was amazing how well we got along with that. Because it was a soft ball, players could throw it at the runners as they went from base to base and not hurt them.

Dolls—Playing with dolls was make-believe housekeeping.

May I—Teams were selected. Steps were given to a player to be taken, but only "May I" would give the player permission to advance. A player moved forward as the game advanced; however, if caught by the caller, the player returned to starting position.

Sling Shot—In those days, if you owned an automobile you knew there were inner tubes in the tires. You could hardly take a trip without having a puncture because there were so many objects and bumps in the roads. People patched those inner tubes until they got beyond the patching stage before purchasing new ones. Boys and girls got the old ones and cut strips of rubber and made sling shots.

THE OLD SCHOOLHOUSE

My first schooling was at Pooles' Cross Roads. I was enrolled in the first grade there, a one-room schoolhouse located at the crossroads of Pooles' Mill Road and the Abanda/Roanoke County Road. I remember it being a rustic building of rough heart pinewood with high windows and a bell-tower entrance. Long desks for students, a blackboard, a pot-bellied stove, a teacher's desk, and a recitation bench were the furnishings.

The large long recitation bench was placed in the front of the room where the teacher would call each class up for recitation. This procedure was a good motivator for preparation, but it could be intimidating. (Perhaps today's classrooms need a recitation bench.) Older students listened to the first- and second-grade children read and recite their lessons. It was good for both groups, and made the older students more apt in the skills of reading, spelling, and arithmetic. The school was pretty well organized in four grades with an enrollment of twenty-five.

I was impressed by the teacher, John Tom Green. Born in 1905, he began teaching at age twenty in the fall of 1925 in a one-teacher schoolhouse. He excelled as an educator, school administrator, and coach for forty-five years and retired as superintendent of Lanett City Schools (1945-1971) at the age of sixty-six. Recently I had the pleasure of interviewing my old first-grade teacher.

Potts: "I am just amazed that you taught me in the first grade and that you are so active today; that's just amazing to me."

Green: "Those were good days back then. We didn't have any money. We had most anything that you wanted to eat and enough clothes to cover us and that's about all."

Potts: "That's about all we had. Well, you made school a good experience. I don't remember any bad. I didn't have any bad experiences with you."

My parents supported the school teachers in their teaching methodology and in all disciplinary actions. I knew if I got in trouble at school, I would have trouble at home. If I got a whipping at school, I would get a whipping at home. My parents were partners with the school teachers and officials in all matters related to their children.

Green: "I've had very few bad experiences in school."

Potts: "I think you're the person responsible for that, not us, but you. I think your gift of teaching and working with people helped you immensely in that."

Mr. Green is a churchman in the United Methodist Church, active in civic activities. I was most fortunate in having such a good teaching model. It was my privilege to recognize him with the Outstanding Educator's Award in the 1993 Alabama Senior Citizens Hall of Fame.

A TIME TO MOVE

In 1929, Papa and Mama decided to move the family from rural Randolph County, where my sisters, brother, and I were nurtured the first nine years of my life. Most farm families failed to prosper in the 1920s; we were no exception.

We kids were ecstatic over the move from rural Alabama, a place of tranquility and hard work, where the sun shown brightly and the moon always had a silver lining. In fact, our piece of rural Alabama was so far remote from town, I was six years old before I realized the sun did not set between my house and Roanoke, Alabama.

"Where are we moving, Papa?" we asked. "We are moving to Shawmut, Alabama," he said. We wondered, "Where is that?" Shawmut is located in east Alabama in Chambers County, adjacent to Randolph County on the south. It is a big textile center, home of the West Point Manufacturing Company, whose mills manufacture Martex towels and Lady Pepperell bed linens.

The 1920s were hard on farmers, and there were no government subsidies. Papa believed he could provide better for his family with a steady job in dairying. I think Papa was tired of farming and thought a change would be good for him and the family. However, we were unprepared for the move. Sharing a house with another family, uprooted from High Pine Baptist Church, thrust into a new culture, and enrolled in a new school system, all radically distanced us from the isolation and security of life on the farm. The solidarity of family was threatened by our move to "the foreign country." We were strangers in a foreign environment with the loss of our freedom. Perhaps, though, the greatest adjustments were laid on my parents.

Papa went to work for Uncle Charlie Bailey, who was in the dairy business. He was married to my mother's sister, Lizzie. In retrospect, I think it was a mistake to have moved from the farmlands of rural Alabama to the Valley. The environment seemed radically different and at times hostile to the lifestyle of our family. We children were so restricted in our play and other activities. The moral values we learned in earlier years were challenged by new friends and my cousins. In addition, we were not accustomed to having so many people around us. We felt so crowded.

Then the Great Depression of 1929 struck, devastating not only the South and the nation but the world. The financial collapse of the nation affected all members of all families. For our family, survival was the greatest concern. Our family members spent the three years after 1929 as transients moving four times as Papa followed his job. He was not ready for the hardships his family was to encounter.

From 1929 to 1933, prices of farm goods fell about 50 percent. Farmers could not pay mortgages and were forced to rent their farms or move. We moved.

The depression was a drastic decline. It was as though business could not pull out of the slump. Buying and selling dropped, causing a decline in production, prices, income, and employment. Chronic illnesses became common, and suicides were frequent. Money became scarce. Businesses and banks failed, workers lost jobs, stores closed, and manufacturing dropped. Bankruptcies occurred, wiping out savings and bank balances. Uncle John Veal and Aunt Mae, my father's sister, lost their savings overnight in a bank closing.

Each of the calamities of the Great Depression hurt great numbers of people, especially people who lost their jobs. Thousands of people lived on charity. I remember the embarrassment of having to take charity from Mr. Morgan, the depot manager in Fairfax where we had moved in 1930 because my two uncles consolidated their dairies. Each school-day morning my younger sisters, my brother, and I would pick up school lunch money from Mr. Morgan. He was a kind and generous man, and his kindness cushioned the heartache of having "to take a handout." We children were grateful, because the lunches filled our hungry stomachs.

The depression caused people to lose faith in themselves and in the future. Society suffered as it spread more unemployment, poverty, and despair. Human suffering became a reality for millions of Americans. I remember corn bread, butter, and sorghum syrup as a regular breakfast at our house for several weeks. We children thought that to be the depth of poverty, but we did not know how fortunate we were. Many died of disease and malnutrition. Thousands lost their homes. The homeless, jobless, and transient obtained food from welfare agencies and religious missions—soup, beans, or stew. Times were hard.

However, Papa and Mama and we four kids managed to stay in good health. Thanks to God and the abounding strength and solid commitment of my parents to each other, we survived those difficult years of the 1930s. Family solidarity was a virtue in our family. Today, I realize how blessed we children were in having a father and mother who struggled in their labors yet never thought about separation or divorce. In fact, there was an unyielding solidarity in my parents' marriage. How marvelous to celebrate their wedded years "plus fifty" and never have to wonder about their commitment to each other.

It is a joy to salute my parents with praise and thanksgiving, but I must confess my pain to the reader for something I failed to do. My sisters and brother planned a fiftieth wedding anniversary for Mama and Papa to be held on a Sunday afternoon. I felt it was more important for me to be in the pulpit on that Sunday, so I did not attend the party. I was wrong. This is one of several conflicts I will not belabor you with. It suffices to suggest that I should have paid honor and appreciation to family; don't neglect giving appropriate and timely recognition and gratitude to family. Once people are in the grave, it is too late. The pain of neglect does not go away, so let me again encourage you to consider your ways and your priorities.

How did my parents' marriage survive? There was a tolerance for imperfections, mistakes, and wrongs. My mother, for example, could be overbearing and demanding, especially in her later years. Illness contributed to this posture. I know there were times when Dad and the

children were not sympathetic. I know this was hard on Dad and my
younger sister and her husband.

The Great Depression made a lasting impression on my life. It was a
very difficult time for Mother and Dad beyond anything I can imagine.
Yet, by the grace of God and our struggles for survival, our family
remained intact. Though the foundations of family were shaken, our
faith remained steadfast in each other. God's provisions were adequate.

I learned many lessons from the depression. First, my faith in God
was strengthened for daily life. Second, my parents never disappointed
me. They were always there when I needed them. Third, I learned the
meaning of frugality, and I trust that my lifestyle today reflects that trait.
Fourth, I am a better steward of my gifts, my life, and my acquisitions.

My memories of life in a new setting are colored not only by hardships caused by the depression, but by a potentially life-threatening
experience as well. I never knew whether the incident was intentional or
not. We lived in the same community with two other sets of cousins.
There were seven boys. Four of the boys were together one day when one
of them shot me in my left leg with a twenty-two rifle. He said it was an
accident, and I gave him the benefit of the doubt. The bullet penetrated
my leg just below the kneecap and came out through the mid-calf of my
leg. I was restricted to bed for days. The doctor administered treatment
and drugs, but I almost lost my leg from blood poisoning. It was serious
and yet, it was as though I was spared for some miraculous reason which
I did not understand. As I reflect on life, it seems to me God had a
protective wall about me for a special mission. Unquestionably, the spirit
of God was upon my life.

Another life-threatening illness, double pneumonia, threatened me
at age seventeen. Since the family did not have health-care insurance, I
was cared for at home. The doctor visited me there and my mother and
a well-trained experienced nurse, Ms. Johnnie Gray, nursed me through
the crisis. The Lord spared me that I might respond to his call upon my
life, which I did. Sixty years later I know my life was spared by the mercy
of God. It is a losing battle when you resist and fight God.

There were other experiences I recall. One involved the boys from
three families, all located within a half-mile of each other. We decided
we needed a place off limits, a place secret to other people, especially our
parents! We agreed to build an earth cave. Site selection became more
of a problem than we had anticipated. We carefully surveyed the land

area and finally, a decision was made; my house would be the nearest to the cave site.

We began excavating by removing red clay from the site. The task took days. Finally, the last load of dirt was dumped. We put a leak-proof roof on the cave. Support timbers were put in place and sub-roofing laid over the support timbers and covered with dirt. Then our cave was secured with a door, one of the greatest challenges. We boys had completed our most ambitious and challenging project. The rewards reassured our privacy.

In our cave, we began to experiment with smoking. In fact, our parents had forbidden us to smoke. My dad was a smoker, very adept at rolling his own "Duke's mixture" cigarettes. Later he became a smoker of Camel cigarettes and would have literally "walked a mile for a Camel," though I don't remember him ever having to do that. My dad had forbidden smoking (and drinking) for other members of the family. In retrospect, I think smoking contributed to my dad's death.

We boys discovered "rabbit tobacco," a weed grown in the sage growth in uncultivated areas of the community. I did indulge, but I never became addicted to smoking nor ever cared for alcoholic beverages. I am glad!

I suppose in many ways our habits were the habits of other youth of our generation. As for me, I am glad smoking and other vices indulged in by the boys were short-lived. I learned the Scripture that said, "Know you not, your body is the temple of God . . ." (1 Cor. 6:19). Drinking, smoking, dancing, and cursing, the cardinal sins of youth in my teenage years, never became habits in my life. I am grateful to the Lord for removing the desire.

We moved the third time in 1934. The second move was from Fairfax to Shawmut. This time my papa's new employer was H. G. Word, owner of Word's Dairy and a faithful member and deacon in the Shawmut Baptist Church. Finally we were in the community where we were to live for the rest of my parents' lives.

There was to be one other job change. My dad went into the auto-motive service-station business in 1953 at age fifty-eight. It was not necessary for us to move, however.

Alas, when my dad made the transition in work from farming to dairying to service-station industries, his church participation became most infrequent. Dairying was a seven days per week business, each day begin-ning at 2:30 or 3:00 A.M. Later, the service station also required seven days.

Perhaps, there were more subliminal reasons for my dad's infrequent church participation. He was not a high-school graduate. I hope I was never embarrassed by that, but I noted the men of the church did not nurture my dad in his faith and church participation. I have met thousands of men in my pilgrimage of faith who are, as my dad, non-participatory in church. It is regrettable when the church does not have "eyes to see and ears to hear." Perhaps there would have been more family church participation had we been in another branch of Christianity, but we were Baptists. We can leave people behind when we become middle-class Christians. My personal response would be different today. However, Papa and Mama were proud of the participation of their children. We were very active in church activities.

Jesus never failed to reach out to the homeless and uneducated; to the sick, dying, and handicapped; to alcoholics and prostitutes; to the poor and the affluent. Should the church not do as much today? Let me hasten to say that many churches do. Compassion was present in the congregation of my home church with its blue collar/white collar folks. Somehow, though, a connection is often not made with so many of our church dropouts.

We moved from Fairfax, where we children had attended the inter-denomination Congregational Christian Church, to an area between Shawmut-Langdale. Shawmut Baptist Church has been our home church since 1932. Rev. Earle Trent was pastor then.

I was converted in a revival meeting with Dr. M. P. Hunt from Virginia preaching. I was in the Junior Department and remember my baptism. The church did not have baptismal robes, so Pastor Trent asked the baptism candidates to wear white. I had a white shirt and my mother bought the white pants for my baptism. I remember how meticulously she prepared my baptismal clothes. They were immaculate.

Pastor Earle Trent, Sunday School teacher Osmus Lanier, the deacons (Oliver, Word, Plant, Underwood, Hollis, and others) and members of the congregation nurtured this young Christian convert in the rudiments of the Christian faith and church fellowship. The women of the church were encouraging, with supportive words and motherly counsel. I love the Bible, God's word, and I love the church, the body of Christ. My commitments compelled my faithfulness.

My teenage years were years of involvement in the church's leadership. Baptist Young People's Union (BYPU) is where I received my first training in speaking before people and praying in public. My Sunday

School teacher, Osmus Lanier, was special. I remember him so well as someone who really cared for teenagers and exemplified the Christian lifestyle as I perceived it as a teenage boy. His walk with the Lord has been steadfast; great has been his faithfulness to Christ and the church. Sixty years have passed and Osmus Lanier continues in his faithfulness.

The Shawmut First Baptist Church has always had a large cadre of men and women found faithful in their love for the Lord and in their participation in the church. Praise the Lord for the great host of laypeople—women, men, and youth undergirding the church. Their work is a witness to their faith in the living Lord and their love for the body of Christ. Today, I envision the great host of saints by the millions filling church pews to hear words from God. How awesome is the responsibility upon the spokesman for God when the saints come together for a word from God.

The discipleship program in the Baptist church has evolved through several formations during my lifetime. I was a member when it was BYPU. The programs and disciplines focused the young people in the church. Later, it became the Baptist Training Union. Adults were enrolled and involved in training and in discipleship. Then another name change identified the program as Church Training Union because all age groups were enrolled. The most recent name change is to Discipleship Training. Whatever we call it, the purpose is unchanged— equipping the saints in discipleship to do the work of ministry.

The Shawmut Baptist Church elected me at the age of fifteen to be the young people's leader in Training Union. I remember my feelings and thoughts about this matter, and although I was a teenager leading teenagers, I gave it my best effort. The Lord was equipping me to be a servant leader. I was struggling with the "call to preach," a struggle that lasted for five years. I remember the feeling of peace and the consciousness of reassurance that possessed me when I said to the Lord, "Here am I, send me." Here is the story.

THE CALL OF GOD

In 1934, I dropped out of junior high school and started working at Word's Dairy, working my way up from the bottom. I literally came up through the ranks, progressing from the job of delivery boy up to managing a route. Why was I a school dropout? Our family needed the money. Although Dad worked constantly, he was having a hard time financially.

Also, I needed some money for personal needs. But, short-sightedness prompted my dropout. Still, God was relentless and faithful, and I was never freed from the sense of call upon my life. God never gave up!

Finally, after two years as route manager, at age nineteen, I made my surrender and commitment to God's call—yes, to the gospel ministry. As soon as I realized there was to be no reversing the call and the Lord had my stubborn will subdued, I said yes and at once I knew there was no turning back, no turning back.

My call to the ministry came on Sunday afternoon in the bottle washing and sterilizing room at Word's Dairy. I remember the beauty of the day— a picture perfect spring day. The morning was spent in Sunday School and morning worship. Mama's lunch was so good (her meals were always good). After lunch I went to work at the dairy, with no idea of the life-changing experience which awaited me. My altar was the bottle sterilizing machine. The call of the Lord was definite—a call to prepare which I have never questioned. That was fifty-six years ago. Through good times and tough times, I return to my "Bethel" for reassurance and encouragement.

The "call of God" became a heavy burden on my heart for five years. I would ask, "Lord, why not my brother; he is so articulate." I made several suggestions to God, but I could never remove myself, my heart and mind, from his call. When I would question the validity of the call, the Holy Spirit was always there to validate its genuineness. Ultimately, after months that seemed like years, I surrendered my life to the call of Jesus Christ:

> Lord, I praise you for salvation.
> I thank you for loving me.
> I am overwhelmed with your call.
> I acknowledge the claim you have upon my life.
> Lord, Here am I! I surrender to your call to ministry.
> I am ready to prepare.
> I am ready to go wherever you lead!
> Lord, I believe preparation is going to be hard.
> I am willing to pay the price, to endure, to become what you will make
>   of my life.
> Lord, what more can I do! What is next?
> Please Lord, do not leave me or forsake me.
> Help me to keep loving you and trusting you!

Mr. and Mrs. Clarence J. Potts on their fiftieth wedding anniversary.

God answered my prayer and I found more, so very much more to life in surrender to him.

A miracle happened in my dad's life when I answered God's call. He drank alcoholic beverages, and this habit was an embarrassment to the family. But he was so proud that his son was to be a minister that from the time I surrendered to the call to preach, Dad gave up alcohol, never again drinking the substance in any form. I was overwhelmed with my dad's decision. His action was so courageous. This miracle in his life was vital in my years of surrender and preparation and a source of strength and encouragement in my life and ministry.

Dad questioned me thoroughly at the time I was considering re-entering school. He, as I, didn't know how in the world I could go back to school, change jobs, and enter Howard College. He became my greatest supporter in my pastoral ministry. Both he and Mama gave out of their needs to help pay for their son's college expenses.

The Training Union ministry of Southern Baptists provided me with challenges and opportunities, some of which I have listed: (1) young people's leader; (2) associate director of Associational Training Union, East Liberty Association, geographically in Chambers County; (3) Associational Training Union director, East Liberty Association; (4) worker in Birmingham Association Training Union; (5) president, State Training Union Convention (Alabama) 1944–1945 and 1945–1946; (6) Maines Rawls and Cynthia Jo Hall invited me to join the State Training Union Department. John Jeffers championed the cause. John made an invaluable impact on my life. He and Jeanette encouraged me in my preparation for my calling; (7) approved worker, State Training Union Department; (8) Dr. Clay I. Hudson, adult director, Training Union Department, Southern Baptist Convention (SBC) invited me to consider being his successor. That was phenomenal and incomprehensible. I could not imagine such responsibility; (9) Training Union worker, Kentucky Baptist Convention, while a student at Southern Baptist Theological Seminary; (10) pastor advisor to the young people in the Birmingham Association where I had pastored; (11) active in Training Unions in churches where I pastored; (12) strong advocate of discipleship training as executive secretary-treasurer, with John Sawyer, one of the ablest and most resourceful persons I have known in the ministry of discipleship, serving as director of Discipleship Training in Alabama.

I was elected by the East Liberty Association to serve as associational Training Union director in 1934. Election to this position of leadership opened the door for me to know the leadership, especially the Training Union leaders of the Alabama Baptist State Convention (ABSC) and the leadership of the Southern Baptist Convention, Dr. Jerry Lambdin and Dr. Clay I. Hudson, director of the Adult Department, Baptist Training Union.

East Liberty Association, Chambers County, was one of the first associations in the state for the Standard of Excellence Achievement. I remember going to the state assembly at Cook Springs for recognition of the Standard of Excellence Achievement when I was Training Union director of the East Liberty Association.

The Baptist Training Union opened many windows of opportunities for me. It started simultaneously with my conversion and my involvement in the Training Union of Shawmut Baptist Church. It was there I prayed my first public prayer and I began my pilgrimage in the discipline of prayer. The church Training Union gave me the opportunity to stand before my Training Union group to affirm my faith. I experienced much anxiety at that time in my life. Let me hasten to say that I am still nervous and emotionally moved when I have the responsibility of speaking to a congregation. The East Liberty Baptist Association gave me the opportunities to grow by providing me with opportunities in leadership. I realized the association exists for the churches. I was intrigued with the interaction and cooperation among the churches. The autonomy of each Baptist church made a profound impression upon me. I learned the importance of equipping the saints to do the work of ministry in the church and the association through participation.

I learned that "The Church" did not give to the Cooperative Program. Rather, cooperating Southern Baptist churches gave through the Cooperative Program in supporting missions around the world. I was asked to give the Cooperative Program report at the annual meeting of the association. I used the reference concerning churches giving "to the Cooperative Program." I don't recall who the denominational worker was who spoke to the report, but he corrected my vernacular from "giving to the Cooperative Program" to "giving to missions through the Cooperative Programs." I think that might have been a man from Nashville.

Nellie Higgins, from Langdale Church, was my mentor in Baptist Training Union work. I became her assistant in the Associational Training Union program and then followed her as Association Training Union director. She was one gifted lady and an exceptional lay leader in the association. She set the pace for quality work in discipleship among the churches. An outstanding church woman, she was known and loved by the laity and pastoral leaders in the East Liberty Association. She could resurrect any dead Training Union and bring renewal to any living Training Union. At the time of Ms. Higgins's retirement in 1990, she was manager of a Baptist Bookstore in Baltimore, Maryland, where she resides.

Other windows of service opportunities were opening to me. I became active in the State Training Union program, becoming the president of the Alabama Training Union Convention in 1944. One thousand attended the convention in 1944. Later, I began to conduct study courses and Training Union enlargement campaigns. I believed the Training Union was the place to be trained to think and speak on your feet, and I still think so.

I shall never forget Mr. Maines Rawls and Cynthia Jo Hall (Pryor). They sensed my zeal for the Training Union, believing it to be the place where a Christian could become equipped to better serve the Lord in the church. Cynthia Jo came from Red Hill, Alabama and was converted and baptized in Refuge Baptist Church. A gifted communicator, she was a dynamic young people's leader and student worker from January 1944 to 1947. Dr. F. M. Barnes spoke to Cynthia Jo when she applied for the job. The Lord blessed her with a good mind and a caring heart, and she dedicated both to the Lord. She maximized her opportunities for service as an able speaker, whether it was speaking from the pulpit encouraging the worshipers in their Christian pilgrimage, speaking in state associational meetings, or leading conferences at state assemblies and at Ridgecrest. The Training Union program and Baptist Student Ministries were based in the same department. Cynthia Jo gave leadership to the Baptist Student Union (BSU) program. She married Samford Pryor, a Georgia Tech graduate in engineering who retired from the space program in Huntsville. The Pryors are the parents of two lovely daughters, Cynthia and Emily.

THE CALL OF GOD

I have always thought of Brother Everette Calvert and Mrs. Mildred Calvert as my spiritual parents in the ministry. They encouraged me through every phase in my response to the call. I loved them and their sons Frank, a distinguished physician, and Robert, a dedicated pastoral leader in Alabama and Mississippi. Mrs. Calvert was steadfast in believing in me. Her words were always encouraging.

I knew a call to serve the Lord was a call to prepare. In retrospect, I am amazed how the Lord directed the plan step by step. Here is what unfolded.

One: I shared my call experience with my pastor lifting the burden of the call. Rev. Hoyt Ayers, who had followed Brother Calvert at .Shawmut, became my spiritual mentor and pastor during these critical years of closure to independence and change in employment and yes, to prepare for ministry.

Two: I initiated conversation with Principal Pennington and Superintendent Amos Kirby at Lanett High School.

Three: I received permission to enter Lanett High School in order to earn enough credits to enter Howard College where my deficiencies would be made up. I attended classes in the morning. As a nineteen year old, I was embarrassed to reenter school. However, the regular students were most affirming, and my teachers became my heroes. I was even selected class president. This schooling experience did much in building confidence and establishing friends.

Four: I resigned my good job with Word's Dairy. My dad had some reservations about this decision, and with good reason. I had excelled as an employee at Word's Dairy and was making a good income. However, my dad never verbally questioned or tried to discourage me in what God had called me to do.

Five: I sought employment with West Point Manufacturing Company at the Shawmut textile mill. James Hollis employed me to work the second shift—3:00 P.M. to 11:00 P.M., five days per week as inspector in the cloth room. Mr. Hollis, a deacon, was a devoted churchman. I had a genuine respect for this quiet man who held a deep faith in the Lord and for the church and who lovingly affirmed young people. His countenance inspired me, and he is still an inspiration to young people. Mr. Hollis became a close, encouraging friend and employer. He was the overseer of the "cloth room" department of the Shawmut Mill. The inspection department was the last place before shipping. My job was to inspect the cloth, identifying any and all defects caused by the weaving process.

Six: After two years at Lanett High School, I had earned enough credits to enroll at Howard College in September 1942. Major Harwell G. Davis was president, and he and Mrs. Lena Vail Davis were friends to all students. I was privileged to be at Howard College during Major Davis's presidency. He was a leader among leaders. I shall never forget the Thursday chapel service when President Davis announced the acquisition of land in Shades Valley on which the new Howard College would be located. "Unbelievable!" or "Not in my lifetime!" many of the students said. But in 1957, the dedication service for Frank P. Samford Administrative Building, the first of many, was held. I was there to witness this miracle, and I was convinced that the new Howard College was emerging because of the multiple gifts that we had in our presidential leadership. Mrs. Davis became a dear friend to Louise and me. Also, their daughter, Betty Davis Eshelman, is a good buddy. An excellent attorney in Birmingham, she's truly a "chip off the old block"—her dad.

Seven: Whom the Lord calls, he is able to equip! My family was my greatest resource through these critical years of my life. When I was accepted at Howard College, my papa and mama decided they could provide $35 a month for my education. I supplemented my income by hopping tables in the college lunchroom and working in men's furnishings during the afternoons and evenings at the downtown Birmingham Sears Roebuck. When I entered Southern Seminary, I transferred my work record from the Birmingham store to the Louisville, Kentucky, store, where I excelled in sales and was offered the position of department manager of customer services. I declined out of concern that my seminary studies might be affected.

Soon it became time to leave for the university. On the eve of my departure for Howard College, my pastor, Hoyt Ayers, had asked me to preach. I shall never forget the sermonic analogy of how Jesus withdrew from the public ministry to pray and teach the disciples. It is necessary for Christians to withdraw for renewal and affirmation through prayer and study. It is imperative for ministers.

It was in this church, Shawmut First Baptist, where I had been nurtured as an infant in the Christian faith. I had become an active participant, doing anything the church asked of me. The adults were very nurturing and encouraging. I loved the people and felt secure in relating to my beloved pastor. The curtain was about to be drawn closed on the most meaningful and memorable formation of my life.

MY FIRST PASTORATE

I had resolved decisions regarding reentry to public school and employment with West Point Manufacturing Company. I began more active participation in the Associational Training Union program, a work which opened doors to the churches. Then the Lord provided an opportunity to preach. The Pulpit Committee from the New Hope Baptist Church talked with me about pastoring their congregation.

New Hope Baptist Church, Fredonia, Alabama.

The New Hope Baptist Church, Fredonia, Alabama, East Liberty Association, extended to me their call to become their pastor in 1941. In praying about the matter, I was impressed to accept the call. Three matters concerned me—first, the awesome responsibility of preaching to the people of God; second, building a community of faith to be all the Lord would have us; and third, providing spiritual leadership to a church through a perilous time, World War II. My overarching concern was reaching the unsaved. I quickly learned that the Holy Spirit would provide the resources.

I remember the pastors in the East Liberty Association. They prayed for me. They encouraged me. My pastor, Hoyt Ayers, and Mrs. Ayers were constant with encouraging counsel, instant in praying for me, and tirelessly patient with me.

There were others: L. E. Kelley, pastor, Langdale Baptist Church, later to accept the pastorate at the great Highland Baptist Church in Florence; Albert Smith, pastor, Fairfax Baptist Church, who gave me five books from his library; Oley Kidd, pastor, Riverview Baptist Church (later, I was to work with him in Birmingham, where he served as director of missions for the Birmingham Baptist Association); Dr. P. P. Baldridge, pastor, Lanett First Baptist Church; Mrs. Virgil M. Gardner and Dr. Virgil M. Gardner, pastor, First Baptist Church, Lafayette; Mrs. B. B. McGinty and Rev. B. B. McGinty, pastor, Riverview Baptist Church and the author of the *History of East Liberty Association*. There were many others. The roll call of pastors and laity who have influenced my life and ministry is extremely lengthy. A great reunion day is coming!

The New Hope Baptist Church requested my ordination by the Shawmut Baptist Church. My ordination service was held on Sunday night, December 21, 1941. The examining council was composed of the pastors from the association. I was examined before the congregation and still remember the awesomeness of the experience. I was scared to death!

Dr. P. P. Baldridge was elected the moderator for the ordination. An erudite man who had distinguished himself as a preacher, he counseled with me prior to the service. He was so serene and confident in demeanor, and he made a statement that I have never forgotten. He was talking about pastors, expectations, and disappointments, and he said, "There is always a place of service for good pastors." I hope I have been a good pastor. Is there a greater compliment that can be given a pastor by his congregation?

I have endeavored never to be a disappointment to God, his churches that I have pastored, my colleagues and friends in ministry, and my family. I'm not sure what difference my response to my concerns for my first pastorate made, but this I know—I learned much about building a community of faith. Today, the New Hope Baptist Church is alive! A beautiful two-story, red-brick structure holds forth where once stood the old wood-frame building with a balcony. Church minutes record that slaves occupied the balcony. This church had a membership of 143, with forty-five Sunday School members, three groups in Training Union, and a pastor's salary of $286.40.

During these transitions in my life, our country was heavily involved in a world catastrophe, World War II. The ravaging destruction and astronomical loss of human lives weighed heavily upon Alabamians, our nation, and the world. We continue to be shocked by this tragedy, with its dreadful waste, including the dropping of the atomic bomb on Hiroshima, Japan, and six days later on Nagasaki. Since then, I have had the opportunity of sitting on the Governor's Holocaust Commission. Each year we commemorate the millions of Jews, Poles, and others who were stripped of their human dignity, forced to march in formations, herded into box cars, hauled to crematoriums, gassed, and burned. A tragedy of tragedies!

And today we cry out, "Oh God! Save us from such atrocities that happened just a few years ago." And then . . . Bosnia, Albania, and Rwanda . . . again the depravity of man is before and within us. There is a balm in our world to make the wounded and broken whole. The balm is Jesus Christ!

CHAPTER 2

Education, Marriage, and Early Ministries

I REALIZED THAT COME SEPTEMBER 1942, I WOULD BOARD the bus in Opelika for Howard College. Fear welled up in me, but thank the Lord and his people, fear never overcame! The climax came when the church recognized me in the worship service on a Sunday night in September 1942, presenting me with a beautiful brown leather bag and accessories for my trip to Howard. The church had entrusted multiple roles of leadership to me. I grew spiritually, mentally, and physically prior to my departure to Howard College, a life-changing experience.

I must acknowledge my love for and loyalty to Birmingham, a city that has fascinated me from my college years. To a boy from Shawmut, Birmingham was a big city. I was captivated with the downtown area: the big department stores, Loveman's and Pizitz; restaurants; banks; office buildings; and the quaint street cars with their multidirectional routes, though the noise factor would probably be considered an environmental hazard today. The mountains were beautiful, overlooking the city.

No sports event excited me more than the annual Alabama-Auburn football game. I remember one year when the game was played in terrible weather—the mountains were covered with snow, with icy conditions on sections of the roads. The spectators, at least where I was, sat on icy seats. Our feet froze, conditions were miserable, but the big game was played out anyway, and we forgot about the weather until the game ended!

But there is more, much more, to support my love and loyalty to the "Magic City." Birmingham was good to me during my years at Howard College. Many Howard students worked in the downtown business community; it was a good deal. The Birmingham business community needed help, and the "preacher boys" provided some of the best labor because they needed the income. The churches welcomed students, and many churches provided us with life-changing opportunities in church growth and development.

The Birmingham Baptist Association helped in providing service opportunities in the Associational Training Union program under the leadership of Roy Johnson, a devoted layperson from Central Park Baptist Church. Roy and Louise Johnson were loving and gifted Christians. My, how they served the Lord and his church! It would be impossible to measure the impact of their ministry in Birmingham Association Training Union work. There were others: Albert and Eva Woodin, Jane and Maurice Williams, Mr. and Mrs. Gilmer.

My praise is continuous. If I lived a hundred years, I would be singing praises to the Lord for the laity in Baptist churches for dimensions of spiritual growth and service to Kingdom causes.

I enrolled in Howard College in September 1942. Because my credentials for enrolling were incomplete, my classification was special student, pending completion of course deficiencies from high school. I removed the deficiencies from my record with hard work and additional courses. I was twenty-two years of age with a robust determination to equip myself to be a fit vessel as a minister, a workman approved by God.

A Scripture, 2 Timothy 2:15, was alive in my soul. "Do your best to present yourself approved, a workman who does not need to be ashamed and who correctly handles the Word of God." Fifty-two years later, I am endeavoring to become that minister approved by God. My testimony is "Praise to the Lord, the Almighty the King of creation! O my soul praise Him for he is [my] health and salvation . . ." (Joachim Neander, *Baptist Hymnal*, 14).

Three jobs and college consumed my time and energies. I worked in the snack bar at Howard, hopping tables during the lunch-break hours. My favorite customer was Dr. Lizette VanGelder, professor of English. She was an attractive, articulate, and resourceful professor in the fields of English and literature. I also worked in the men's furnishing department at Sears Roebuck and as a student pastor in two churches. All

"Old Main," Howard College campus in East Lake.

three jobs were necessary for paying my bills and for my education at Howard College. All my bills were paid in full upon graduation.

On the Howard College campus, Renfroe Hall became my home. There were two young men to a room. A common bath-restroom was located on each floor of the boys dorm. Meals were served in the dining room. Our stay in Renfroe Hall was short-lived because the Naval V-12 Training Program came to the campus in 1943 and the naval students took over the dorm. However, the civilian male students objected very vociferously, and emotional and irrational conduct took over the last night of our stay in Renfroe. I'm sure we had our student leaders, but it was as though every resident was involved in a rowdy all-night party. Our wonderful housemother, Polly Bookman (Mrs. George J.), had to turn disciplinarian for one night. She was great, but thoroughly disgusted with such conduct. I didn't blame her.

The dawning of the new day was our day of reckoning. We had not thought about accountability, but we got the message early from the president's office. My memory fails me on details, but I feared expulsion. We were not expelled; however, we had to satisfy the punitive damages. Major Davis was disappointed in us and that was enough for me. He chastised us, reminding us of our responsibilities as Christian young men. We had acted without reason or substance; we had upset our housemother. We pledged our cooperation and apologized for our inappropriate conduct. We also apologized to our dear housemother, Mrs. Bookman.

Recovering our good sense and realizing the reason for the Naval V-12 program, harmony and understanding returned to the student body and lasting friendships were developed between students in the Naval V-12 program and the civilian students. We realized the value of the Naval V-12 program, both financially and for student enrollment but more importantly to the lives of the students enrolled in the Naval Training Program and the defense of our country.

Alas, I had some personal guilt. A dear personal friend, who had all the bright promise a gifted youth could have, was killed in action, a gunner on a B-29. As I remember, the draft board classified me 4-D because I was a ministerial student and serving as a pastor at the time. I have some regret, especially when I think of my friend and brother, Charles Strother.

Following expulsion from Renfroe Hall to make room for the V-12 program, I rented a room from the Pates in the fall of 1942. Their home in East Lake became my home for three of my years at Howard College. East Lake was a prime residential area of the city—beautiful homes, a lovely park and lake, well-manicured lawns, beautiful flowers, gracious people, and strong churches. Children respected their fathers and mothers. Husband and wives married for life. Families were neighborly and caring.

The neighborhood churches of East Lake were Ruhama, Lakewood, Eighty-fifth Street, Lake Highland, and East Lake Methodist. They were places of strong fellowship. Mr. and Mrs. Pate and daughter Margaret lived next door to the Ruhama Baptist Church, which was the student church and a center of student activities for those who lived on campus at Howard College. The College Department at Ruhama occupied one floor of one wing and had strong department leaders and good teachers.

Dr. J. C. Stivender was pastor, an exceptionally gifted preacher with outstanding mannerisms. He stood tall in the pulpit, all six feet six plus of him. I thought his stature reached the summit, both physically and spiritually.

Ruhama Baptist Church taught me a lot about departmentalization of Sunday School and Training Union. I had not been a member of such a large church before. The pastor and his people demonstrated what the relationship should be in building up the body of Christ. Their tie of love was strong and binding.

In addition to hopping tables in the college lunchroom and working part-time at Sears during my freshman year, I had other doors for service open. Dr. A. Hamilton Reid, vice president of Howard College, befriended many preacher boys by getting them before churches and offering other mission opportunities. He opened three doors for me: student summer missionary, Cahaba Association; pastor at Mt. Vernon Baptist Church, Lookout Mountain; and member on the Board of Ministerial Education. Dr. Reid and Dr. James Chapman, professor and chair of the Religion Department at Howard, were responsible for my summer 1943 assignment in the Cahaba Association, Perry County. Both were generous in recommending me to serve the churches of the association as a student summer missionary. I accepted what was to be one of the best learning experiences of my life.

Excited at the prospects of beginning my summer work, I packed my one piece of luggage, the luxurious brown leather bag that my home church, Shawmut, had given me when I entered Howard College. Almost everything that I owned was packed in that bag. Since I could not yet afford a car, my transportation was the Greyhound bus from Birmingham to Marion, Alabama.

The Associational Missions Committee supported the Summer Missions program. They met with me in Marion at the Siloam Baptist Church. Dr. Harry Dickinson, pastor of Siloam and my supervisor for the summer, called the committee to prayer for their new summer missionary. I shall never forget the prayer room. We gathered around the historic table where the Board of Domestic Missions (now the North American Mission Board of the Southern Baptist Convention) was organized in 1845. Members of the Missions Committee affirmed me as student summer missionary and prayed for me as the work began. The inspiration and spiritual strength that came to me in the meeting were sources of hope and encouragement during the summer. The meeting had special significance for me, a special time of consecration as I laid my life on the altar of the Cahaba Association and the churches.

My assignment was multifaceted: coordinating Vacation Bible Schools, teaching the youth, speaking in the churches, visiting in the homes, and whatever else was needed. I was to be in a different church or churches each week. It was not unusual to spend the night and take each meal in a different home each night. The ladies in the churches provided my meals and frequently I was in one home for lunch and a different home for supper. I learned to appreciate food—all kinds of food.

The student summer missionary was supposed to build up the churches through strengthened leadership roles with youth, enrichment of youth, and providing the organization and leadership for the children's programs. The host pastor and/or his designee were to work with me in identifying my task. I was "all things to all the churches." The summer provided me with opportunities of inestimable value to my ministry. I learned to appreciate the laity in the churches by living in their homes, eating their food, sharing life's experiences. (What would our church be without the people in the pew?) I learned much about servant leadership, and I learned to appreciate convention leadership. And I learned the Vacation Bible School motto: "I will do the best I can with what I have for Jesus' sake today."

Exhausted, I returned, via Greyhound bus, to Birmingham at the end of the summer. Now, occasionally, I return to Marion. I attend church at Siloam Baptist Church where my son, David, and his family are most active. I always make a visit to the prayer room and stand for a few minutes in quietude and prayer, remembering some of the devoted women and men of God—Rev. Percy Bamberg and his gracious wife; Rev. Martin, pastor at Uniontown; and Jack Rogers, layman at Siloam, all full of love, counsel, and inspirations. Brother Bamberg touched the lives of the countless saints who attended his funeral service.

WOODLAWN BAPTIST CHURCH: 1943–1944

During my second year at Howard College, I had the unique opportunity to work with Dr. D. I. Purser, pastor of Woodlawn Baptist Church. Dr. Purser needed an assistant pastor to help with visiting and to give leadership to the RA boys. Two members of Woodlawn, Pauline Shepherd and Hazel Morrow, knew about me through the State Convention Training Union program and work, and my service as a student Summer Missionary in Cahaba Association. They recommended me to Dr. Purser, and he contacted Dr. James Chapman, professor and chairman of the Religious Department at Howard, enquiring about that Potts fellow.

I am glad it was Dr. Chapman who was approached for a recommendation. He talked with me about the challenges at Woodlawn Baptist Church, and with his encouragement I made an appointment by telephone to see Dr. Purser. I was responsive to this extraordinary man. He impressed me with his commitment to pastoral leadership and preaching. His conversation revealed his spiritual and Biblical depth, and I remember thinking he must be an exceptionally gifted pulpiteer—

he was. His demeanor was unusually informal, and his pulpit area was different, containing only two chairs and a small table. Dr. Purser did not preach from a lectern, feeling it was cumbersome for sermon delivery. Instead, he used the small table to lay his Bible on, leaving adequate space for freedom of movement and eye-to-eye contact with the congregation.

Dr. Purser was an astute sermon builder. I have not known a preacher to be as adequately prepared upon entering the pulpit. Possessing a well-disciplined mind, he considered preparation of the utmost importance in preaching the gospel effectively. To Dr. Purser, preparation for preaching meant

Dr. James Chapman.

that mind and heart must be attuned to the leadership and power of the Holy Spirit. Preparation came through prayer, study, and a draft of the sermon. His sermons related to the needs of the congregation. He knew people, and they knew he loved them. His preaching was dynamic, persuasive, and brief—he packed into twenty minutes what most preachers take thirty to forty minutes to say. When he stood to preach, the people were enthralled and inspired by his compelling sermons. From my perspective, the sermons were masterpieces.

Did the congregations come? Absolutely! I remember the church being packed. Dr. Purser left Woodlawn in 1946, accepting a call from Parker Memorial Baptist Church in Anniston, one of the strongest churches in Calhoun County and the State Convention. By that time, I had already left Woodlawn, having been called to Union Grove Baptist Church in 1944. He wanted me to go to Anniston with him, but the call to preparation was still before me.

Looking back, I value my time of service with Dr. Purser. As his assistant, I learned much from him about decorum, integrity, and the church. Woodlawn Baptist Church, with a church membership of approximately

2,100 in 1943, was one of the strongest and largest churches in Birmingham. It was not only noted for distinguished and dynamic preaching, it was strong in Christian education. Bible teaching in Sunday School was exceptionally life changing. Trained teachers and officers held weekly meetings. The Woman's Missionary Union (WMU) gave strong support to mission education, preaching, and giving. People attended Church Training.

In the 1940s, however, proposals for change were being made, proposals designed to increase outreach by introducing small classes and new methods of teaching, including discussion. This was the era when the Baptist Sunday School leadership in Nashville and Montgomery were determined to break up some classes by using the grading system. More classes and more departments meant more building space to accommodate more people. There were, however, some classes well entrenched in the lecture method. Also, large men's and women's classes prevailed, with the adult members taught by strong-minded and great-spirited women and men.

Dr. Frank Wood became pastor of Woodlawn Baptist Church following Dr. Purser. He was a big man in stature, with a very strong-willed personality. One of his goals was to grade the Sunday School and thus break into the structure of the large-membership classes. He was tenacious in his commitment and was consumed with his objective. Although he succeeded in his mission, the report is that the prize was costly to his health, and the lives of many church members were never the same.

The battle of grading the Sunday School was costly not only at Woodlawn but also in other churches across the Southern Baptist Convention. Many of the large-membership Sunday School classes had become mini-churches within the churches. The class might have a teacher who was not supportive of the pastor and/or the church program. These classes oftentimes had their own treasury and would decide how the money was spent and how much to give to support the church budget.

Occasionally, a large-membership class did not always encourage attendance at the worship service, resulting in a distant relationship with the rest of the congregation. Men and women would have church in the Sunday School. Many of these classes would have gifted speakers or lectures coupled with special programs; class members felt they had been in a worship service in Sunday School.

UNION GROVE BAPTIST CHURCH

Rev. Robert Woody recommended me to the Union Grove Baptist congregation. Robert, from Chambers County, graduated from Howard College in May 1944. He served the church during his college years, endearing himself to the people. He loved his people and provided quality pastoral leadership. He married Jean Yates, daughter of Dr. Kyle Yates, professor at Southern Baptist Theological Seminary.

Union Grove is located on beautiful Sand Mountain near Crossville, Alabama. The mountain is one of the most densely populated and productive agricultural regions in rural Alabama. Agriculture dominates the landscape; it does not take much land for family livelihood.

The Union Grove Baptist Church is a member of the DeKalb Baptist Association. The church has a good history of Christian education, providing capable teachers and officers. The deacons served faithfully in their responsibilities. The congregations believed the church facilities should be adequate with good maintenance. When I became pastor in 1944, the church reported a membership of 231. The pastor's salary was $616.00. However, there was more, so much more! Individuals and families showered me with love, meals, housing, and gifts. The years 1944, 1945, and 1946 were filled with exhilaration and usefulness. The church family was most gracious in providing for their pastor.

I spent many nights at the home of Roy and Mary Davis. They had a lovely teenage daughter, Bobbie. I would ride the Greyhound bus to Collinsville, transferring to the mountain run of a small bus company, getting off at the Davis home. Other families assisted with the logistics of my travel responsibilities. I shall never forget "red-eye gravy" and country ham at Mary's table on Saturday night.

The Lord blessed the ministry! There was a wonderful fellowship among the people, and they were most supportive of their "Howard College Preacher Boy."

The Union Grove Baptist Church celebrated their Centennial Anniversary August 21, 1994. The Church Planning Committee honored me with an invitation to preach the Centennial sermon. The service of celebration was followed with dinner and fellowship. You don't find better food, by any measurement, than you find on Sand Mountain. More importantly, I noted hallmarks of faithfulness, pathways of righteousness, and a lot of love prevalent today as it was fifty years ago, and a much larger congregation and enlarged facilities.

MT. VERNON BAPTIST CHURCH

Dr. A. Hamilton Reid attended the annual meeting of the DeKalb Baptist Association in 1945. After the morning's program, I visited with Dr. Reid during the lunch hour. "Earl," he said, "there is a church in need of a half-time pastor across the valley from Sand Mountain—the Mt. Vernon Baptist Church, which is located in the Lookout Mountain Association. Would you consider another half-time church?" My response was, "Yes!" I always considered Dr. Reid as the person who gave me my start in the Alabama Baptist Convention and pastoring churches.

Mt. Vernon Baptist Church was founded in 1874. It was a participating church in the association and maintained a strong BYPU. Today the church is one of eighteen in the Lookout Mountain Association. It has been blessed with faithful laypeople: the Joe Glaznor family, the John Cleland family, the Morgan Barclay family, the Masseys, and the Benefields. I remember the Benefield family. Let me tell you about one faithful steward, Mrs. Lexia Benefield, mother of Rev. T. A. Benefield. On August 18, 1994, Mrs. Benefield turned ninety-two years of age. She resides in a nursing home in Gadsden, Alabama.

The Every Member Canvas, a church stewardship emphasis, was launched in the 1930s. The purpose of the Every Member Canvas was for every church member to be visited by a canvassing team who would explain the biblical concept of giving in support of the church's programs. Each member was asked to sign a pledge card giving the amount pledged on a regular basis. Each member would receive a packet of envelopes.

The Canvas team visited Mrs. Benefield. She and her family, like multitudes of Baptists in Alabama, were poor. The depression of the late 1920s and early 1930s had wiped out their financial resources and jobs. A canvasser said he knew Mrs. Benefield would be unable to participate. Her response was her testimony of faithfulness to her church. She said, "I'm a member of Mt. Vernon Baptist Church, and I want to pledge ten cents per week." Mrs. Benefield received her packet of envelopes. She sold eggs and butter to the rolling store weekly so that this wonderful mother and faithful servant of the Lord could give her pledge. What did Jesus say about this kind of giving?

> Jesus sat down opposite the treasury and saw how the people put money into the treasury. And many who were rich put in much. Then one poor

widow came and put in two mites, which make a quodrans. So He called his disciples to Himself and said to them, "Assuredly I say to you that this poor widow has put in more than all those who have given to the treasury; for they all put in out of their abundance, but she out of her poverty put in all that she had, her whole livelihood." (Mark 12:41–44)

Great was the faithfulness of Mrs. Lexia Benefield. Amen!

LOUISE

My marriage to Arvie Louise Green on August 6, 1946, was unquestionably one of the most wonderful experiences of my life. Louise was not only a spouse, but a partner in ministry. Our marriage began that way and ended that way with her untimely death.

She was born on February 6, 1920, in Boligee, Alabama, located west of Eutaw in Greene County. Her parents were James Taylor Green ("Pa"), a farmer, and Pearl Hitt Green ("Ma"), who managed a hotel and dining room. At that time, there was considerable traffic into and through this small west Alabama town, especially by rail. Ma had an enviable reputation in the culinary arts. She knew how to prepare delectable meals, palatable to the tastes of young and old. It paid to be on time for meals at Ma Green's, because her tables were always crowded. Louise's parents were saints of God, active in the community and the Greensboro Baptist Church.

After Louise's graduation from Eutaw High School, her parents made a bold move from Boligee to Auburn, Alabama, to benefit the education of their two children, James Austin and Louise. Pa worked for Auburn University and Ma ran a boarding house, for which she always had a waiting list. Among the students, her cooking became known as "the best."

James, who excelled in soil conservation work for the state, married Leola Pierce of Eutaw, an exceptional teacher in math. Louise graduated from Alabama Polytechnic Institute (Auburn University) in 1939. During her college days, she was very active in the Baptist Student Union.

Davis C. Woolley was BSU director at Auburn at that time and was very influential in her life. She took an active part in student activities on campus and in Auburn First Baptist Church. After graduation, she taught social studies at Handley High School in Roanoke, Alabama.

Louise accepted the position of BSU director for Appalachian State College, Boone, North Carolina, from 1940 to 1941 where her leadership made quite an impact on the students and faculty. In 1941, she returned to her alma mater, Auburn University, as the first female BSU director at this great university, where she served for six years. There she excelled in her ministries to students and to the First Baptist Church family.

I met Louise at Sunday night fellowships at Auburn during 1941–1942. I really don't recall what precipitated the invitation to the youth from our church at Shawmut to attend youth fellowships at Auburn, but I do remember these delightful and enjoyable functions. Later, our paths crossed at state Training Union assemblies, which were held at Judson College. The Training Union assemblies were ideal not only for state assemblies but also for dating, and Louise and I began to date. The campus provided many places for developing relationships: the Judson parlors, the rose arbor, the lodge, and the spacious campus.

Earl and Louise pictured with wedding party.

Reception following the wedding.

While I was a student at Howard College (1942–1946), Louise and I corresponded. Occasionally, perhaps once a month, I would buy a Trailways bus ticket from Birmingham to Opelika where Louise would meet me or have someone pick me up.

Surely, the best experience that ever happened to me was on August 6, 1946, when I was privileged to stand at the altar of marriage with Arvie Louise Green. Dr. Hoyt Ayers officiated. The wedding was at First Baptist Church, Auburn, Alabama. I shall never forget this wonderful church. What fellowship and what joy prevailed in the congregation. Louise had endeared herself to the students and church family. She filled the pulpit when Pastor Edwards was ill or out of town. Her presence and messages, filled with hope and inspiration, were well received by the congregation. Being the person in Christ that she was and being in the role of BSU director, there was no problem with Louise speaking to the church family. Pastor Dr. Edwards was a faithful supporter of Louise's role of leadership in the church.

Ladies of the church decorated for the wedding. The altar was beautifully decorated with smilax, white gladiolus and other white flowers, and
a beautiful, white satin aisle cloth. Also, the ladies planned the reception,
which was the ultimate, lasting until 11:00 P.M.

Louise and I left the church for our honeymoon, which took us to
Louisville, Kentucky, where we did some house hunting prior to my
entering the Southern Baptist Theological Seminary in September.

I shall never forget my schedule for the ensuing days. Revivals and
Vacation Bible Schools in the summer of 1946 were scheduled in each of
the churches that I was pastoring at the time in Alabama—Union Grove
Baptist Church, Crossville (Sand Mountain), Mt. Vernon Baptist
Church, and Highberger (Lookout Mountain).

SEMINARY DAYS

To God be the glory for all the blessings bestowed upon Louise and
me. The Lord honored us with beautiful provisions from our parents,
churches, and friends. However, I still shudder when I recall the situation at the time of our departure from the train terminal in
Birmingham for Louisville. There I was with a gracious lady, my wife, all
the earthly possessions we owned (except many of the beautiful wedding
gifts), and $200 in my pocket. Neither of us had employment or the
promise of employment in Louisville, comforted only by the confidence
that he who called was sending and would provide. Louise's mother had
an enormous faith. She told us the Lord would provide, and he did. And
for all who shall find themselves in similar situations, he will!

Within the month, Louise was employed to teach social studies at
Atherton Girls High School in Louisville, where she taught for four years.
Needless to say, the Louisville school system was strong in academics, one
of the best in the country.

I transferred my work at Sears Roebuck in Birmingham to the Sears
Roebuck in Louisville in men's furnishings. That was a good experience.
It was a gift from the Lord, and it helped with our financial responsibilities. Later I was transferred to customer service, where the personnel
director offered me the director's job. I wanted to say yes. I enjoyed
responding to the needs of and exchanges with our customers, but it
would have put some restrictions on my seminary training and studies. I
did not accept the offer.

I remember one particular experience that Louise and I had while we were in Louisville. We shared a kitchen and living-room space with another couple, which wasn't always the ideal situation. One night, I was awakened by smoke coming under our bedroom door. I shouted to Louise to get up because the the house was on fire! As I followed the smoke down to the living room, I called the same instructions to the man with whom we shared the house. His wife was out of town at the time. His reply of "Let it burn" amazed me. Downstairs I discovered the source of the fire to be an overstuffed chair. Without thinking, I picked up the chair and threw it out the front door. I praise God that I was not seriously burned that day. Later, Louise and I realized that the fire was started by a cigarette that had been left in the chair by our housemate.

I was a student at Southern Baptist Theological Seminary from 1946 to 1949. Dr. Ellis Fuller was president. Dr. and Mrs. Fuller had come to Louisville from Atlanta, Georgia, where Dr. Fuller had pastored Atlanta First Baptist Church. Mrs. Fuller became a dear friend to my wife, Louise.

Dr. Fuller was an excellent preacher. His life in Christ was most meaningful to the students. I recall a reference he made in chapel. When he asked Mrs. Fuller to marry him, he said to her that she would have to take second place. "Christ has first place in my life. You will have second place." She accepted his proposal.

Our seminary experiences were enriching, inspiring, and challenging. We had some great men of God who were skilled in preaching and teaching the Holy Scriptures and other church-related courses. Henry Turlington was one of my favored seminary professors. His field was New Testament. Dr. Clyde Francisco was one of the outstanding men of the day in the field of Old Testament interpretation. Others were equally equipped and men of deep spiritual faith and practice: Dr. J. J. Owens, Dr. James Witherspoon, Dr. Morton, Dr. O. T. Binkley, and Dr. Edward A. McDowell. Dr. Gaines Dobbins was uniquely and remarkably equipped for his field of study and training in church administration. I continue to refer to *The Church Book* and Dr. Dobbins.

I remember many of the discussions led by this man, Dr. Dobbins, a prolific writer as well as a professor of deep faith, love for the church, and commitment to equipping preacher boys. I mention one. The class discussion focused on conflicts within the church—the causes, facilitating, and resolving of conflicts regarding church polity and practice.

An Alabama class at Southern Seminary standing in front of Mullins Hall in the late 1940s.

Following a lengthy discussion, Dr. Dobbins made this statement, "Well, young gentlemen, you need to remember there will be some church fusses that will not be resolved until there are some first-class funerals." There was laughter.

The student body, members of the faculty, and president were men and women of deep faith in the Lord. We had an enriching community of faith on campus. The campus, known as "the Beeches" because of the magnificent beech trees which dominated its landscape, was special— for scholarship, fellowship, churchmanship, discipleship, and Lordship prevailed there in the 1940s.

My dear wife, Louise, was very active in the campus organization for a minister's wife, and she developed lasting friendships. Two of the most meaningful were her friendships with Mrs. Ellis Fuller, wife of the president, and Mrs. Gaines Dobbins, wife of the renowned professor in church administration. They were special ladies to Louise.

The trustees were trustworthy men and women of deep faith in the Lord, the church, the Holy Scripture, and the Southern Baptist

Convention. The seminary grew numerically, academically, and spiritually, and Southern Baptists praised God for their flagship seminary. Faculty members excelled in teaching the Holy Scriptures, unquestionably the Word of God. I was proud! Alas, many of those cardinal principles of faith and practice have passed.

RETURN TO THE PULPIT, YOUNGER'S CREEK

A call to pastor came as I began my second year at the seminary in Louisville, Kentucky, for Younger's Creek Baptist Church, one of the older churches in the Elizabethtown-Boston communities. Our ministry was blessed at Younger's Creek. The late Dr. T. L. Holcomb had pastored this church when he was a student at Southern. Dr. Holcomb served as executive secretary-treasurer of the Baptist Sunday School Board until June 1, 1953, and then was elected executive secretary-treasurer of the Southern Baptist Foundation in 1953.

At this time I bought my first car, a 1941 Packard business coupe. It had class! It was an added blessing to have transportation, enabling us to expand our pastoral ministry. However, we continued to ride the city transportation system in Louisville.

Younger's Creek was good to us and for us. This congregation showered us with love. The church compensated us for our ministry. The people, especially the ladies, would give us food on Sunday that would feed us for the week. The Baptist polity of Southern Baptist churches in Alabama worked the same and as well in Southern Baptist churches in Kentucky.

I learned Biblical principles about pastoral leadership: Be pleasing to the Lord as a servant leader; do more than is expected of you; see each person as someone special; be trustworthy. I also learned a lot about Kentucky people from my Younger's Creek experience. I helped the men folks in their chores. We spent a lot of time on the church field in the summer. Louise and I loved the people and they loved us.

Jim and Dora Douglas were special friends. Louise and I were frequent guests in their home when we had long events and pastoral responsibilities. Jim was a Kentucky farmer; that meant he grew tobacco. When it was time to cultivate his tobacco. I offered to help, although I had never been in a tobacco field.

He taught me a lot about growing and harvesting tobacco—about the pruning process, where the shoots are snipped away from the main stalk, and about the worming process. You probably have seen those big, fat, long, green worms with a horn. They had to be pulled from the tobacco and killed by stepping or stomping on them, which was awful. When the tobacco reached the proper maturing stage, it was cut and hauled by wagon and hung, stalk by stalk, in the tobacco barn for maturation, a process requiring considerable attention by the grower. Then it was ready to market and sell at auction. Of course, for Jim and me this was before we knew the health hazard of tobacco. I think, though, that we had always known smoking could not be conducive to good health.

I graduated from Southern Baptist Theological Seminary in May 1949. Louise and I decided to move to the church community near Elizabethtown, Kentucky. The Younger's Creek family was glad. We moved into a new bungalow near the intersection of Tunnelhill Road and Bardstown Road, which was ideal for us. Louise took joy in moving into new housing with every move we made the rest of our married life. How blessed we were!

I had applied for a county system teaching assignment at Rineyville High School. After we decided to move to the church community, I was accepted to begin teaching in September of 1949 and became the home room teacher for grade eleven. The students were quality youth, presenting me with a great challenge. My responsibilities were three-fold: teaching English/literature, supervising the library, and producing a stage play. I approached the teaching assignment with some apprehension, but I developed a special relationship with my students. I also enjoyed the third phase of my assignment: practicing with the students for the stage production. The play was a big hit. We gave three performances, and each was a sellout. It was difficult to break away from the students in the spring of 1950. They gave me a big going-away party and presented me with a pair of lovely table lamps, which are still in use in my house after forty-five years.

The ministry at Younger's Creek went very well. However, we were Alabama born and reared. We appreciated our home state and our families, and many, many of our friends were in Alabama. Louise and I wanted to go home. However, we had to sever ties and leave behind friends and colleagues in ministry that we seldom would see. Louise and I would miss the places and people in Kentucky, but the Lord had work for us back home in Alabama, at McElwain Baptist Church.

CHAPTER 3

McElwain Baptist Church

McELWAIN BAPTIST CHURCH, LOCATED ON MONTEVALLO Road over the mountain from Birmingham's Southside, was built in 1895 in a rural community surrounded by pastures, farms, and beautiful country homes. The first church was a small, wood-frame building located on property where the W. B. Baker Memorial Chapel is now located. The community was known as the McElwain community, named after W. S. McElwain, who had come to Birmingham from Chattanooga, Tennessee, to establish the first ore mill in the Southeast. In 1864, Mr. McElwain, who was determined to provide iron to the Confederacy, put into operation a stone furnace in the woods along Shades Creek. The first cannon cast for the Confederate government was cast in the Irondale furnace. After the furnaces were destroyed by Wilson's raiders, McElwain went north where he had contacts and raised funding to rebuild the furnaces. In 1866, the furnace was in full operation, the only furnace operating in the state. The Irondale furnace reached its high point with the Confederacy; now it is but a memory, but the name McElwain has endured to the present.

A migration of residents from the Northside, West End, and Southside areas of Birmingham was underway by the mid-twentieth century. In 1949–1950, new residential developments of single-unit houses were under construction in Crestline. There was a verbal war between the cities of Mountain Brook and Birmingham pursuant to incorporation of the area, ending with some trade-offs between the two cities. A line was drawn—one section was taken in by Mountain Brook and another section was taken in by Birmingham. The McElwain community became part of Birmingham.

The W. B. Baker (a charter member) family moved over the mountain from Birmingham's Southside where senior Mr. Baker, his wife, and children were members at Southside Baptist Church. Here, they established a dairy farm, which later functioned as a processing plant. The Bakers were charter members of McElwain Baptist Church in 1895 and were still very active in 1950.

Dr. Vernon E. Davison, a professor of New Testament in the Department of Religion at Howard College, became interim pastor of McElwain Baptist Church in 1949. He knew me from classes at Howard College and my Training Union work in Alabama. Dr. Davison said to me, "Earl, the church needs a pastor who, one, has college and seminary training; two, is family oriented; three, can get along with people; four, can keep his hands off of women; and, five, can give leadership in the transition from a small-membership church in a rural community to a fast growing church in the suburbs." He suggested my name to the Pulpit Committee chaired by Mr. Ed Baker, son of W. B. Baker. Mr. Baker contacted me, inviting me to come visit the church and preach.

The door opened to McElwain when the congregation extended a call. I felt the leadership of the Holy Spirit and accepted the call without reservation and with no timetable for longevity. There was contentment and peace in my heart and Louise's. We had labored faithfully and with full measure through our seminary pastoral experiences.

Although I had teaching responsibilities as well as a congregation in Kentucky, my school superintendent at Rineyville School in Kentucky was willing to release me from my contract at an early date. I became pastor of McElwain Baptist Church on April 15, 1950. We had come home.

Little did I realize I would spend the next twenty years of my life with my family at McElwain. My, how the Lord blessed his church and people: "Great things He taught us, Great things he did."

I knew McElwain Baptist Church had a good foundation in the Scriptures and Baptist polity, a thoroughgoing Southern Baptist mission program, and an openness to the emerging new church field. Brother

Ed Baker, a good man full of faith, was superintendent of the Sunday School. He served for thirty-eight continuous years as Sunday School superintendent, always maintaining his vision for reaching people, his enthusiasm, and his commitment to the teaching of the Holy Scriptures. Sunday School attendance was on an escalating scale—upward (and continued so for twenty years!). The small congregation had a mind-set and heartbeat for the people—all the people. Newcomers were entering our community almost weekly, and visitors were present every Sunday, but neither the pastor nor the people viewed this as undesirable. Members of the congregation who had been there for decades welcomed new people. There was room for them in this extraordinary family of faith.

"We never did it that way!" became a reference that provoked laughter. The church family got so caught up in the mission of the church that several years would pass before there would be a cessation of buying land, planning and building new buildings, raising levels of giving—first by giving ourselves—and reaching more and more people.

Louise was pregnant with our first child when we moved to Birmingham in April. Our son was born July 1, 1950, at the South Highland Infirmary. He was given the name David Earl Potts and has borne the name quite well. Three years later, April 26, 1953, our daughter, Elizabeth Louise Potts, was born at the same hospital, during the Training Union hour, with the same doctor, Dr. Bateson, attending Louise at birthing.

Louise and I loved our two children. We knew they were special gifts of the Lord. We endeavored to be a good family by precept and example, with great support and encouragement from the McElwain Church family. The church shared our interest in and emphasis on children. Children's activities, in terms of leadership, resources, and facilities, were given priority.

In fact, I always thought the McElwain Community and Church were good places to rear children. There were community activities, home style, where dads and children would gather in "the pasture" for baseball. Everyone got to play. The games were primarily for dads and sons, but the girls could play as well. We usually had a crowd, which meant that there were always substitutes available. The front lawn at the pastorium became the place for football where David and all his friends would gather to play. I didn't have much of a lawn, but the boys had great fun.

Libby and her friends enjoyed playing with their dolls in the playhouse.

During all this play, Louise's watchful eyes were always present, but the children always had room for using their imaginations in creating make-believe play and in designing their own toys. I remember stick horse riding, outdoor swings, the playhouse, homemade ice cream, cookies and Kool-aid. Laddie, our beautiful collie, was present for many of these activities. He was most protective of the children when they were playing outside, keeping them out of the street while playing with them.

I was very proud of my family. I had a wonderful wife and terrific children whom I enjoyed. Helping David with the basics of baseball and football was one of my favorite activities. Libby was Daddy's "little girl." She especially enjoyed crawling in bed with Dad and Mom.

Louise and I always emphasized family celebrations. These joyous days revolved around birthdays and holidays: New Year's Day, the Fourth of July, Thanksgiving, and Christmas. Birthdays were always big events with our family. Festive meals, gifts, and expressions of love were showered upon the honoree. Christmas celebrations were special, attended by children, parents, and grandparents. Gifts were exchanged with much anticipation, excitement and expectation. Alas, we miss those gatherings.

Libby and David Potts.

David and Libby.

David and Libby.

David, Earl, Libby, and Louise.

Emphasis on these special days was a tradition started by my parents and Louise's parents. Christmas dinner and Christmas trees at Ma and Pa Green's were beautifully meaningful. Also, I remember delicious Christmas brunches with my parents. Sister Fannie and her husband, Bob, prepared these special times, which to our family were touches of heaven on earth.

We had time for family vacations. Usually my family of four would plan for a week away. We always enjoyed planning for these times together. We had great fun in the mountains of North Carolina and Tennessee and at Gulf Shores. These were times of celebration of family and renewals in the Lord and with each other.

I am glad our son and daughter grew up in a loving church family, lived in a developing community, and attended and graduated from a good school system, the McElwain Elementary and Junior High Schools and Ramsay High School. Furthermore, I am thankful our children enrolled in Samford University (Howard College), where both graduated from this outstanding Baptist school.

The growth of McElwain Baptist Church in the early 1950s had the attention of the pastor and deacons. Church growth discussions—numerical, structural, and spiritual—dominated the agendas for deacon meetings, church business meetings, and budgeting.

McElwain Baptist Church, 1950.

Building expansion is one measurement of church growth. Ah, we sought divine wisdom and spiritual empowerment for the challenges facing a growing congregation. I knew most of the young adult couples coming into the McElwain Baptist fellowship were becoming more heavily financially obligated—with payments on housing, furnishings, and automobiles. Many couples were beginning their families, adding more financial obligations to already tight budgets. Louise and I could empathize with these young adults. We were in the same boat, though we had no mortgage payments.

However, there was another phenomenon present in the congregation: men and women maturing in their faith and practice who loved the Lord and the church and were committed to leadership in the church family and to giving. These young adults were rising leaders in the work places. They were giving of themselves first of all, and of their resources, in all areas of church growth and expansion. The ministry of stewardship became more prominent.

Expansion of facilities began in 1952 with the construction of a two-story educational building (a small four-room annex to the church building had been built before I became pastor). The church was given permission to use the McElwain School facilities on Sunday morning for adult classes. The nursery was moved into a seven-room residence next door to the church.

Meanwhile, a long-range Church Building Committee was appointed to address long-range and short-range needs. The committee submitted the report to the church in 1954. The church asked the committee to revise the plans, especially in reference to land areas. The church was praying! The church family was excited! Church services and meetings were exhilarating! Church membership expanded!

The year 1955 was pivotal for McElwain Baptist Church for two reasons. First, Mrs. W. B. Baker, affectionally called Mother Baker, and the only living charter member of the McElwain Baptist Church (1895), gave five acres of land for church expansion. This was prime property located directly across Montevallo Road from the church. Second, the church approved the long-range plan, drafted by the long-range planning committee and the architectural firm, Davis, Speake and Thrasher, that would accommodate 1,200 in Sunday School upon completion. The Church Architectural Department of the Baptist Sunday School Board, Nashville, Tennessee, provided consultants.

The first phase of the new plan was completed in 1957. There were two units built—the church office suites and the nursery building, and the temporary auditorium-fellowship hall. Educational space was provided for two Adult Departments. A cornerstone was laid at the time of dedication.

Two additional educational units and the 1,200 seat auditorium were completed and in use by 1967. These facilities were essential for church growth. Additional property and three additional residences were purchased adjacent to the new worship center and nursery building.

The church was engaged in buying additional land and/or building a new building every two years from 1953 through 1970. These were monumental tasks for the church family. The church grew!

Why did the church grow? There is a reference in the Holy Scriptures that puts in focus the answer for me—Ephesians, chapter 4. The passage is an exhortation to unity:

> . . . walk worthy of the vocation where you are called, with all lowliness and meekness, with long-suffering, forbearing one another in love; endeavoring to keep the unity of the spirit, in the bond of peace. There is one body, and one hope of your calling; one Lord, one faith, one baptism, one God, and Father of all. . . .

Listen to this:

> . . . but unto every one of us is given grace according to the measure of
> the gift of Christ . . . and . . . gave some pastors and teachers . . . for the
> perfecting of the saints, for the work of ministry, for the edifying of the
> body of Christ . . .

Amen! Amen! What a tremendous passage of Scripture that sets in focus
my task as pastoral leader. My task was people-centered! All the necessary components were present for building the church. We were
endeavoring to bring all elements under the lordship of Jesus Christ.

I have identified the building components already. Some people may
believe buildings are not essential to building the church. I believe
adequate facilities are not only desirable but needed to provide a gathering place for the church family.

I worked from the premise of prayer and divine leadership empowerment in leading the church family to pray. We took the time over a period

of months to pray for the Lord's
revelation. "Lord, what would you
have this people first of all 'to be'
and secondly what would you have
the church 'to do' in this community?" The fruits of praying for
divine direction, studying the Holy
Scriptures, engaging a long-range
planning committee, and reaching
people for Christ were priorities for
the church family. The new worship
center brought the people closer to
God and to one another as family.
We moved from two morning
services to one unified worship
service.

Leadership training became a
priority with the church. (It had to
be then, and it has to be now.) I
knew the task would require
persons who were already trained
to do the work of training the laity,

and we enlisted those who were equipped. There was a compelling program of leadership training being fostered by the Sunday School Department of the State Board of Missions. So we asked Louise Potts, Kellar Dick, and Glendean Swearingen to spend a week at Shocco Springs. They were trained, returned to the church all fired up, and did a fabulous planning job on the structure for the Leadership Training Department. The classes were challenging and required a commitment to attend on Sunday mornings, Sunday nights, and Wednesday nights for nine months. Our skilled and enthusiastic teachers were Bible scholars who offered a program that was biblically based and doctrinally sound, that emphasized methodology and Baptist polity. At the conclusion of the course, each graduate was presented a document of certification.

I would rank this commitment of the church to leadership training a priority. As a result, the church always had church leaders equipped for vacancies in the ever-enlarging organization. This was one of the many workable and effective components in building the body of Christ taught to me by my seminary professor, Dr. Gaines Dobbins.

I believe the church must make a decisive resolution regarding the ministry of visitation and soul-winning. The ministry of visitation was discussed in church administration class at seminary in 1944–1945 with Dr. Dobbins leading the students. Several plans were mentioned: Monday night visitation, telephoning, hand-written communication, remembering special occasions and special needs, and meaningful worship. Dr. Dobbins suggested that the plan be based on the needs of people. His reference to need got my attention. I applied this approach in a modified way in my seminary pastorate. I thought trying it in smaller congregations would help me and it did. I pursued the plan at McElwain. Simply stated, it is whenever-whomever-wherever a need is identified (examples: sickness, hospitalization, marriage, graduation, birthday, anniversary, new job, death), there is need for visitation/contact ministry from the church family.

Hospital visiting became one of my most effective and appreciated ministries among the church family. I would always visit my parishioner patient the day of surgery before the preoperative process began. Many times I was at the hospital from 4:30 A.M. onward. We would have a Scripture reading, pastoral thought, and prayer. Seldom did I sit with the family through surgery, but I assured the patient and family I would check on them later, either by phone or personal visit. No member of the congregation, to my knowledge, was critical of my practice of hospital visitation. Most people experience illness at some time in life, and there is a spiritual and emotional need when it occurs.

I have referred to four components in building the church: facilities, leadership training, the ministry of visitation/reconciliation, and the ministry of stewardship development. The children's ministry is another component. The magnitude for this ministry varies. The ministry to children is urgent where there is a large number of young adult families. This was true at McElwain.

Here, I have additional high praise for my wife, Louise. Children were her first love. She believed every child should have good beginnings in childhood, that the foundations for life were established in preschool years. Every child, she said, needs lots of hugs, much attention, and training through the early years of life. "Train up a child in the way the child should go, and when he is old he will not depart from it" (Prov. 22:6).

McElwain Baptist Church built a strong base for viable ministry to preschoolers and their families. Its childhood-education ministry began in 1954 with care, Christian principles, an excellent curriculum/discipline, and imminently qualified teachers. John and Frances Carter of the Department of Education at Howard College and Louise were instrumental in planning and launching the preschool/kindergarten workshops at Samford in the 1950s. These workshops were available each summer, attracting teachers from all over Alabama and from other states. The McElwain kindergarten was used as one of the models for the workshop each year.

The music ministry was another essential component of the growth of the church. McElwain Baptist Church has a rich heritage of good music, with many talented people contributing to the program. A number of students from Samford University—Billie Jean King, Charles Woods, Dick Barrett, and Perry Scott—served in the music ministry. John and Sarah Preston came to McElwain from Southwestern Baptist Seminary.

In 1967, Gene and Faye Black came to direct the music and remained for many years. Dr. Black was professor of music at Samford University and dean of the Music School. The A Cappella Choir, one of the best college choirs in the nation, has been under his direction for many years. Faye Hamilton Black, an accomplished pianist who played for some of the most renowned artists in the country, was an able assistant to her husband. The people loved both of them.

McElwain's worship services were enhanced with good music, lifting the hearts and minds of the people to God in praise and wonderment. I appreciated those who led our music; we were blessed with the best. We were also blessed with good accompanists, who are essential to worship. Mrs. Edna Reynolds Watkins was an excellent organist-pianist for forty years. "Miss Edna," as she was affectionately called, was a graduate of Howard College and Southwestern Baptist Theological Seminary, where Dr. Isaac Reynolds, her uncle, was head of the Music Department. Dr. William Reynolds, her cousin, was head of the Music Department of the Baptist Sunday School Board. Miss Edna died on June 26, 1996. Her funeral service, conducted at McElwain Baptist Church, and the music were a worthy tribute to this gracious and loving lady.

The seventh phase of expansion at McElwain Baptist Church, the new worship center, was completed in the spring, with the bronze marker in the foyer identifying the historic year, "1967 A.D." That is all it has on it, but that is enough! The theme for the dedication service of the center expressed clearly the feelings of the church family: "Built to the glory of God, and the spiritual enrichment of mankind."

In 1970, I had been at McElwain for twenty years. During that year I invited Dr. Bagley to be our guest for lunch and to visit the new pastorium, which had been constructed under the direction of Fred Watkins, an exceptional craftsman. Every detail had to be right, or Fred would rework it until it was right in his mind. The resulting house was more than adequate in every detail. In fact, this was the second house he had built for the Potts family. We had outgrown the first one at 1220 Dunston Avenue, but it was not to be so with the second house. It was a lovely two-level structure with 5,500 square feet. I had desired a house with a large area in which groups could be accommodated, especially friends and church groups, and this house was great for both family living and accommodating groups, especially youth.

This was the house I wanted Dr. Bagley to see. It was on the tour of the house that Dr. Bagley asked me the question, "Earl, would you be interested in coming to Montgomery?" I didn't think so! There were so many reasons why I wasn't interested in going to Montgomery. McElwain Church was a wonderful family of faith. There was a lot of love in the fellowship, and after twenty years of ministry, I knew the people.

Despite my unwillingness to leave my beloved McElwain congregation, Dr. Bagley's question did spark a question in my mind as to how long a pastor should stay in a pastorate. Surely, above all else, the response to this question must emerge from fervent, sincere prayer. A timetable cannot be established by the pastor or the church, especially in Southern Baptist churches.

Dr. Gaines Dobbins, in Southern Seminary classes, had indicated that the first pastorate after graduating from seminary should be for five years, the second for six to ten years, the third for ten to twenty years, and the fourth up to retirement. I had some questions about this time sequence, but in retrospect it is a good procedure because the response from the congregation engages the pastor and church leadership, especially deacons, in an experience of review, evaluation, and decision.

My first seven years at McElwain passed quickly and without the thought of moving entering my mind. I think we were so caught up with the congregation building the church that there was no thought of my work being finished so early. The seven years had been demanding. Pastoring is hard, rigorous work! I rejoice in Christ who gave me no encouragement to leave. Little did I realize the consequence of my decision would be another thirteen years of productive ministry at McElwain for a total of twenty years. However, the decision was of the Lord.

So, Dr. Bagley's question was appropriate for me to consider prayerfully. His question was, "Would you consider coming to the Convention Office in Montgomery?" The conclusion of the matter is that the door opened and I entered. The decision process was short and decisive. Again, I had peace in my heart and mind about the decision.

Dr. Eljee Bentley said, ". . . the church celebrated twenty years of pastoral leadership in June 1970 and in September Potts was gone!" That is true. Let me be candid—my pastoral ministry at McElwain Baptist Church was a good experience for my family, an experience for which I shall ever be grateful both for me as pastor of a great people and for my wonderful family. There is a niche in my life filled to overflowing in thanksgiving for the congregation of that church.

Yet, I owed a thoughtful and prayerful evaluation process to the congregation. There were the "mountaintop" experiences inspiring us outward and upward in this pastor/people relationship. There were the times when we were in the valley, when fewer people were uniting with the church, when attendance had leveled for periods of time, with the completed building cycle. Perhaps there were other considerations. My preaching, for example. The people had affirmed my preaching! They loved and supported me, their pastor, and my family and other staff

McElwain Baptist Church Worship Center, 1997.

ministers and their families, a love they demonstrated. Never once was there an overture from them to suggest that it was time for the me to go. Nevertheless, I acted on my belief that the church family needed a preaching ministry that would minister to their spiritual needs, that would nurture the believers into further depth and growth, and would "feed my sheep" as Jesus said in John.

I realize this aspect of my chronicle is confessional, which has some pain to it. But I feel I need to be confessional at this point. I need to be confessional for those young pastoral leaders who will come after me. I don't feel that I was this way, but we preachers can become complacent. We can rationalize our inner thoughts and convictions. We can become passive. We can blame others, especially the people, if things are not going well. For ministers in the church and in church families, a new beginning is appropriate.

I believed it to be a junction in life and in my ministry for a new beginning. The Lord had opened a door, and I thought it right for me to enter the door for review and evaluation by Dr. Bagley and the appropriate committees of the State Mission Board. However, our son, David, was a student at Samford University, and our daughter, Libby, was a senior at Ramsay High School, Southside, Birmingham. Transferring to another school system in a new community created much anxiety and concern, but I knew that going to Montgomery was the right decision despite the difficulties.

Directing Alabama Baptists' Church Ministries Division

DR. CHARLES CARTER, PASTOR OF THE SHADES MOUNTAIN Baptist Church, was a member of the Administration Committee and the Baptist State Executive Board in 1970. He was chairman of the Personnel Committee bringing the recommendation on July 31, 1970, that Earl Potts be elected as director of Church Ministries Division to fill the vacancy left by the retirement of Dr. Claude T. Ammerman. Charles Martin, pastor of Parker Memorial Baptist Church, seconded the motion. The salary was $13,298, as classification per group seven. The benefits included a housing allowance, annuity, and insurance.

I knew that Claude Ammerman was a gifted leader, and I soon found out that he was known as the staff poet. I must say he always had the poem for the occasion. Dr. Ammerman served as the first secretary to head the newly established Church Ministers and Retirement Department beginning on December 7, 1958. He was a dear friend from the time of his pastorate at First Baptist Church of Troy, Alabama. I was in his church for a Church Training week of study and fellowship with him and Mrs. Ammerman.

Dr. and Mrs. (Annette) J. O. Colley, life-long residents of Troy, are active members of First Baptist Church. I asked Dr. Colley what it was about Dr. Ammerman that kept him at First Baptist of Troy for nineteen years as pastor. Dr. Colley said, "Dr. Ammerman was a good man, good preacher, good pastor, and a faithful friend to the Alabama

Baptist Children's Home. He always had a calming disposition and lived life as it came." Members of the Colley family of Troy have maintained active participation in leadership roles and financial support of the Alabama Baptist Children's Home for decades. Mrs. Annette Colley, a capable and devoted leader, served as chairperson of the board of directors.

Dr. Ammerman was a native of Kentucky, a graduate of Georgetown College, and a proud theology degree graduate of Southern Baptist Theological Seminary. He was convinced of the importance of the annuity program of Southern Baptists and worked diligently to increase the number of pastors and churches who participated in the program. There were 622 churches and 487 pastors in the ministers' plans from Alabama in 1958. When he retired in 1961, there were 900 churches and 960 pastors and ministers of music.

I had some big shoes to fill succeeding Dr. Ammerman. I think I never quite did fill them, but I was honored to follow this exceptionally disciplined man. I was fortunate to have him as a friend. He was a rare human being.

How did the Potts family feel about moving? We were leaving behind so much in the church, community, and the Birmingham Baptist Association. Our roots were deeply embedded in the Birmingham community, the public school system, the religious community, and the churches, especially McElwain Baptist Church.

The transition from Birmingham to Montgomery was not terribly hard on Louise and me. However, this was not true with the children, especially Libby. She was a senior in high school, a difficult time to consider a change of location, and there was no way she could see the wisdom of our decision to move. I remember the conversation Libby had with Dr. George Bagley. She and Louise were house hunting in Montgomery when they stopped by the Baptist Building. Libby walked into Dr. Bagley's office. Dr. Bagley asked Libby how she felt about moving to Montgomery and began to tell her what a good place it was to live. Well, Dr. Bagley should not have said that, because Libby let her feelings be known without reservations. It was not good, but Dr. Bagley was still most charitable.

Libby ended up returning to Birmingham for her last semester of high school, graduating from Ramsay High School in 1971, where David had graduated in 1969. Dr. and Mrs. Black let Libby live in their house for her last semester in high school. Gene and Faye were most gracious in making this possible for Libby.

Daughter Elizabeth (Libby) Louise Potts is a special lady to me. She was daddy's little girl, and I endeavored to give her special attention when she was a child. Following in her mother's footsteps, she chose early-childhood development as her major area of study at Samford University, where she graduated with her B.S. degree in 1975. She taught kindergarten in the Birmingham school system from 1975 to 1977, then enrolled at Southern Baptist Theological Seminary, receiving her M.R.E. in 1979. Professors significant in her pilgrimage at the seminary were Dr. Allen Graves, Dr. Frank Stagg, Dr. Clyde Francisco, Dr. Bill Leonard, and Dr. Walter Shurden.

Libby returned to Alabama in 1979, working in the child-development ministry at Woodlawn Baptist Church in Birmingham for a year. In 1980, she was offered the position of staff member at Spring Hill Baptist Church, Mobile, where she worked with singles, senior adults, and college students. She remained there for four and a half years, until 1984. She then became interim campus minister at the University of South Alabama for a year, where students rallied to her leadership, blessing her life as she gave of herself to the students.

The year 1985 was a pivotal year for Libby. She accepted leadership responsibility as associate director with the Christian Life Commission of the Baptist General Convention of Texas. Dr. William Pinson was her executive director. Dr. Phil Strickland was director of the Christian Life Commission. Her colleagues and associates were fine people in their commitments and gifted leadership. Libby enjoyed working with singles and senior adults in the churches and associations across the Baptist General Convention of Texas. Her time there was the best of times for her.

Back to our move: God was good, and we did adjust to our new home. Now, twenty-seven years later, we completely enjoy living in Montgomery. But the transition to Montgomery was bathed in prayer, patience, and perseverance. We acknowledged that moving would deprive us of several things of great importance: experiencing our daughter's senior year in high school in Birmingham, investing our lives in McElwain Baptist Church, and cutting off our deep roots in Birmingham's civic, governmental, and religious communities. Severing spiritual and emotional ties was difficult, but I had made a commitment to begin working with the Convention Office in September 1970.

The McElwain Church had been most generous in housing, providing the family with three different houses during our twenty years at

McElwain. Graciously it permitted us to stay in the pastorium until we could get housing worked out in Montgomery. It took a lot of work, energy, prayer, and money. My savings were meager. From the time that Louise and I married, our family had lived in a pastorium. We never owned a house and therefore had no equity. This is one good reason for the church to consider providing a housing allowance to the members of the church staff. The pastor and other staff members need to build equity for future housing, especially in retirement.

The transition from the pastorate to the office in Montgomery was a huge challenge for me at home, in the community, and in the work place. There were days of frustration in getting reestablished and redirected— it was so different from the pastorate. I thought, then, that the most strategic ministry was in the local church. I still believed that when I retired twenty years later from the State Board of Missions.

Dr. and Mrs. Bagley were supportive and encouraging, not only in my new assignment as new employee, but in providing bed and breakfast! They shared their beautiful new home with me until I could get accustomed to Montgomery and secure living accommodations. They would not accept any monetary consideration. I must say that the short period of time with them was very much like being home. They had not been in their new home very long, and there was work to be done, especially on the new lawn. Dr. Bagley wanted to get it established before the winter rains. I volunteered to help him in the afternoon after work hours, and we made good progress. In fact, we agreed we made a good team, a relationship that I was to appreciate for fifteen subsequent years. We believed if our lives could be shaped into a team doing lawn work, we could become a team in State Board of Missions work. And we did!

The experiences of sharing such gracious hospitality in the home of George and Helen Bagley for a few weeks were memorable. Dr. Bagley, Helen, and I developed a kindredness in teamship, fellowship, and working relationship. Mrs. Bagley was most appreciative of my efforts assisting in the work and life of Dr. Bagley. We all forged a lasting friendship that, though later tested and challenged, endured.

These were to become in many respects the best and the worst of years—the best in work performance, in collaborators, in work supervision, and in postretirement enjoyment. Ah, by the way, I knew the employee, that's me, had much to learn about Alabama Baptists and the work of the Alabama Baptist State Convention. After years of service and ministry with the convention, Dr. Bagley had a deep sense of owner-ship in the convention. We handled the situation rather well, though I know it was difficult for him.

Louise and I made serious attempts to buy a house, but we were unable to consummate a contract. We were praying, trusting, and waiting. After several weeks, I leased an apartment in one of the transi-tional communities in Montgomery. The rent was reasonable and the furnishings acceptable. I learned much about mortgages during these weeks of living in rented properties.

It was October and housing was on my mind and heart. The children and Louise were in Birmingham. One day, glad tidings came from a realtor in Montgomery. He was indeed a messenger from the Lord, Ollie Emfinger. He said to Louise and me, "I have a lot in Carriage Hills. I will sell you the lot. I will build you a house, and I will help get you a loan." We were somewhat ecstatic to put it mildly, believing this was the proposition we had been searching for. ". . . Again I say wait on the Lord" (Ps. 27:14b).

Emfinger was a board member of the Federal Savings and Loan Association office in Montgomery, where we ended up getting the loan to build and buy our house. One of the five banks in Montgomery had turned us down for a loan, the worst financial blow I had ever had. In fact, it made me mad. It was a bad judgement call by the CEO of that bank. The funding was approved by Federal Savings, and I never missed a payment. Thanks be to God and Alabama Baptists!

Some of the laymen from McElwain Church helped me with the down payment. I shall forever be grateful to Robert Freeman, Fred Watkins, Kellar Dick, Bob Mallory, and Ed Baker, and the congregation of McElwain Baptist Church for their generous provisions to me and my family.

The house foundation was laid in late October 1970. Mr. Emfinger had our house ready for the family to move into during the last week in December. Christmas 1970 was an unforgettable week. Try to imagine putting furnishings and all things from a 5,500 square-foot pastorium into a 2,000 square-foot house. After twenty-one years in Birmingham, the Potts family, including Laddie, our beautiful and aged collie, moved to Montgomery. Not only was our address changing, but our world was in revolution.

I didn't realize the strength of attachment between David and Laddie. We had no place prepared for Laddie, assuming he would stay put around the house and on the lot we called home. We were wrong. One Saturday afternoon, Louise and I went to visit Dr. and Mrs. Hoyt Ayers, dear friends and former pastor. We were gone about three hours. On returning, we missed Laddie. For two weeks Louise and I searched and followed up every lead that came along. Finally, I found Laddie dead on the railroad tracks about half a mile from our house. It was a sad time. When I told David, a sophomore at Samford at the time, about

Laddie's death and whereabouts, he wanted to go to the site. Oh my, I thought. Yet, I had no choice. We retrieved Laddie's remains into a plastic bag, placed them in the trunk of my car, and buried them in the backyard of our house. Today, a red brick marks the site.

My first act in Montgomery was to review the purpose of the Alabama Baptist Convention. It was necessary for me, a new staff member of the Executive Board, to have an understanding and a working knowledge of the convention purpose. I took the purpose statement apart, phrase by phrase. I found it to be a statement which had undergirded Alabama Baptists for 147 years.

> The purpose of the Alabama Baptist State Convention shall be to promote the preaching of the gospel in Alabama and throughout the world; to promote ministerial and Christian education; to publish, if desired, and distribute Christian literature including the Bible; to organize and promote all phases of work fostered by the convention; and to aid any benevolent or moral movements it may deem promotion of God's Kingdom. (1970 *Annual* of the Alabama Baptist State Convention)

That purpose never escaped my attention during my tenure with the convention.

My observation affirms the unchangeable nature of the convention's reason for being: the commission mandate from the resurrected Lord.

There is little deviation or change in the convention purpose in 1997 from the purpose adopted by the founding convention in October 1823, a tribute to the convention founders. I know for a fact that since 1970, whenever a Review-Planning Committee for future emphases and programs was appointed, the convention purpose underwent scrutiny by the special committee.

The new assignment was an awesome challenge for me! The men serving as departmental directors were not at all sure of me serving as division director. However, that never posed a threat to me at the time. Also, I knew each of them, knew they were persons of integrity and of Christian principles. It took time for me to learn about their work, but they were patient with me. I think in the six years working together, I was accepted as a colleague. The respect was mutual. We were a team, with minds to work, and a love for the Lord and Alabama Baptists. I found that each director served in the leadership responsibility out of a sense of call of the Lord to the greatest challenges of ministry. Each

Alabama Baptist State Convention staff, 1973.

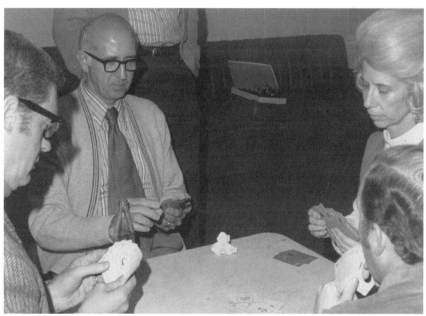

Staff retreat, 1972.

man's job had a hold upon his life. Otis Williams, John Moon, Jon Appleton, H. O. Hester, Billy Nutt, and David Richardson will always have a distinctive niche in my heart.

I came to the employment of the Executive Board of the Alabama Baptist Convention believing strongly that the decision was affirmed by the Lord and under the leadership of the Holy Spirit. I came to the Convention Office with an openness to do whatever I was called upon to do. I had confidence in the leadership of the executive secretary-treasurer. I believed I could assist him in his work load. Dr. Bagley was gracious in entrusting me with some big assignments. I knew that I had a lot to learn, and I wanted to be a good student who could learn quickly. I wanted to measure up to the expectations of the Lord, of Dr. Bagley, of the Executive Board, and Alabama Baptist pastors and laity.

There were major differences in my ministry at the Convention Office from my ministry as pastor of a local church. I soon realized my responsibility had been extended to the churches of the Alabama Baptist State Convention, all three thousand plus, and the associations.

CHURCH MINISTRIES DIVISION-DIRECTOR'S OFFICE

The work programs of the Church Ministries Division were what I identified as the extended ministries of the church, rather than being directed toward the development and promotion of the church program organizations. The departments and directors were: Associational Missions, Billy Nutt; Evangelism, Otis Williams; Ministry to Special Groups, H. O. Hester; Campus Ministries, Jon Appleton; and Retirement and Insurance, John Moon. One of my assignments was to correlate and promote the ministries and programs of the five departments of the Church Ministries Division. Each department was unique, but each related to the whole. This distinctness was evident particularly in the funding process. A primary assignment was coordinating the budgeting processes within the division and the office of executive secretary-treasurer in developing and coordinating new ministries initiated by the executive secretary-treasurer. I presented budget requests to the Administration Committee, defending any request challenged with the assistance of the department director. Another assignment was to assist the departmental directors in performing their tasks and to be a channel through which the local churches could seek assistance in extending their witness and ministry to the whole world.

Each department had business with the Home Mission Board, though annuity and insurance related specifically to the Annuity Board of the Southern Baptist Convention. The Church Ministries Division related to the Home Mission Board in programming, planning, and interdepartmental coordinating in assisting the churches and associations in reaching America for Christ—a bold mission, challenging enough to keep every pastor and member of staff and the State Board of Missions team members exhilarated in anticipation and in participation. I believed the mission tasks of each church should: (1) identify and fulfill the church's mission to glorify God in her place and time; (2) understand the nature of the community to which she is sent; (3) undertake the mission to which she can most effectively reveal the Kingdom of God; (4) relate to her association in cooperative missions planning; and (5) determine interrelationship with the entities of the Southern Baptist Convention.

ASSOCIATIONAL MISSIONS

Billy Nutt said, reflecting upon his pastoral ministry in Pike and Washington Counties, ". . . We had our ups and downs in Washington County. I was asked to preach the doctrinal sermon in the annual meeting of the association. I decided to preach a message on the Baptist Association." The messengers took note of the sermon. Several preachers requested copies because of the relevance of the sermon to some issues of concern in the association. The sermon influenced state leadership, namely, George Ricker, director of Associational Missions Department, to invite Dr. Billy Nutt to assume a major role in the Crusade of Americas as director of a state-wide religious census with more than 75 percent of the state population participating in the survey. As Billy shared this experience with me, I recalled that the modern missionary movement was launched by a sermon preached at an association meeting by William Carey: "Attempt great things for God, expect great things from God." Since 1967, Dr. Billy Nutt has been a leader in the Associational and Cooperative Missions Department.

It was a new day for a new beginning when state missions leadership gave formation to partnership planning. The concept was embraced by both associational and state leadership with a deep sense of purpose and appreciation. I think the times have passed, and I hope, buried never to be resurrected, when directors of Associational Missions are perceived to be implementers of Southern Baptist and state missions plans and programs. Or to put it another and perhaps plainer way, directors of Associational Missions are not to be perceived as field hands, but rather as colleagues and partners in mission advance.

The Associational Missions Department of the State Board of Missions is a partnership with the associations in (1) identifying ministers needs; (2) planning strategically to meet the needs; (3) providing counsel, personnel, finances, and resource materials; (4) offering orientation and training opportunities; and (5) scheduling orientation sessions for new pastors and other church staff members. Associational Missions is most strategic to the mission accomplishment of the local church. Alabama is blessed with visionary and consecrated leadership in seventy-five associations.

EVANGELISM

The Evangelism Department was led by Otis Williams during the 1970s. God blessed Alabama Baptists in extraordinary ways under his leadership: Alabama reached and baptized more people in that decade than any other state nationally, except for Texas. In 1970 alone, 28,615 persons were baptized into Alabama churches; in 1972, 31,981. There were churches reporting 200 professions of faith. Otis Williams said to the 1971 convention, "There is a new movement of the spirit of God across our state and many of our churches are reporting revivals!" A renewed emphasis upon the role of the laymen in witnessing was very evident in the churches. Lay evangelism schools, about 500 in all, were planned in every association in February and March of 1972.

Amazing! How did it happen? There was a refreshing presence of the Holy Spirit within the family of Alabama Baptists. Literally, the laity arose from the church pew to be trained in a lay evangelism school to go forth sharing their faith experience of grace. The Lord blessed the laity with fruit for their witness. Pastors were revived with a new sense of the Holy Spirit's presence. Church members got right with the Lord and with one another! Evidence of awakening was moving across the state.

A large number of our laypeople and a sizable group of the pastors were praying, confessionally asking the Lord to forgive our sinful ways and renew a right spirit in our lives. Second Chronicles 7:12,14 states: ". . . I have heard your prayers, and have chosen this place for myself and as a house of sacrifice . . . and my people who are called by my name humble themselves and pray and seek my face and turn from their wicked ways, then I will hear from heaven, will forgive the sins, and heal their land."

Hundreds of laypeople found joy in witnessing and sharing their faith with lost people. College students were huddling in prayer groups on college campuses across Alabama; students shared their faith, and students were saved. Summer missions volunteers increased. Financial resources were stretched.

Equipping members of the congregation to do the work of ministry is an exhortation to inclusion for the local church congregation. The task of equipping the laity is never finished and is always active.

Let me focus on the challenge of equipping the men and boys in the church for mission achievement. The task begins in prayer and continues in the experience of prayer. In 1969, Dr. Bagley approached me about the possibility of filling the vacancy in the Brotherhood Department of the convention. Having prayed about the matter, I was led not to consider it. Why would the executive secretary-treasurer of the Alabama Baptist Convention turn to the pastoral leader of the McElwain Baptist Church as a possible candidate to fill the vacancy in the Brotherhood Department of the Alabama Baptist State Convention? I believed then, and the opinion is unchanged, that it was because of what the men and boys of McElwain were becoming in Christ and what they were doing in missions. There was present in the congregation a body of men and boys responding seriously to the biblical challenge of building the fellowship and unifying the body of Christ.

Jimmy Paul and Jimmy Pharr made a great team in leading the Birmingham Baptist Association in great brotherhood rallies. I remember an occasion when the Central Park Baptist Church was packed out for a soul-winning rally. What an inspiration to be a witness to fifteen hundred men marking their Bibles in the plan of salvation. What a sight. What great sounds in praise and adoration.

During the same time frame, Dr. Bagley asked about my interest in campus ministry. There was a vacancy in leadership in Birmingham. Reverend Mac Johnson, pastor of Clayton Street Baptist Church, filled the office of Brotherhood/RA director from April 1, 1969, until his untimely death on May 24, 1990, ended his admirable and effective long-term service. His fruits bear record to unprecedented expansion and growth in the men/boys ministry. He was a remarkable man for God who gave himself unreservedly. Mac's dear wife, Eleanor, died prematurely. Those of us in the Baptist family who knew them miss their presence among us today.

There was also a vacancy at Troy State University. Jon Appleton, State Campus Ministries director, recommended that Elbert Williams be considered to fill the vacancy. Elbert had proven himself as a BSU director in the Birmingham Campus Ministry, and I perceived him to be ideal for the ministry in Troy. It would provide him a new beginning and an opportunity to transfer his ministry in leadership to a campus with a large and growing student enrollment in need of an experienced leader for the ministry.

Ralph Adams was the president of Troy State University at the time of Elbert's tenure. Student enrollments, campus expansion, and growth in endowments/alumni giving increased significantly under Dr. Adams's leadership.

I had the opportunity to give support and affirmation to Dr. Adams's successor. I had met an exceptional young man, Dr. Jack Hawkins, president of Talladega School for the Deaf and Blind. Dr. Hawkins was a very compassionate person and gifted and intelligent leader. He impressed me with his rapport and care for the student body at Talladega. Learning that Dr. Hawkins was on the list of candidates for president at Troy State University, I communicated with the governor of the state, the honorable Guy Hunt, whom I had met and been with on several occasions while he was governor. In fact, Governor and Mrs. Hunt honored me on the occasion of my retirement from the office of executive secretary-treasurer. I continue to hold Governor Hunt and Helen in high esteem and appreciation.

Dr. Hawkins was named the new chancellor of the Troy State University systems and is currently rendering exceptional leadership with integrity. I claim proudly the friendship of him and Mrs. Hawkins, both active in the First Baptist Church, Troy. Dr. Hawkins teaches in the adult division of Sunday School.

One of the largest cooperative efforts in evangelism was supported in 1973 by 130 religious bodies in the United States. The theme was "Calling our Continent to Christ." The slogan for the year was Key 73.

Simultaneous revivals took place in southern Alabama in March and northern Alabama in April. Drooping hands were strengthened; hearts discouraged were exhilarated in Christian fellowship; minds were renewed in Christ! More than 8,000 persons attended the 1973 Evangelism Conference in Mobile alone.

Perennially, the State Evangelism Conference draws more pastors, church staff members, and laypeople than any other State Convention meeting. The program always exalts Christ with great preaching, Bible study, and music.

The list of preachers at the Evangelism Conference reads like a who's who of preachers: John Bisagno, R. G. Lee, Wayne Ward, Jack Stanton, Carl Bates, Vonder Warner, Manuel Scott, Stephen Alford, E. V. Hill, Vance Havner, C. B. Hogue, Sam Cathey, James Pleitz, Claude Rhea, Leighton Ford, Bill Tanner, Adrian Rogers, and John Haulik.

Youth evangelism conferences were sponsored by the Department of Evangelism. Attendance was great, numbering into the thousands. Special guests have included youth leaders; among them was Miss America 1975, Shirley Cothran. Summer youth revival teams were enlisted, trained, and sent out to conduct youth revivals and youth rallies in the churches during the summer. The youth revivals are conducted in the churches and are, occasionally, associationwide.

Associational evangelism conferences were sponsored by the associations across the state. Thousands of laypeople from the churches and pastors really believed evangelism to be the continuing priority of every believer and every church. Otis Williams says, "Evangelism is the heartbeat of Alabama Baptists."

SPECIAL MISSIONS

H. O. Hester said that the commanding words of the Great Commission were taken seriously by the Department of Special Missions. Sharing the gospel with every creature means working with deaf, retarded, and illiterate people, National Baptists, Southern Baptists, Native Americans, Koreans, Spaniards, Arabians, Chinese, and other internationals. Members of the staff shared the gospel regularly with people from the aforementioned groups. David Richardson and his spouse, Patsey, were classified as missionaries to the deaf, retarded, and illiterate, under joint sponsorship of the Executive Board and the Home Mission Board. In 1976, thirty-two churches sponsored the ministry to the deaf. This ministry was enlarged to include illiterate and retarded people: in the year 1976 there were 234,498 Alabamians with hearing impairments, 30,832 deaf Alabamians, and 110,000 Alabamians with some form of retardation. One out of ten adults was a nonreader. Ministries fostered to serve these groups included camps, the portable teletype machine ministry, Shocco conferences, and interpreters conferences. David Richardson is often called to interpret for deaf people in hospitals, doctors' offices, courts, and any other situation where there is need.

The cooperative ministry with National Baptists is a shared ministry of fellowship and inspiration, primarily at the annual human relations conference at Shocco Springs. Such notables as F. G. Sampson, Ray Robbins, and Robert Bradley were conference leaders, preachers, and singers. This department advocated the formation of joint InterBaptist Committees with representatives from the Baptist conventions and from the associations.

H. O. Hester sought out National Baptist students preparing for the ministry. He encouraged them and assisted them in finding scholarship funding for their education. The Home Mission Board and the Alabama Baptist State Convention gave graciously in scholarship support. The department assisted with Vacation Bible Schools, camp programs, programs for students preparing for the ministry, and in-training revivals. It helped with providing scholarships and planning programs of cooperation among conventions. The publication *Directions* was edited and printed by this department with Mrs. Delma Warner as chief editor.

Reverend and Mrs. E. R. Isbell served as missionaries to the Native Americans in Washington, Mobile, and Escambia counties. Ten churches and missions served the Native American population, which numbered 6,000. Major emphasis was given to Vacation Bible Schools and youth camps for the children and youth; the latter provided leadership and resources by the Alabama Woman's Missionary Union. All the Native American churches and missions gave in support of missions through the Cooperative Program.

The foreign mission appointment service was held in Mobile in 1973 and many Native Americans and their pastors attended. Their hearts were stirred by the testimonies of missionaries and their spirits quickened to give support to their new vision. That year, Mrs. Albert Smith taught the foreign mission study and Mrs. Burma Leggett taught the home mission study. Woman's Missionary Union is always on the cutting edge of missions advance: studying missions, praying for missions, and giving in support of missions.

It was my joy to work with the Mobile Baptist Association; Gerald Blackburn, Mobile association's director of missions; Dr. Billy Nutt, and leadership from the Home Mission Board in securing an ideal site, just off Interstate 10 at Texas Street for the International Seamen Ministries Center, with state mission funds and local funding. The site has four acres of land and a $250,000 facility. This is a great missionary work. The churches of the Mobile Association have given sustained support to maintain this vital mission station with a global outreach. Churches like the Plateau Baptist Church gave a new bus to the mission in 1974. The bus transports seamen from the ships to the Mission Point and returns them to the ships.

The international seamen ministry began in the Sage Avenue Baptist Church when Q. T. Curtis was pastor. Vernon Simpson, a member of the Administration Committee, provided background information and reports, and clarified the ministry to the Administration

Committee. Internationals in Mobile pointed out that the Sage Avenue Church could not sustain the vital ministry alone; the ministry multiplied so rapidly that more space, more trained leadership, and more funding were needed. In a meeting of the Administration Committee, Dotson Nelson moved that an appropriation of $4,800 be made to Mobile Baptist Association for the seamen ministry and that the Mobile Association involve itself not only in administering the work, but in financial support as well. Clinton Wood seconded.

The Mobile Association accepted the mission project and provided leadership. The Home Mission Board shared in the mission through the cooperative agreement with the Alabama Baptist State Convention. Churches from across the state provided leadership for Vacation Bible School and revivals. Woman's Missionary Union of Alabama has been faithful in support with leadership and resources through the years, co-sponsoring camps and leadership training, rallies, mission studies, and outreach.

Dr. Ivan de Souza, who spoke nine languages, and his wife served as missionaries to seamen from more than one hundred countries annually. More than seventy-nine different languages were spoken by the seamen who came to the International Seamen Center.

From 1971 to 1976, there were 1,435 recorded professions of faith. A significant dimension of the seamen ministry was the referral or follow-up ministry with the new Christians. Dr. de Souza, his staff, and volunteers from the Mobile churches referred the name and vita on each person to our foreign missionaries in each of the converts' native countries. This helped each convert grow as a Christian by being discipled by missionaries and churches in that home country. Bibles and literature were distributed in the native language, if possible.

Mobile Association also operated Camp Citronelle. Family week is a great event at the camp, with families coming together for fellowship, Bible study and preaching.

CAMPUS MINISTRIES

The Department of Campus Ministries was placed in the Church Ministries Division when the organizational structure of the State Board of Missions was changed from departments to divisions. Campus Ministries was the single largest ministry based in the State Board of

Missions in four areas: personnel, facilities, ministries, and department budget (with the exception of annuity and insurance). This ministry is directed to college and university campuses throughout Alabama.

There were some concerns and differing views toward campus ministry on the part of some local churches, associations, and the State Convention. I viewed these as challenges with enormous potential, provided there was openness to cooperate. Unfortunately, this was not always the situation. Frequently, the BSU director or campus minister experienced the impact, in other words, caught in the middle.

Campus Ministry is a good example of why there is the need for a State Convention. Quite simply, the challenges, needs, and ministries are greater than any one church and/or association. The magnitude of Campus Ministries in collegiate communities commands a response from local churches, associations, and the State Convention. I think, also, the national convention is needed.

In Alabama, Campus Ministries expanded into a network with all the colleges and universities in the state. There were, in the 1970s, forty-one undergraduate/graduate colleges and universities in Alabama. Thirty-seven percent of the 120,000 student population was Baptist or Baptist preference.

How do Alabama Baptists reach out to all forty-one campuses? Begin where you are. That is what we did in 1971. Following several weeks of conversations, praying, and interchanges, a formation statement was developed by directors of Campus Ministries and division directors.

The Administration Committee met in Montgomery, Baptist Building, December 2, 1971, with Convention President Lambert Mims, layman from Mobile, presiding. Dr. Bagley requested that I be recognized for a proposal regarding Campus Ministries. The proposal called for the development of a single state program of campus ministry to all schools of higher education relative to personnel, facilities, and ministries to be directed by the Campus Ministries Department of the Executive Board. I regard this as one of the most important decisions made in the period from 1970 to 1976.

Another factor in single program development was campus ministry on African-American campuses. At the meeting of the Administration Committee May 24, 1972, Rev. Jack Mason, chairman of the Convention Study Committee and the Personnel Committee, reported that the Administration Committee was studying and reevaluating the board's student program as it related to African-American students.

Unfortunately, on July 20, 1973, death claimed Reverend Mason, the pastor of York Baptist Church, York, Alabama, Bigbee Association. He was the son of O. D. Mason Sr., who also pastored York Church. Together, this father and son faithfully served this wonderful family of faith. Dr. Leon Ballard is now pastor of York Baptist Church and currently serves as president of the Alabama Baptist State Convention.

There were other dynamics present in implementation of a single Campus Ministries program. Population growth in college and university towns meant new churches were needed there, but more churches were being established in urban-metro areas.

This task of developing a single program had several facets, some of which had stubborn systemic factors, for example, the lassitude in the Student Department in the Baptist Sunday School Board and the fragmentation caused by various components of the campus ministry program in the State Board of Missions, such as adequate funding for campus ministers' salaries, ministries, and programs, and the need to intentionally focus on students.

However, Jon and I were given latitude and support from the leadership of the state Executive Board. We were released to move forward. The main objective was to have leadership presence and student-faculty focused ministries on each of the colleges and universities in Alabama. A second objective, where the need could be justified, was to provide a BSU center and/or update the center facilities already in place.

The task was enormous. I commend the leadership of Jon Appleton and his readiness to be consumed by the twofold project. The rewards were gratifying, and Campus Ministry was set on course for making a major difference in kingdom advance in Alabama. The momentum has been sustained through the years by a team of campus ministers par excellence. Among the campus ministers in the 1970s were Charles Barnes, Rodney Ellis, Robert Ford, Glenn Gring, Ruford Hodges, Peggy Masters, Walter Porter, Oxford Smith, James A. Warren, John W. Tadlock, Elbert Williams, Shirley Richardson, Jesse Wood, Gertrude Thorpe, Mike Avant, Martha Anderson, and Peter Parks.

The members of the Administration Committee were encouraging with their comments and perceptive with their questions. Approval of the proposal set in motion extensive processes with far-reaching implications, up to the twenty-first century. There were also immediate implications.

Jacksonville State University was requested as a site for a new BSU center by Dotson Nelson, chairman of the Properties Committee. Miriam Jackson, secretary of the Administration Committee, was dean of students there. The proposal to purchase land for a new BSU center at Jacksonville State University was approved. Wallace Construction Company was awarded the construction contact for $152,566.

The First Baptist Church, Jacksonville, Alabama, is a remarkable family of faith. The pastoral leaders and members of the congregations have always responded to the invitation of the Alabama Baptist family for leadership responsibilities. We miss John Norman, a strong advocate for student ministries and equally supportive of ministerial students. He served on the State Board of Missions and was chairman of the Convention's Programs Committee for the Sesquicentennial Celebration.

Student work at the University of Montevallo, including the student center, also needed attention. Executive Secretary Bagley, director of Campus Ministries Jon Appleton, and I as director of church ministries, assessed the project and reported back to the Properties Committee, chaired by Dotson Nelson. The convention had already given $80,000 toward the construction of a student/education building at Montevallo Baptist Church. The Administration Committee heard the request from the Properties Committee for the purchase of property in Montevallo and directed campus ministry to be based in a residence adjacent to the main campus. Renovation and expansion were necessary, transforming the residence into the BSU center.

Simultaneously, landscaping was completed at the new BSU center in Jacksonville State University. Bob Ford is senior campus minister at Jacksonville, having excelled in campus ministries, always sharing counsel, guidance, and encouragement with his students.

A resolution was passed for the Baptist Center building in DeKalb Association—the Home Mission Board gave $25,000 toward the project and the convention gave $10,000. The Baptist Center would provide space for activities related to junior college and migrant work, and office/conference space for the association.

Executive Secretary-Treasurer George Bagley encouraged moving as expeditiously as possible in adding BSU centers at Livingston (West Alabama University) and the University of Montevallo. On January 24, 1972, the Administration Committee approved purchase of property for a BSU center at Livingston University (now University of West

Alabama) for $17,500. It is now one of the most attractive and accom-
modating centers. Asa Green, president of Livingston University at the
time, was a strong advocate of campus ministry. His leadership made
possible an ideal building site located on the main traffic artery, highly
visible to all the campus.

Historically, the Baptist Student Union was the link for the students
between college and the local Baptist church, which was perceived to be the
college church in the community. For example, Ruhama Baptist Church in
Birmingham was known as the college church for Howard College. In
Auburn, the college church was the First Baptist Church, which invested
thousands of dollars in facilities, programs, and leaders for the college
students. Louise Green Potts was BSU director at Auburn University. The
following is a list of known persons in Auburn BSU serving full time in a
Christian vocation who were influenced directly by Louise Green Potts,
according to Dr. John Harvey Thomas and Dr. Charles Martin:

James Bartley, Th.D., foreign missionary; Sarah Smith Bohanon, campus
minister; Marie Golson Cheyne, foreign missionary; James Ellis,
preacher; Mary Hazel Ford Moon, foreign missionary (deceased);
Frank P. Forwood, Th.D., pastor/teacher; William Sewell Garmon D.R.E.,
seminary professor/teacher (deceased); Charles L. Martin Jr., D.D.,
foreign missionary/pastor/camp minister; Robert E. Hall, home
missionary; George F. Hocutt, preacher; Evelyn Whitman Hocutt,
preacher's wife; Patty McCoy Horton, church secretary; Leonard G.
Irwin, preacher; Roy Isbell, campus minister; Louie Verle Warren Isbell,
campus minister; W. J. Isbell, D.V.M., state brotherhood secretary;
Nell Hammond Isbell, wife; Howard Johnson, preacher, Hutterian
Brethren; Marion Rushton Johnson, Hutterian Brethren; Jamie Jones,
Ed.D., campus minister; Beverly Childs Jones, campus minister;
Harold Malone, Ph.D., teacher/counselor; Harold Massey, Ph.D., Ed.D.,
counselor/teacher; Beth Martin Massey, wife/teacher; J. Leon Marsh,
D.R.E., seminary professor; Virgil O. McMillan, foreign missionary;
Donabel Pitts McMillan, foreign missionary; Gerald Naylor, Ph.D.,
preacher/teacher; William R. Norman, M.D., medical missionary;
Lois Williams Norman, medical missionary; Bonnie Walker Nutt,
preacher's wife; Hankins Parker, D.V.M., preacher (deceased); James L.
Pharr, preacher (deceased); J. Earl Posey Th.D., foreign missionary; John
Harvey Thomas Jr., Th.D., Ph.D., preacher/teacher; Helen Williamson

Thomas, preacher's wife; Mary Jo Thomas, preacher's wife; William O. Thomason, D.R.E., education work, Baptist Sunday School board; Mary Roberts Thomason, education worker's wife (deceased); Roy Timberlake, preacher; Anita Harris Timberlake, preacher's wife; George Underwood, preacher; Marie Rhodes Underwood, preacher's wife; Claudia Weinman, preacher's wife; Barbara Weaver Winn, preacher's wife; Clinton Wood, preacher; Warren Wolf, campus minister; and Louellen Hovey Stephenson, artist, BSSB.

There were good relationships between the local Baptist church and the colleges or universities all over Alabama. Campus-ministry leadership encouraged local church participation; thus, there was a gradual shift from the one college church concept to multiple churches. Campus ministers were encouraged to support the association of churches through visitation and to be supportive of the ministries work of the association. A Campus Ministries Committee, or an areawide committee, functions in the association where there is campus ministry. The local churches are very much involved in this strategic ministry. The students make returns by their support in giving time, talents, and money.

Campus ministry was expanding. More students and faculty were becoming involved, primarily because of the leadership of state director, the local campus minister, and the great host of student leaders serving on BSU councils and committees, many of them our key church leaders in churches across America and especially in Alabama. This living witness speaks to us from the church pew.

More participation meant more students responding to summer missions, community missions, and the ministries of the Alabama Baptist State Convention. The Alabama Baptist State Convention encouraged and supported this involvement.

I, along with Jon Appleton, encouraged a student presence on the Administration Committee and the State Board of Missions. These groups approved representation; five students were elected to serve as observers and nonvoting members on the State Board of Missions. The state president was to serve on the Administration Committee. The presence of students on the State Board of Missions and the president sitting on the administration speeded the process of change.

The decision to develop a single program for campus ministries necessitated an evaluation of campus ministry to African-American and other ethnic students. The summary of the matter was to embrace all colleges and universities and all ethnics into campus ministries. Students and campus ministers are numbered among the forerunners touching the lives of all people in the name of the all-loving, all-caring Lord Jesus.

In January 1972, Ruford Hodges, campus minister in Birmingham was transferred to Huntsville-UAH. It was Ruford who initiated linkages with Alabama A & M. He has gone full cycle. Currently, he is state director for Campus Ministry.

In January 1973, a pilot project in campus ministry was established in the tri-association areas of DeKalb, Marshall, and Etowah—the Northeast Junior Colleges of Snead-Gadsden-Boaz. The three associations became partners in planning financial support.

Pastor Newell Massey, chairman; Mrs. Roy Nelson; and Mrs. Charlie Walker, Etowah Association worked in developing this pilot project, along with Jon Appleton, the director of missions, and campus ministry representatives J. E. Morton, Marshall Association, and Clifford Black and Rodney Elliott, DeKalb Association.

A decision significant to campus ministry in Alabama was made in the November 29, 1973, meeting of the Administration Committee. Mr. Oxford Smith, who was campus minister at Auburn University, was elected associate campus minister in the Campus Ministries Department. Oxford is an anchor and valued minister for campus ministries in Alabama. A personal friend, he encourages all persons whose lives intersect with his. I've said to myself often, "When the one great scorer comes to write against his name, he writes not whether we won or lost, but how we played the game." Oxford is valiant, courageous, untiring, and capable, a key leader in the strategic campus ministries. It was my joy "to walk the walk" in Christian service with Oxford Smith. He is a person who joyfully took "the towel" as servant. I recall it was Jesus who took the towel and washed the feet of the disciples.

The Administration Committee in March 1974 extended an offer to First Baptist Church, Auburn, to pay the church $100,000 for the BSU center properties. The offer was taken under advisement by the deacons at Auburn's First Baptist Church and Pastor John Jeffers. Pastor Jeffers responded to Dr. Bagley's letter.

Subsequently, Pastor Jeffers notified the executive secretary-treasurer and Administration Committee that on July 7, 1974, the congregation at First Baptist Auburn would vote on the proposition. The vote to sell was approved by the congregation. There were some provisions in the event that the State Board of Missions ever decided to sell.

The congregation and pastoral leaders of Auburn First Baptist are dear to the writer's heart. I thank God for my every remembrance of this family of faith. After all, it was at the altar of First Baptist Church where my bride Arvie Louise Green and I were married on August 6, 1946. This congregation planned everything—rehearsal dinner, bridal parties, reception, altar decorations—as expressions of love and appreciation for Louise Green.

Students with outstanding academic records and campus activities gave leadership to our state student programs. For instance, in 1973, the vice president of State BSU was Jane Rice, senior at Jacksonville State University and the reigning "Miss Alabama." The state president was David Garst, an outstanding graduate of Auburn University. Some of us can remember that Dr. David Matthews, president of the University of Alabama, served as state president when he was a student there. He continues to champion the causes of BSU and the ministries.

Numerous improvements were made on student centers. For example, in July 1975 the Baptist Student Center in Birmingham was refurbished. Other student centers needed work, also. New facilities were added, and Campus Ministries was expanded for the purposes of reaching students and faculty for Christ, strengthening churchmanship, and extending the kingdom.

In 1975, twenty-nine persons were serving as Campus Ministry staff. Sixteen of them were full-time employees, two were interims, eight were volunteer directors, and three were on staff of the Baptist Schools.

Retreats and conventions were always inspiring. The 1976 Fall Convention was held at First Baptist Church, Auburn. One thousand students participated in the convention program and activities. The Spring Retreat was in Shocco Springs. Students were exhorted to become more Christlike on their campuses. A record number of student summer missionaries (forty-nine) were commissioned to mission service for the summer, and in fact, the number of student summer missionaries increases each year.

The students and campus ministry leadership amazed me by raising $19,000 for their summer missions program in 1975. All kinds of projects engaged the students and the funding for summer missions multiplied fourfold.

A transition of leadership in campus ministry occurred in 1976. Jon Appleton resigned on December 31, 1975, as state director to accept the pastorate of First Baptist Church, Athens, Georgia. Dr. Charles Martin,

Alabama Baptist Campus Ministries, 1975.

pastor of Parker Memorial Baptist Church in Anniston, Alabama, became state director on June 29, 1976.

Campus Ministries Division, one of the nation's most comprehensive programs for students, is a great tribute to Alabama Baptists. The department defines the purpose for campus ministry to be ". . . to lead students to commitment to Jesus Christ as Savior and Lord and to nurture them in the Christian faith and life."

RETIREMENT AND INSURANCE—JOHN MOON

John Moon brought expertise of a very practical nature in working to provide adequate retirement income for church, association, and convention personnel. Dr. Darold Morgan became president of the Annuity Board of the Southern Baptist Convention on March 1, 1972. The Annuity Board funds are held in trust for persons contributing to retirement plans or to use to pay monthly benefits. The funds are invested for the largest possible returns in keeping with safety or monetary and morality factors.

Each member participating in the plan began receiving a personalized statement in 1971, a dream come true. The statement shows members' benefits and coverage in the retirement-fund insurance programs.

In 1971, $4.8 million was paid in benefits. In fifty-three and a half years, the total benefits paid have amounted to $86.9 million. Four hundred and twenty-two persons received relief grants amounting to $68,869 in the first six months of 1971.

I would encourage all the churches to participate in the retirement programs of the Annuity Board to the fullest. The staff members' and pastors' benefits at retirement are determined by the contributions of the church, the pastors or staff members, and the State Convention. Pastors and staff ministers should be included unless they are in some other retirement plan. The Baptist State Conventions provide one-third with each ordained minister's basic plan. In 1975, the State Conventions affiliated with the Southern Baptist Convention to spend over $4 million each year for their pastors and ministerial staff.

The most remarkable way to describe the ministry is "helping hands." A new retirement program was drafted in 1976, when 1,341 churches and associations with 1,781 employees participated in the retirement program in Alabama. The program is more realistic for SBC church employees retiring in today's society.

CHURCH MINISTRIES DIVISION OFFICE

Created for greater efficiency and effectiveness, the division structure of the State Board of Missions was in place when I joined the staff in 1970. The Church Ministries Division was one of three divisions of work at the time. The Church Development Division and the Business Management Division were the other two divisions.

The responsibilities of the executive secretary-treasurer expanded with the growth of State Board of Missions programs and ministries, increasing the supervision responsibility of the executive secretary-treasurer. This new structure worked well; each department had access, if needed, to the office of the executive secretary-treasurer. With time and experience, the structural relations were refined, and confidence developed between the department director and the division director.

The division structure was in place until 1984, at which time I became executive secretary-treasurer. Having served as division director, I had observed certain strengths and weaknesses. The strengths included: an intermediary who could make many decisions in consultation with department director, disencumbering the executive secretary-treasurer from multitudinous decisions; a workable chain-of-command for the executive leaders; and the potential of expediting the work. Perhaps the most obvious weakness was that the department director did not have direct access/dialogue with the executive officer, in this case the executive secretary-treasurer. At times the department director desired dialogue with the executive secretary-treasurer and the division director was not needed at all.

Yet within a few short years, six to be exact, the Executive Committee and president and Dan Ireland, chairman, were conversing about the need for an assistant to the executive secretary-treasurer. This matter will be discussed later.

The commitment of the Church Ministries Division was to the people: seeing people, hearing people, listening to people, touching people, serving people, winning people, and nurturing people.

In addition to the four major departments of the Church Ministries Division, other areas of ministry and witness involvement were church and state issues: drug abuse, Christian citizenship, resort ministries, the state legislature, the retired, the bereaved, the migrant labor force, homes, churches, and associations.

The work of the division's director by 1976 was multifaceted: He or she would (1) assist departmental leadership in planning and implementation; (2) assist the office of executive secretary-treasurer as assigned by the executive secretary-treasurer; (3) serve as state director of Missions to Home Mission Board; (4) coordinate disaster relief for convention; (5) serve as liaison to Vietnamese refugees; (6) coordinate work of Christian Life and Public Affairs Commission; and (7) relate to Baptist chaplains in Alabama.

DISASTER RELIEF

I was given another responsibility when Executive Secretary-Treasurer George Bagley designated me as the coordinator for the Disaster Relief Ministry of the Alabama Baptist State Convention, one of the most commanding ministries in 1970. My first assignment was to survey the needs caused by disaster and report on Alabama. Sunday, June 24, 1973, was designated as Disaster Relief Sunday, with churches taking a special offering for the new ministry.

The Alabama Baptist Disaster Relief Ministry mitigates the suffering of humanity due to natural disaster. Resources for this ministry are provided through the Alabama Disaster Relief Fund, which was established on June 25, 1973. The Disaster Relief Ministry was designated for all people and was interdenominational.

There were severe disasters in Alabama in 1973, 1974, and 1975. More than $400,000 was distributed out of the Disaster Relief Fund, with more than 800 families receiving direct assistance in food, clothing, household items, and funding. There was major damage and/or complete loss to twelve of our churches. A lot of love, praying, shelter, provisions, first aid, food, and clothing were given from the generous hearts of Alabama Baptists as the church pew responded to humanitarian needs.

The Alabama Convention was one of the first state conventions to develop a disaster relief program. Our convention was also one of the first to develop a *Disaster Relief Manual*, in December 1974. The manual was a guide for the churches, associational Disaster Relief Committees, and our state Committee on Disaster Response.

I also worked closely with Emergency Preparedness for the State of Alabama and the Department of Human Resources on state and national levels. These two state agencies were magnanimous in working with state-wide denominations and church groups. A network of Disaster Relief Committees was established in each association. I salute the state of Alabama Emergency Preparedness Department and the Department of Human Resources for their efficiency, skills, and expertise in organizational management, and their compassionate response to the citizens of our state when there is a sustained loss from natural disaster. The state personnel were super in coalition development. I had the privilege of occupying the chair for the religious community in the Department of Emergency Preparedness for several years.

It was hurricane Fredric, a major storm, that ravaged Mobile in 1981 and the coastal areas of southern Alabama, causing enormous losses. This catastrophic hurricane catapulted the State Board of Missions into developing and putting into service, at a cost of $85,000, a major disaster relief van with the capacity to serve 5,000 hot meals per day, and had a 500-gallon water tank, a communication system, refrigeration, ice makers, and sleeping accommodations for a disaster team of six, complete with shower and toilet.

Disaster relief check to Doug Dortch.

BAPTISTS CAN WORK WELL TOGETHER

An outstanding example of cooperation among church, association, convention, and the Home Mission Board was the creation of the Baptist Center in DeKalb Association, in Rainsville, Alabama. Sand Mountain is one of the most densely populated areas and one of the most agriculturally productive per acre in Alabama. Irish potatoes and tomatoes are two of the lead crops. Harvesting the potatoes and tomatoes necessitated labor, usually provided by migrant workers. They would enter southern Alabama from Florida, harvesting crops as they migrated north.

Work was plentiful during the harvesting season, but housing for families was woefully inadequate in most places. Migrant families lived in chicken houses renovated and connected to utilities. Child-care facilities were unavailable. Other circumstances caused shortages of accommodations and services.

DeKalb Baptist Association decided to address these needs. Milton Pope and Vela, with other association leadership, approached the State Board of Missions with a list of the needs and a request for help, including funding for establishing day-care ministries and provisions for a Baptist Center. The Department of Associational Missions got involved. We developed a projection for the Baptist Center Project. DeKalb Baptist Association and the adjoining associations (Marshall, Etowah, Tennessee-River, Lookout Mountain, and Cherokee) were invited to participate with volunteer personnel and funding.

The Christian Social Ministries Department at the Home Missions Board was presented a copy of the prospectives. The center would provide space for ministries and activities for the children of the migrant workers, husbands, and wives. Deliberations were held by all participating entities and the response was good. The Home Mission Board provided $25,000 to be paid in two $12,500 payments; the Baptist State Executive Board pledged $10,000, in two $5,000 increments. The DeKalb Association and the adjoining associations also provided funding for the partnership in ministries. The Baptist Center would provide the following: (1) space for leadership training, (2) space for day care for children and related ministries, (3) space for Howard College Extension Center with other associations participating, (4) office space for DeKalb Baptist Association, and (5) training conferences, "how-to" conferences, and Christian social ministries.

The Baptist Center Building was built, using much volunteer labor. The SBC leadership presence of Dr. Clovis Brantley, director of Christian Social Ministries, Home Mission Board, greatly facilitated the project. Dr. Brantley was a remarkable Christ-like human being and was most helpful with the project. Dr. Billy Nutt, of the State Board of Missions, was a catalyst in the project. The building was a gift from heaven, providing valuable space to missions support.

THE SESQUICENTENNIAL CELEBRATION 1973

One of the most exciting things which occurred during my years in the Church Ministries Division was the Sesquicentennial Celebration in 1973. It was such as joy to commemorate 150 years of service.

Baptist forerunners set forth their intention to follow the historic biblical truth laid out in the Great Commission of Jesus Christ our Lord. There were fifteen of those forerunners—"delegates," they were called—from missionary societies from churches in seven counties in Alabama. Their historic meeting was held in Salem Baptist Church, Greensboro, Alabama, on October 28, 1823.

Today, Salem Baptist Church is doing well and has a membership of African-American Baptists. They cooperate excellently with the National Baptist Convention in missions and education.

The delegates hammered out what Baptists would do in response to the Great Commission: (1) promote missions, (2) promote religious instruction throughout the state, (3) improve the education of gospel ministers, and (4) aid the benevolent views of the General Convention of the Baptist denomination in the United States in extending the benefits of the gospel to the heathen. With minimum modification, the objectives have survived more than 171 years.

For twenty years prior to the sesquicentennial year, the convention adopted programs to advance missions. These Advance Programs led up to the "program of work beyond 1973" which was adopted by the convention at the historic 150th Anniversary Celebration.

The first Five-Year Advance Program was in effect 1952–1956. Alabama Baptists responded to the church and denominational goals with renewed enthusiasm. Mission gifts toward the Cooperative Program increased 116 percent. With the second Five-Year Advance Program, 1956–1961, there were increases in Cooperative Program giving, with a larger percent going to mission causes of the Southern Baptist Convention. The third Five-Year Advance Program, 1962–1966, set forth more baptisms, new churches, and missions, and saw increases in church memberships and organizations, the circulation of *The Alabama Baptist*, and Cooperative Program giving.

The next Advance Program lasted seven years, 1966–1973, ending in the Alabama Baptist sesquicentennial year. Baptist heritage, Baptist doctrines, and Baptist faith and message were the emphases. A measure

The Alabama Baptist State Convention marker.

of success was reported in goals set by the convention for educational organization, auxiliaries, and the Department of the Executive Board.

Mr. Lambert Mims, layman from Mobile and president of the ABSC, appointed a committee on planning beyond 1973. The committee was chaired by Lamar Jackson; members were Wicker Hutto, Hugh Chambliss, Mrs. J. W. Triplett, Arthur Walker, Drew Gunnells, Q. P. Davis, Raymond Scroggins, Q. T. Curtis, Ex Officio Walter Nunn, and George Bagley.

The committee began its assignment by having at least one committee member representative in attendance at twelve district listening sessions across the state. Pastors, laity, entity representatives, and Executive Board members were urged to attend at least one listening session. The purpose was to open the planning process to the Alabama Baptist family.

There were three parts to the procedure in reporting what the record showed: (1) church data and characteristics, (2) population data, and (3) recommendations. Characteristics broke down this way:

    I. What church members said
        A. Listening services
        B. Listening sessions summary
    II. What denominational leaders said
        A. Director of missions
        B. Institutions and agencies
        C. Executive Board staff members
    III. Recommendations

The Beyond 1973 Committee presented one of the most, if not the most, comprehensive reports at the 1972 convention. The churches and associations were encouraged to study the report under the caption of the following question: "How can our church and/or association implement the recommendation and findings of the report?"

A BIG TENT AND A COTTON PATCH

The Convention Program Committee, chaired by Dr. John Norman, pastor of First Baptist Church Jacksonville, Alabama, gave leadership in planning for the Sesquicentennial Celebration. The 1973 convention program was a celebration of praise to the Lord for his providential leadership and for the joyful privilege of serving him for 150 years. Dr. Walter Nunn, president, presided over this celebration. There was an unfaltering commitment to the challenges of the Great Commission by the family of God called Alabama Baptists.

Feel the spirit that hovered over First Baptist Church, Tuscaloosa, Alabama, and the big tent, seating 4,000, erected on the founding site of the Alabama Baptist State Convention, now a cotton patch, in Greensboro, Alabama. Experience the joyful enthusiasm that brought thousands of Alabama Baptists to their feet in the Colosseum of the University of Alabama, in thunderous applause for the Birmingham Symphony Orchestra, the combined choir from Judson College, Mobile College, and Samford University, and the magnificent pageant, "The Vision Glorious."

DAVID AND BETH'S MARRIAGE

It was during those years in Church Ministries, on June 30, 1973, that my son, David, married Beth Bloodworth, a fine and attractive young lady. She and David were high school sweethearts at Ramsay High School, where they were both excellent students. I think they had heart-felt feelings toward each other for quite a few years.

David played football for Ramsay in the position of quarterback. His coach, Thompson Reynolds, was a mentor. There was a wonderful bonding between coach and student; in fact, Coach Reynolds had a good yet demanding rapport with all his players. Playing football was a good experience for David, except that in one game he was tackled from behind and sustained a major knee injury which necessitated surgery. He bears the marks of that injury today.

After high school, Beth enrolled in Auburn University. David thought he would go to Auburn as well, but in late summer he decided instead to go to Samford University if it wasn't too late to register. He was accepted. While at Samford, he was a member of the A Cappella Choir under the direction of Dr. L. Gene Black. In a Harold Hunt production of *You're a Good Man, Charlie Brown*, David played Charlie Brown. The production was well received by students, faculty, friends, and President and Mrs. Leslie Wright.

While Beth was at Auburn and David at Samford, they both made new friends and, in fact, dated other people. I think the bond between them was never broken through four years of college. Following graduation, they were dating again.

Louise and I received a call one night from David. He wanted to drive down and talk to us about getting married to Beth. Louise and I gave our blessing and would hear more about the matter when appropriate. We were very happy for our son and our future daughter-in-law. At that

Shannon, Kristin, Beth, and David Potts.

time, David was working in admissions at Samford University and Beth was teaching at Riggins Elementary School.

The wedding date was June 30, 1973, at McElwain Baptist Church. Beth and David planned for a beautiful and meaningful experience. The wedding was a church family occasion. The church family had a vital interest in and support for the groom, whom they had helped raise from birth.

David and Beth are the parents of two beautiful daughters, Kristin, a sophomore at Judson College, and Shannon, a senior at Marion Academy. Their parents provide the girls with love, counsel, and affirmation. For me one of the most difficult aspects of Grandmother Louise's premature death is her absence from the "growing up" of her two granddaughters. Oh, how she loved Kristin and Shannon. She would be proud to see them now. In fact, sometimes I think that she does see them.

CHAPTER 5

Serving alongside Dr. George Bagley

I RECALL THE CONVERSATION DR. DANIEL IRELAND HAD WITH me regarding the person who would become assistant to the executive secretary-treasurer. "Earl," he said, "we are looking for someone who is qualified to be the assistant to Dr. Bagley in carrying the workload, yet someone who would not be a candidate to succeed him as executive secretary-treasurer. Are you interested?"

I felt I could immerse myself in the role of assistant for two reasons. One, I had been assisting Dr. George Bagley since 1970, and secondly, I had no desire to succeed him as executive secretary-treasurer.

There was another factor. The Baptist State Board of Missions was to consider a retirement policy for Baptist State Board employees later in 1983. The new policy would identify age sixty-five as the normal age for retirement. I had been working on this document. In fact, the first reading review was before the Administration Committee. I was planning redirection in my ministry at age sixty-five because I am an advocate of the retirement policy at this age. There is a provision that makes it possible for a board employee to continue employment beyond sixty-five at the request of the State Board of Missions. This is an important stipulation because, like serving in pastorate, you can stay too long.

Then in the meeting of the Administration Committee on July 29, 1976, Chairman Dan Ireland expressed the need for an assistant to the executive secretary-treasurer. Harlice Keown made a motion and

Returning from mission trip to Latin America, 1976.

Gene Nail seconded to instruct the Personnel Sub-committee and the Organizational Evaluation Sub-committee to consult with Dr. Bagley about the employment of an assistant. Dr. Bagley stated that he had not encouraged hiring an assistant because he did not want the organization to be criticized for being too top heavy. After discussion, the motion carried.

In a subsequent meeting of the Administration Committee, the Organizational Evaluation Sub-committee, chaired by Frank Wells, brought a recommendation that an assistant be employed to work with Dr. Bagley. Dan Ireland identified the position on the organizational evaluation chart. He stated that, through the years, many responsibilities had been added to the workload of the executive secretary-treasurer, with no provision for assistance.

He indicated the person would be an administrative assistant to the executive secretary-treasurer. Harlice Keown pointed out that Dr. Bagley did not ask for this; it was the request of the Administration Committee.

The question was raised about a job description for the position. The response was that the job was exactly as the title implied, a general assistant to the executive secretary-treasurer. The initial funds for the job were to come from the contingency fund. The motion passed unanimously and a job description was developed with the following principal functions:

To assist the executive secretary-treasurer of the Executive Board in all
matters relating to that office;

To relate to and assist in all administrative responsibilities as needed;

To authorize expenditure of funds; co-sign all checks;

To handle any mail as needed;

To attend to details relating to committee meetings;

To assist in developing the budget;

To act in behalf of and represent the executive secretary-treasurer on
such occasions as may be necessary and as requested to do so;

To assist with research for articles, speeches, and information as needed;

To handle investigation and recommendation for aid on pastor's salary
and purchase of property; and

To assist in any other matters that may be assigned by the executive
secretary-treasurer. (Administration Committee *Minutes*, 1976)

This new venture was justified, explained, and satisfied through
prayerful and orderly steps. Any new initiatives in the convention are
generated from various sources, the foremost being the ministry needs
in the local churches, associations, or convention at large, needs rising
from the expansion or the need for expansion of the kingdom of God.
(The Disaster Relief Program is illustrative of what I mean by need.)

In the first step, the ministry is identified. Ministry needs may
surface in a conference, or perhaps, circumstances indicate a need. An
example is a natural disaster: flooding, fire, tornado.

In the second step, research is conducted to identify the need to see
if there is sufficient evidence which merits further consideration.

In the third step, a rationale is identified from which a statement of
purpose is developed. The statement of purpose is critical to further
action.

The fourth step is review and consideration by staff leadership and the
executive secretary-treasurer. This step is highly beneficial in gathering
further information and staff evaluation.

The fifth step involves the Organizational Evaluation Committee of
the Administration Committee. If the proposal reaches this level for
review and evaluation, it is highly likely the proposal will go to the
Executive Committee.

The sixth step involves the Personnel Committee, provided
personnel is needed for implementation. An alternative to adding new

personnel would be directing the proposal to leadership and programs already in place.

I began the assignment of assistant to the executive secretary-treasurer with anticipation and the wholehearted belief that I understood my role. I knew Dr. George Bagley well. I was to assist him with his multiple assignments and responsibilities. We had been working together for six years and I anticipated six more together. By that time, I would have my sixty-fifth birthday and expect to retire.

Already, I had been functioning in the assignment in directing committee assignments. There were nine standing subcommittees of the Administration Committee: organizational evaluation, personnel, Shocco Springs, disaster relief, aid on pastor's salary, properties, employees retirement, constitutional study, and world hunger.

There were also short-term committees appointed after consultation with the executive secretary-treasurer. For all committees, I would prepare tentative agendas and resource materials for review, editing, and approval by Dr. Bagley. The secretary would then prepare the agendas and resources for committee meetings. I would assist the executive secretary-treasurer as needed in his preparations for meetings with the boards and commissions for convention agencies and institutions. Other assignments related to: Colloquium on Christian Higher Education, Alabama Baptist Historical Commission, associational annual meetings, associational and State Convention leadership conferences, and Christian Life and Public Affairs.

There were tangible mission initiatives developed for sharing the gospel with all the world: Bold Mission Thrust, Mission Service Corps, Good News Alabama, doubling the Cooperative Program, and launching the ministries programs of the 1980s. A major assignment for all staff personnel was planning and launching Bold Mission Thrust, a mission strategy of Southern Baptists to share the gospel with all the world populations, especially those who had never heard the gospel of Jesus Christ, and to provide every person an opportunity to participate in a New Testament worship fellowship. Indeed, this *was* a bold mission thrust. Never had we had a more compelling challenge before the Southern Baptist Convention.

Alas, the energies, resources, and commitments of Southern Baptists began to erode through the sinister one, Satan, who diverted us from the first priority (Matt. 28:19–20). Bold Mission Thrust never reached its full potential, and in many endeavors we faltered in the mission mandated by God. Bold Mission Thrust reports were made to the Southern Baptist Convention. Although the reports were courteously received and approved, the program lost momentum to the power struggle in the Southern Baptist leadership.

"Again, if the trumpet does not sound a clear call, who will get ready for battle?" (1 Cor. 14:8). Uncertain sounds were being generated among Southern Baptists. The Bold Mission Thrust reports to the messengers at the Southern Baptist Convention began sounding like brass and clanging cymbals. Our leaders were interested in and committed to a renaissance in leadership, an issue that lingers, but in the process, love lost her way. The laity from our churches knew what was happening—they usually do!

I assisted the office of executive secretary-treasurer in drafting a business and financial plan, later to realize it needed more refining. This was done by drafting the personnel manual and the operating manual for the State Board of Missions. I felt much better about the two additions. I also helped review, restate, and complete guidelines and bylaws.

Earl Potts presents goals of Bold Mission Thrust.

In those days, travel to the meetings of the Executive Board was by suggested travel groupings from geographical locations across the state. Travel groupings were utilized for the convenience of board members and for financial feasibility. The executive secretary-treasurer was an ex officio nonvoting member of all committees and work groups. As needed, the assistant was available to the executive secretary-treasurer.

The annual meetings of the Alabama Baptist Convention required much prayer, planning, and preparation. Special task forces needed assistance in expediting assignments. The secretaries and I would organize the logistics for the legislative prayer breakfast, luncheons, and important gatherings with the Executive Board members and the legislators begun by Dr. Bagley.

I interfaced with the legislators and governors on matters of proposed legislation. I personally knew Governor George C. Wallace, who was present for the dinner in honor of my election as executive secretary-treasurer, and Governor Guy Hunt, who was present when I retired as executive secretary-treasurer. I still believe him to be a godly man with integrity. Governor Jim Folsom and Governor Fob James are friends. I could be rather definitive in thoughts and judgements, but I believe it suffices to observe that serving as governor or in the legislative body carries awesome responsibilities and requires accountability.

TIME TO LISTEN

During my time as assistant to the executive secretary-treasurer, a particularly timely and needed event was the inauguration of listening sessions in 1981. The plan called for sessions in each of the twelve districts of our state. The sessions were open to all Alabama Baptists, with no restraints placed on discussion, and were recorded, transcribed, and translated in ministries and activities after contingencies were considered. These public hearings created strategy and implementation demanding of the time, energies, and expenses of the convention and entity leaders. They also affirmed the need for renewed efforts and determination for magnification of the Sunday School, the agent of Bible teaching and study in our churches.

I recall the listening session that was held in district three—Anniston—at Parker Memorial Baptist Church. The session went well.

When it was over, the hour was late and it was a long drive to Montgomery. There were five of us in the car: Andrew Tampling, George Bagley, Ellis Bush, Jim Glaze, and I—I was driving. Going south on Highway 21 from Anniston to Talladega, I began speeding. The state trooper clocked my speed at, well—it was too fast. I got a ticket. I was embarrassed over the incident. That was the only speeding ticket I got during my twenty years with the convention. I learned my lesson.

Remembering who we are as Christians and remembering what we are to be about helps enormously in times of transition. As I made my transition from my old position to Dr. Bagley's administrative assistant, I began to think of the uncertainties we face in the midst of change and realized anew that we can be secure, even when life's foundations are shaken. In thinking about this, my thoughts were directed to the Scriptures. The mind and heart yearn for religious teachings and ministries that have biblical foundations both in the Old Testament and the New Testament. God speaks specifically of this in the Old Testament when he said,

> And these words, which I command Thee this day, shall be in Thine heart. and thou shalt teach them diligently to the children and shall tell of them when they sittest in Thine house, and when Thou walkest in Thine way, and when Thou layest down and when thou risest up. And Thou shalt bind them for a sign upon Thine head, and they shalt be as frontlets between Thine eyes. (Deut. 6: 6–8)

One of the most penetrating New Testament references is

> . . . all authority is given unto me in heaven and earth, therefore go and make disciples of all nations, baptizing them in the name of the Father the Son and the Holy Spirit. Teaching them to observe all things that I have commanded you. . . . (Matt. 28:19–20)

The Testaments are replete with references to the divine imperative of observing the authority of Jesus, baptizing disciples, and teaching all things that Jesus commanded to be taught. This is a teaching as relevant, if not more so, today than the time it was uttered by the Lord. One clearly evident observation is the biblical foundation for the church.

LOUISE'S ILLNESS

An eclipse in my life at that time was the discovery of Louise's illness. It was a typical, hot July day in 1981. The sun was bright with a brightness that makes your eyes squint. I had promised David and his family that Louise and I would ride with them to Lake Martin. My son and I were interested in securing some lake property. David's neighbor had a lot and cabin on Lake Martin which was available if David wanted it.

Suddenly, and without previous warning, Louise was very passive about the whole thing. She made no comment about the cabin or property. I had a horrible feeling that something was wrong. It was not like Louise to have no comment on matters, especially something on matters involving family life and resources. We completed our inspection of the property and drove over to Kowaliga to have supper before returning to Montgomery. There the alarm was sounded. We were seated awaiting the waitress to take our orders. In conversation, my dear wife, Louise, using the masculine gender, asked, "Did he order?" as she pointed to our youngest granddaughter. Things happened fast. I suggested we return to Montgomery immediately. I don't recall what I said, but indicated to Louise we were going directly to the hospital. Our family doctor for twenty-four years, Dr. William Crum, was there, and he called in a neurologist. The long process began—tests, observations, and listening occupied our family for several hours. Ultimately, many, many days later, the diagnosis was delivered—leukemia.

There were many consultations with Dr. Crum, the neurologist, and Dr. Harry Barnes, an oncologist. Dr. Barnes endeared himself to our family. He is a most empathetic person with the highest of ethical standards and practices, a skilled and knowledgeable professional.

I knew very little about what was ahead of us. The children and I supported Louise in her desire to remain in Montgomery for all medical procedures and treatments. She was able to continue work for several months as Mission Friends director for Woman's Missionary Union. Dr. Mary Essie Stephens, executive director of WMU, was an empathetic and supportive friend during this difficult time.

Occasionally, Louise and I discussed her health. Each of us had experienced remarkably good health with few medical problems.

However, we had discussed life support systems in one of our conversations. Each indicated to the other the desire not to be sustained on life support to keep us breathing when the quality of life had deteriorated to the level of no return.

The day would come in Louise's illness when the children and I were faced with this painful decision. Though I had nurses around the clock with her for several weeks, I was with her daily and witnessed her deteriorating condition. It was painful to see her vigor and vivaciousness disappear. I would have gladly borne the suffering for her! The days passed.

Louise Potts.

THE ISSUE OF EXECUTIVE SECRETARY-TREASURER

After years of devoted service to Alabama Baptists, Dr. George Bagley announced that he would retire from the position of executive secretary-treasurer in 1983. At the 1983 convention in the Montgomery Civic Center, Alabama Baptists paid honor and expressed appreciation to Dr. George and Helen Bagley with a special tribute and a beautiful reception.

The Search Committee chairman presented guidelines to be followed by persons making nomination for executive secretary-treasurer: (1) each recommendation for the position of executive secretary-treasurer should be presented in writing, typed, if possible, and signed by the person, making sure that the recommendation is accompanied by a resume and (2) recommendations may be made to any member of the Search Committee or sent to Chairman Troy L. Morrison, Twelfth Street Baptist Church, Gadsden, Alabama.

Morrison solicited continued prayers for the Search Committee and that the committee proceed as expeditiously as possible. The committee, said the chairman, "approached the assignment with a sense of awe and humility, concerned that they find God's choice for executive secretary-treasurer." The committee reported on procedure:

1. the Search Committee made contact with all State Conventions, institutions, and agencies of the Southern Baptist Convention;
2. contact was made with all Convention Search Committees across the Southern Baptist Convention having just recently elected an executive secretary-treasurer, requesting guidelines followed by the Search Committee;
3. a get-acquainted meeting was held by the committee to get acquainted with each other, to receive a charge from the president, and to review committee responsibilities;
4. the committee worked on a draft profile for the office of executive secretary-treasurer;
5. the committee would meet in March 1983 with divisions, directors, department directors, and executive officers of convention entities;
6. recommendations from eighty-three different individuals involving thirty-three different individuals were reported received by the committee as of May 20, 1983 (later the number was eighty-seven).

As assistant to the executive secretary-treasurer, two projects were consuming my time: the employee manual for the State Board of Missions and the employee manual for all employees of the State Board of Missions. The projects were under the supervision of the Personnel Committee of the Administration Committee. I, of course, had other responsibilities.

The Search Committee for executive secretary-treasurer met monthly, sometimes bimonthly, from the beginning of the search. For the record, let me say I was not privy to any of the proceedings, including meetings, of the Search Committee until the chairman requested me to meet with the committee.

Members of the Search Committee were Mrs. Rob Bennett, Louisville; Rev. John Foster, Andulasia; Rev. Lonnie Byrd, Mobile; Mr. William Lane; Rev. Ted Brock, Selma; Rev. B. C. McGohon, Birmingham; Rev. Gilbert Barrow, Montgomery; Rev. Joe Bob Mizzell, Tuscaloosa; Rev. Gary Carver, Huntsville; Dr. Dotson Nelson, Birmingham; Mrs. Maurice West, Phenix City; and Mr. Steve Tondera, Huntsville.

The Search Committee came with an interim report to the meeting of the Administration Committee and the State Board of Missions on the afternoon of September 8, 1983. Chair Harrell Cushing reordered the agenda with committee consent placing the Search Committee report first. Dr. Troy Morrison, chairman of the Search Committee, was recognized to make the report.

Dr. Morrison indicated the committee felt led to a specific and particular individual. However, it became evident that the individual was not the one whom God had chosen at this time. In order for the program of work to continue, and for some continuity to occur beyond January 1, 1984, the committee made the following recommendations:

1. the Search Committee of the Baptist State Executive Board recommends that Dr. A. Earl Potts be called to the position of acting executive secretary-treasurer of the Baptist State Executive Board, and that his tenure begin on January 1, 1984;
2. the committee recommends that Dr. Potts serve until a recommendation is made by the Search Committee and the new executive secretary-treasurer is employed by the Baptist State Executive Board, and that all responsibilities as vested in the office of executive secretary-treasurer be assigned to the position of "acting executive secretary-treasurer" effective January 1, 1984.

Robert Calvert, pastor of First Baptist Church, Piedmont, Alabama, and member of the Administration Committee, seconded the motion. Could it be? The maker of the motion was the little boy for whom I cared when his dad, E. Calvert, was my pastor. Now he was a member of the Administration Committee, seconding the motion for me to become acting executive secretary-treasurer.

After expressing commendations for me and my appointment to this position, Chairman Morrison stated that the Search Committee intended to move forward in this attempt to find God's man for the position. He further indicated that my call would be null and void if the permanent replacement could be recommended prior to January 1, 1984. Such procedure would prevent gaps in leadership, and the work of the Baptist State Executive Board would be continued with a smooth transition in 1984. The Executive Board affirmed unanimously the recommendation by the Search Committee. Dr. Morrison, bringing the recommendation to the Baptist State Executive Board, stated that the interim period would not be of extended duration, but was necessary in order to ensure appropriate leadership and a smooth transition.

The chairman moved that the report in its entirety with the specific recommendations be adopted. Dr. Edgar Arendall seconded the motion. There was no discussion or objection to the report—it and the recommendations were approved unanimously. Chairman B. C. McGohon expressed appreciation to Dr. Morrison for serving as the chairman of the executive secretary-treasurer Search Committee, and to the members of the committee for their work. The chair expressed appreciation to me for my years of service and willingness to serve in this new capacity if called upon to do so on January 1, 1984. McGohon recognized me to make a response to the board.

At the Search Committee dinner, I was introduced as the interim executive secretary-treasurer as the "Duke of Earl." I was presented a nicely framed certificate with a gold seal affixed to it. Also, there were gifts from each member, which are in my prized collection to be given to my great-grandchildren.

How does one give maximum effort to job performance without projecting the image that you want the job?

The Search Committee was diligent in its search for the new executive secretary-treasurer. I knew interviews were being conducted. I understood the election of an executive secretary-treasurer would make null and void the need for an acting executive secretary-treasurer. I knew in my heart I had not sought the office of executive secretary-treasurer. A lot of time was given to prayer and consultation with staff associates and confidants and the Alabama Baptist leadership.

The ramifications of the decision came together in mid-December 1983. The Lord willing I would greet the New Year with a readiness to move full speed ahead. There was work to do, and it would be done decently and in order. Fellow staff members were exuberant in their response. There was a bonding in our staff leadership as each staff member was charged with excitement and expectation. It was a team effort!

We suffered the loss of a strategic team player during the 1983 Christmas season in the person of Jim Bethea. Staff members and their spouses were gathered at the Governor's House Motel, Constitution Hall, for the annual staff Christmas dinner fellowship. The occasion was special—Dr. and Mrs. Bagley were being honored by the staff on their retirement. We "passed the hat" for donations. A Special Gifts Committee had been chosen to purchase the gifts for the Bagleys. We had decided to give Dr. Bagley the fisherman's dream—boat, trailer, gear, the whole bit. Jim Bethea and Sam Granade were responsible for getting the rig from an outlet in Arkansas to the Governor's House. The evening was proceeding fabulously well until Jim Bethea was stricken very suddenly with great pain and displayed difficulty breathing. Several staff members rushed to his aid. Emergency services were summoned, CPR was administered, and he was taken to the emergency room. We prayed, but alas, Jim had suffered a fatal heart attack.

The sudden death of our friend and colleague, Jim Bethea, left us with heavy hearts. His memorial was a fitting tribute to a man who made his mark on the family of Alabama Baptists, especially the RA boys and counselors in churches all across Alabama.

MAJOR LEADERSHIP TRANSITION

A major leadership transition occurred during 1983 with the retirement of six Alabama Baptist leaders. Their absence was conspicuous at the January 1984 meeting of the State Executive Board. A resolution communicates the thoughts and memories of Alabama Baptists for these leaders:

Whereas, six Alabama Baptist leaders have come to the time of retirement at or near the end of 1983

Whereas, each of them is held in highest esteem for their illustrious service totaling more than one hundred years to our convention

Whereas, under their respective leadership the mission of Alabama Baptists has continued to prosper, and whereas these are:

Dr. George E. Bagley, Executive Secretary-Treasurer of the Baptist State Executive Board, 1963–1983; Dr. Mary Essie Stephens, Executive Director, Woman's Missionary Union, 1954–1984; Dr. Sam Granade, Director, Church Minister Relations, 1980–1984; Dr. J. Lamar Jackson, Director, College Endowment Program, 1980–1984; Dr. Otis Williams, Director, Evangelism Director, 1966–1983; and Dr. Leslie S. Wright, President, Samford University, 1958–1983.

Be it therefore resolved, that the messengers assembled for the annual session this November 16, 1983 in Montgomery, thank God for the

Task force on envangelism, 1978–1979.

profound impact these servants have had in our churches and in our lives, that we express our deep and abiding gratitude to them and to their families for their loving support and that we offer the prayer that God will grant them many, many years of fruitful ministry among us.

I would add amen to the resolution as we came to the January meeting.

Two thoughts permeated my mind and heart. I desired to create a climate into which the new executive secretary-treasurer could step without encumbrances, so that he could perform his tasks faithfully. Secondly, I wanted to do a good job for the Lord's people called Alabama Baptists during the transition period. I wanted to do a good job in faithfulness and appreciation to partners in ministry, the staff members.

I prepared for the Executive Board meeting with some trepidation. The report of the acting executive secretary-treasurer was right up front on the agenda. I spoke of my responsibility as it related to the local church, the convention's entities, the Executive Board Staff, and the Southern Baptist Convention, identifying concerns and challenges, special missions, churches in transitional communities, language missions, work with National Baptists, and endowment programs. Also, I revealed the priority concern of my heart—reaching people for Christ and his church.

CHAPTER 6

Transitioning into Executive Leadership

THE STATE BOARD OF MISSIONS HAD POSTED JANUARY 1, 1984, as the beginning for interim executive secretary-treasurer of the State Board of Missions and the Alabama Baptist State Convention. I have always taken beginnings seriously. The importance of "getting started" in new ventures has momentous possibilities, challenges, and implications. Achievement or failure is often determined by the manner of start-up.

Just as every child needs a good beginning, every marriage merits a good beginning, and every church should have a good beginning. A good beginning with a new executive secretary-treasurer was very important. I was desirous that the interim period be dynamic. Each new business endeavor should carefully analyze its needs in the marketplace and the availability of resources for those needs. Good homes are built upon viable relationships. Families stay together when there is openness, tough love, a vital faith life in Jesus Christ, and devotional prayer time and church time.

Staff personnel were exuberant in mind and spirit, and we began the New Year with high hopes. A special chapel assembly was called the morning of January 3, 1984, following the New Year's holiday. I stood before the staff with some trepidation. I knew all the members and was glad to be one of them. Courage prevailed—I experienced a special presence of the Spirit of God, a peace in my heart through the ministry of the Holy Spirit. There was an unpremeditated spontaneity among my colleagues and fellow associates, a spirit of readiness for the challenge. I knew from that hour together that the Lord was going to work his marvelous work and he was going to accomplish it through each member of the team.

Enthusiasm prevailed—the work was begun with joy, in an environment of openness and trust. We found some restraints could be removed once our expectations were identified and relationships established.

I have always functioned best in an environment of trust and openness. There have been some circumstances when I was disappointed with myself and others. I have never been content with blaming the frailties of humanity for failures and disobedience. Neither do I buy into the philosophy, "The devil made me do it." Yet, I readily confess, "where sin abounds, grace abounds much more . . ." (Rom. 5:20). To acknowledge my humanity is to acknowledge at times, "when I would do good, I don't . . ." (Rom. 7:19).

I believe the State Board of Missions was at a juncture where staff personnel could be entrusted with bold expectations for good job performance; therefore, work assignments were revised and clarified. Each staff member knew the job expectations because each was involved in crafting these expectations. Time clocks were removed—the workday was to be governed by the integrity of all employees.

My philosophy of leadership of the staff stressed the importance of working together as a team, with each team member assuming individual responsibility in job performance. Therefore, teamwork was not a threat to any member of staff, although adjustments in work assignments were made within the staff.

Additional adjustments were considered for the Administration Committee and State Board of Missions, such as (1) the auditor interpreting the audit to the Executive Board with full accountability to prevail with the State Board of Missions, (2) the appointment of an Investment Financial Review Sub-Committee with the utmost confidence in the director of business management, and in the executive secretary-treasurer (I thought more Executive Committee members should be involved in investing funds), (3) the refinement of reporting to the larger Baptist family with full reports and audits made available to Alabama Baptist churches, and (4) continuing the listening session concept of providing opportunities for input into the life and work of Alabama Baptists.

I had great expectations for all the ways in which the Lord would work in us and through us for this brief interval of time. The word "transition" took on a new and graphic meaning to me. We were aware of the transitory nature of the assignment.

I was acutely aware of some "signs" of the times. The most conspicuous sign declared boldly, "Remember our heritage!" Alabama Baptists are people who need to be aware of their heritage of faith and practice. There were ministry priorities we could not forget, loyalties to which we would cling in our progressions, especially the preeminence of Christ.

Frequently, the line from *Flanders Field* by John McCrae came to my mind when reflecting upon linking the past with the present, a procession which has been continuous from 1823: "To you from failing hands we throw the torch; be yours to hold high." Each member of the team was a torch bearer.

I believe Alabama Baptists were in a posture like the Apostle Paul in Philippians 3:13 to press on ". . . forgetting those things behind and reaching forth to the things before. . . ." Staff personnel remembered the strengths of our predecessors. We were ready, and we did press on by immersing ourselves in bold mission advances. We laid claim to the promises of God and remembered the strengths of those who had gone before us.

My first report to the Baptist State Executive Board as interim secretary-treasurer was made against the backdrop of their heritage and hope. I pledged my efforts in building strength upon strength, and cycling out the paraphernalia. I saw my responsibilities as primarily twofold: to create a climate into which the new executive secretary-treasurer could enter at any time with a pledge of my support, and to perform faithfully the tasks of the office to the best of my ability with God as my helper. Furthermore, I identified the local church as the most important entity in Baptist life. Other Baptist entities of Christian higher education, child care, senior life, missions information, and communication are linked in the partnerships of heritage and hope with the local church. I hasten to acknowledge the importance of the convention with its position statement on authority:

> While autonomous in its own affairs, the Convention disclaims all right of exercising authority over any church, association, or convention, recognizing the independence of the churches and the autonomy of all Baptist bodies. (ABSC Constitution, Article III)

My first report to the Administration Committee consisted of the following thoughts and actions:

1. being sensitive and responsive to the needs of the churches,
2. preparing the way for the new executive secretary-treasurer,
3. conducting weekly meetings with division directors,
4. meeting with all staff members—stressing working together as a team,
5. having the independent auditor for the convention report directly to the Baptist State Executive Board,
6. identifying the need for an investment-financial review subcommittee.

Elree Waddell, reporting for the Organizational Evaluation Committee, recommended that a Communications Department be established. Joe Bob Mizzell, chairman of the Personnel Committee, recommended Robert Duck as director of public relations. The recommendations were approved, opening the window for this department's services to be expanded and enhanced.

Steve Tondera, chairman of the Properties Committee, presented recommendations for acquisition of property and construction of a BSU Center in Huntsville, a two-year extension on use of a mobile unit on the Montgomery site of a proposed BSU Center, repairs to the Baptist Building in Montgomery, and the purchase of a car for the use of the acting executive secretary-treasurer. The Administration Committee approved all recommendations.

Mrs. Carolyn Miller, president of Woman's Missionary Union, auxiliary to ABSC, shared plans for honoring Dr. Mary Essie Stephens, executive director of WMU. Dr. Stephens served in the office for thirty years and was honored at a special retirement celebration March 20, 1984, at First Baptist Church, Huntsville, Alabama. The Alabama Baptist family was invited to attend this special recognition and say thank you to a special lady who served the Alabama Baptist mission faithfully. Mrs. Miller requested $10,000 toward a gift and to help defray expenses for the retirement celebration. Dr. Dotson Nelson moved that the request be granted—the Administration Committee approved the motion unanimously.

My first meeting with the Baptist State Executive Board in the office of acting executive secretary-treasurer was held at Samford University, January 23, 1984, at 10:30 A.M. It was an amazing experience. I felt solemn awe in my soul. Several factors contributed to this feeling. I was in the presence of pastoral and lay leaders, as I had been before, but never in this role.

I knew all these people, but not in the relationship of leader among leaders. There were many gifted people present: Dr. Hudson Baggett, editor of *The Alabama Baptist*; Dr. Thomas Corts, the new visionary president of Samford University; Dr. Tom Collier, executive director extraordinaire of the Alabama Baptist Children's Home; Dr. Leslie Wright, eminent past president of Samford University; Dr. N. H. McCrummen, stalwart president of Judson College; Dr. U. A. McManus, president of the Baptist Foundation of Alabama; Dr. Mary Essie Stephens, missionary statesperson and executive director of the Woman's Missionary Union; Dr. William Weaver, founding president of Mobile College; Dr. George Jackson, faithful director of the Howard College Extension Division; and Dr. Vernon Yearby, experienced past president of the Baptist Foundation of Alabama. Others who were present included: Evan Zeiger, Beth Wheaton, David Potts, Neal Nichols, Jack Brymer, Cathleen Lewis, and my colleagues and associates in the work of the Baptist State Executive Board, all equally gifted in their respective roles of leadership.

I must confess my inadequacies to the challenges before me. I felt somewhat dismayed as the acting executive secretary-treasurer, somewhat frightened to be sitting at the table where the venerables had sat: Dr. D. F. Green, Dr. L. E. Barton, Dr. F. M. Barnes, Dr. A. Hamilton Reid, and Dr. George Bagley. Furthermore, as the acting executive secretary-treasurer, I was not supposed to be in the chair.

The enormous responsibility in planning the suggested agenda for the meeting was intense to the point of being scary, but then a blessed peace came upon me. I remembered, "When I am afraid, I will trust in you. In God whose word I praise, in God I trust; I will not be afraid, what can mortal men do to me?" (Ps. 56:3–4). Furthermore, I had some capable associates: James Glaze, Gaynelle Young, and Don Watterson. Again, a consoling thought was the realization that the responsibility was a shared responsibility. We had a great team for mission achievement with the Alabama Baptist family.

PARTNERSHIPS—NIGERIA AND ALABAMA

The presence of Alabama Baptists in Nigeria was interpreted by the Nigerian Baptists as proof that fellow Baptists cared about them, loved them, and prayed for them. The missionaries in Nigeria rejoiced in the Nigeria-Alabama partnership formation. The sights and sounds of

Nigeria are unforgettable and astoundingly uplifting. The Nigerian people are kind, generous, gracious, sensitive, and hospitable. Even in 1995, the Baptists of Nigeria in a predominantly Muslim area were dedicated to the Lord and excited about serving Christ and sharing Christ with those around them.

Political developments in Nigeria raised concern for the Alabama partnership with Nigeria. I recall twenty-six students, faculty members, and Marla Corts from Samford University were scheduled for departure when the news came through that military forces had ousted the democratic civilian government. I called some of our Nigerian missionaries in Kano, Lagos, and Kaduna. Their response was encouragement to proceed with departure. I talked with Dr. Akande, executive secretary of the Nigerian Baptist Convention, and his response was the same. Missionary W. A. Cowley coordinated the mission trip for the Samford group.

Among the Alabamians who participated in the evangelistic crusade were Larry Davis and family (I shall never forget their love), Roger Willmore, Don Marsh, Rick Marshall, Kenneth Clements, Phillip Wise, James Shoemaker, Ed Walters, and Ron Summers. They went to Ogbomosho, Kanduna, Ede, Owerri, Port Harcourt, Oyo City, and Lagos. The needs of the Nigerians were for medical personnel and hospitals, ophthalmologists, urologists, orthopedic surgeons, plastic surgeons, ENT specialists, psychiatrists, prosthetists, anesthesiologists, general surgeons, medical maintenance repair technicians, dentists, construction workers, artists, music teachers, and student workers.

Subsequent to the closure of the partnership in mission with Nigeria, the Foreign Mission Board, SBC "acclaimed the Nigeria/Alabama partnership as the most fruitful partnership in long term, in conversions, baptisms, discipled church growth and new churches started." Many great experiences lay ahead of us with our national and international partnerships. Working on this partnership in 1984 was a joy.

DISSEMINATION OF INFORMATION

I began my interim responsibilities with a desire to keep Alabama Baptists informed about the work of the executive secretary-treasurer's office. Questions necessitate response, especially if the question is related to the State Convention, Executive Committee, or State Board of Missions. Oftentimes, response requires further exploration and the

Wallace Henley and S. T. Ola Akande, Nigerian Partnership, 1985.

appointment of a committee. B. C. McGohon, chair of the State Board of Missions, appointed a Committee on Dissemination of Information. This committee was made up of Chairman Elree T. Waddell, Billy Hunt, Bob Carter, W. R. Harrison, and Doug Olive.

"Henley and Potts call for openness with information about Convention," headlined the January 26, 1984, issue of *The Alabama Baptist*. I believe information should be provided to the inquirer. Furthermore, I believe the recipient of the information should be responsible with the information received. Dr. Hudson Baggett, editor of *The Alabama Baptist*, agreed that dissemination of information is of great importance to our constituents.

Listening sessions were sponsored by some associations. For instance, Clarke Baptist Association hosted listening sessions for its churches, with both ministerial and lay leadership present for open discussion, questions, and responses. I, Jim Glaze, and Robert Duck were present as employed personnel of the State Board of Missions. Fred Lackey, vice president of the State Convention, represented Convention President Walley Henley.

All questions received responses from the convention. Several pastors expressed concern over the lack of information on the salaried employees of the Board of Missions. I believe, however, that giving carte blanche to the distribution of information, especially about employees of the Board of Missions, would be inappropriate and cause unnecessary relational problems. Questions regarding information on personnel employment, salary, and benefits, however, are appropriate.

Dr. Lackey affirmed the openness of the convention president and the Personnel Committee. The group was assured that there was a plan in place for receiving information and that the plan would be reviewed, and, if needed, refined.

The Executive Committee of the State Board of Missions is conscientious with employment policies and procedures. Job descriptions receive careful review and approval once the position has been justified by the Organizational Evaluation Committee, the executive secretary-treasurer, and the Personnel Committee.

Job assignment is carefully evaluated by the Organizational Evaluation Committee for approximately one hundred employees. The job assignment is approved upon recommendation of the Organization Evaluation Committee by the Executive Committee and the State Board of Missions.

The executive secretary-treasurer initiates the search for persons qualified for ministry assignment. Then, the prospective employee appears before the Personnel Committee and the executive secretary-treasurer. During the interview, the committee always asks the prospective employee to share personal testimony of conversion, faith in Christ, and divine call to ministry. The job description is reviewed with the candidate.

When these steps have been followed with prayer and deliberations, the candidate is excused from the meeting while the Personnel Committee evaluates the credentials, qualifications, and divine calling of the candidate. Then the Personnel Committee invites the candidate to return, and the chair of the Personnel Committee declares the decision of the committee to the candidate.

All executive personnel, department directors, and campus ministers are approved by both the Executive Committee and the State Board of Missions. All department associates are approved by the Executive

Committee. All secretarial staff, house, and maintenance personnel are employed by the executive secretary-treasurer upon recommendation of the department director.

Meanwhile, the executive secretary-treasurer, the Personnel Committee, the ex officio convention president, and the chairman of the Executive Board carefully review salary-scale grades and benefit proposals for every employee. The salary scales and benefits are approved by the Executive Committee and the State Board of Missions.

Early upon becoming executive secretary-treasurer, I reviewed job descriptions, salary benefits, and schedules for secretarial personnel associates, house maintenance, and employees at Shocco Springs. Several employees deserved salary adjustments, especially secretarial personnel and personnel responsible for building operations, maintenance, and housekeeping both at the Baptist Building and at Shocco Springs. All employees at Shocco Springs were brought into the retirement and health insurance benefits plan of the State Board of Missions. This action was long overdue, as this matter had been a lingering concern for several years. When I completed the evaluation reviews with the assistance of supervisors, I presented my findings and proposals to the Personnel Committee, who in turn presented them to the Executive Committee and the State Board of Missions for review and consideration.

I believe the reader will affirm the thoroughness of the process. The work of all employees is reviewed and evaluated annually by the executive secretary-treasurer and supervisors. In addition, I invited the director and associate director of business management to sit in on the evaluations, and put all salaries, travel expenses, and benefits under their watch and the watch of the executive secretary-treasurer. I also had the administrative assistant to the executive secretary-treasurer record the evaluations.

The personnel committee has full information on all employees for the annual review. Reports are made to the Executive Committee and frequently to the State Board of Missions. I believe the salaries and benefits for the employees of the State Board of Missions are equitable and fair (and I have high expectation of personnel in job performance). Salary information is available to Alabama Baptists and can be obtained by consulting the convention annual, Executive Board members, and the executive secretary-treasurer.

REACHING PEOPLE

The theological principle states, "People are first in the love of God. People are first in the mission of Christ. People are first in the mission of the church. People are first in the tasks of worship, evangelism, discipling, Bible teaching, and stewardship mission." The ultimate priority of reaching people is lodged in the Commission of Matthew 9:35–36 and 28:19–20. Steps of the theological principle for reaching people are listed below:

Step 1—Linking the association with the convention to reach people: On April 2, 1984, I communicated with all the directors of Associational Missions regarding three urgent concerns. First, I acknowledged the amicable relationships among the directors and State Board of Missions staff personnel. However, I believed attention was needed in the planning and funding phase of our work. I felt a missing link (phase) in planning if Alabama Baptists were to reach the people, develop discipleship, and strengthen mission support.

With much praying the first of the discussions of the partnership planning process began. The process resulted in what has been acclaimed as one of the most strategic planning processes in Alabama Baptist life.

A forum of openness and frankness prevailed. Each director of missions, convention staff person, pastor, and church leader provided input without being intimidated or interrupted. The partnership planning concept was endorsed unanimously by key leadership. The following are examples.

Tom Roote, director of missions, Birmingham Baptist Association:

> I think the idea of annual state staff and director of Missions' "get togethers" is outstanding . . . using the knowledge of director of Missions about local churches and coupling it with state resources in planning could forge a better total effect. Thank you for ushering in an era of understanding.

George Y. Williams, director of missions, Etowah Baptist Association:

> Thank you for the invitation to attend the meeting on April 26 for the state staff and the association's director of Missions. I thought the

meeting was very good and the beginning of a new era among us in the work of Alabama Baptists.

Herbert Palmer, director of missions, Russell Association:

Thank you for the meeting of cooperative planning. Would it be helpful to add one other step to the process by bringing together a representative church council group, representatives from churches with different size memberships?

T. A. Benefield, director of missions, Sand Mountain Baptist Association:

. . . There seems to be a new challenge and new thrill in this work. Your declarations of first priorities are very encouraging. We are in the people business.

Bob Franklin, director of missions, Montgomery Baptist Association:

. . . The possibility of some joint planning between the state staff and director of Missions is a welcomed move, and I believe will strengthen us all. It would give director of Missions input into areas where we consistently need help. Thank you for your concern for reaching people.

Hugh Chambliss, director of missions, Madison Baptist Association:

Thank you for the important and helpful meeting we had together yesterday. It seems to me a lot of things surfaced that will be beneficial to all of us as we seek to work together through the association and the State Convention.

Dr. Darrell Robinson, pastor, Dauphin Way Baptist Church, Mobile:

It is especially meaningful to me the way you are available to pastors of any size church. I think this is vitally important for the fellowship of the convention. I am thankful, also for the strong emphasis on the strengthening and growth of the local churches.

Tom Kyser, pastor, Old Spanish Fort Baptist Church:

> I am excited about your thrust in evangelism and trust that our state
> will somehow make it priority.

Step 2—Reaching People Forum: Reaching People Forums were
held in six strategic geographical locations in Alabama—Monroeville,
Troy, Selma, Birmingham, Decatur, and Gadsden. Andy Anderson,
Harry Piland, Don Watterson, and I spoke to the theme. State Board of
Missions staff and directors of missions did hard work in putting
together the program and getting the people to participate. Plans to
reach people and to help people reach dreams were the key elements in
programming.

Forums for churches on sharing ideas for implementing growth by
size of Sunday School enrollment were held in strategic geographical
areas. The numerical breakdown is as follows: total participants from
local churches—pastors/staff/lay leadership: 464; total participants from
associations—directors of missions and staff: 40; total of all participants:
504; number of churches represented: 283; churches by Sunday School
enrollment categories: 0–299: 140; 300–499: 62; 500–749: 33; 750–1,499:
41; 1,500–up: 7. In addition, thirty-four associations responded for
people's search training.

Growing churches are always involved in four actions: (1) establishing initial contacts with unchurched people, (2) establishing
meaningful relations with unchurched people, (3) maintaining a planned
harvesting program to win those with whom relations are begun, and (4)
assimilating converts into the church body.

Step 3—Our priority: reaching people is all that is involved in individuals coming to faith in Jesus Christ. It means the church involving
more people in meaningful Bible study through the Sunday School, discipleship and church training, missionary education and involvement
through Brotherhood and WMU, music ministry, worship, outreach, and
mission support. Reaching people embraces Christian growing in the
fullness of Christ.

Major church events dedicated to reaching people are events whose
concepts are applicable and relevant today—the decade of the ministers.
Different forms and different methods may be used; however, the events
are generic yet strategically important to reaching people. As in the

Rallying Theme, "To whom much is given, of him much is required."

God always has had pastors equipped to proclaim the gospel, reach people for Christ, and equip the believer. Alabama Baptists are a people of God to whom much has been given. Also, consider the laity leadership here. Laypeople fill the church pews Sunday after Sunday, week in and week out. They love the church, the body of Christ, supporting the mission of the church with tithes and offerings and assuming leadership roles and servant leadership responsibilities.

I believe the local church is the most strategic body for kingdom advance. A devoted pastor and an equipped congregation form a formidable team challenging the powers of Satan, advancing the effective kingdom of God, and nurturing humanity with caring love. Having said that, I believe the Lord laid the burden for reaching people upon the hearts of pastors and the laity.

The convention emphasizes reaching people, developing believers, strengthening missions, giving of our sons and daughters and our resources, and starting churches, all timely commandments for the churches in the mid-eighties. Still, the defining statement for emphasis is *reaching people.*

I believed from the time of my ordination to the ministry through decades of service to this date that the Sunday School in the church provides the dynamics for winning people to the Lord and his church. To build a standard Sunday School is to put in place the plan for reaching more people for Bible study, for salvation experience through nurturing love.

I have been in Sunday School for seventy years. My first class was in a one-room church, but there was sufficient space for a Sunday School. It required innovation; remember this was 1923, before folding doors and partitions. The concept was there, however. The pastor and church leadership divided the one-room church building into classrooms, using wire supports for curtains. The pews were used for seats and the teacher stood between the church pews. During the summer months, children's classes were held in the shade of oak trees. But, we had Sunday School.

Our Sunday School lessons were printed on Scripture cards, each with a memory verse and a beautiful and colorful Bible picture. The teacher expected each student to memorize the verse and quote it when called on. I found out you could learn a lot of Scripture during the years from Sunday School cards.

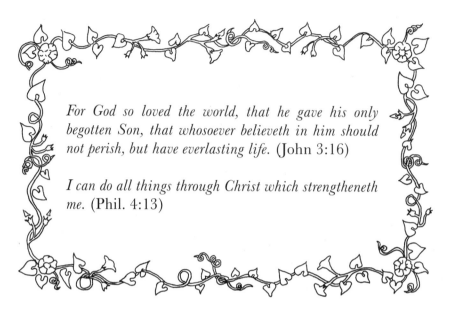

For God so loved the world, that he gave his only begotten Son, that whosoever believeth in him should not perish, but have everlasting life. (John 3:16)

I can do all things through Christ which strengtheneth me. (Phil. 4:13)

Dr. Don Watterson, associate to the executive secretary-treasurer and a leader in reaching people, reported to the Baptist State Executive Board on January 23, 1984, that from 1940 to 1983 one of seven persons in Alabama was a member of an Alabama Baptist church. By 1950, one of six was a member. By 1960, the number was one of five and by 1970, one of four people.

Dr. Watterson reported that the churches were in a holding pattern since 1970. He asked where Alabama Baptists wanted to be by 1990 and stated that in the year 2000, unless we decide where under God we ought to be, we will not know how to plan to get there.

One of the most important actions for the churches is to come to a renewed awareness of and commitment to strategies that enable us to reach more people. In 1960, we had one Baptist church for every 1,155 people in the state. From 1960 to 1980, we had a net increase of 216 churches.

A story goes that when John Ed Matthison was beginning his first pastorate, his father, a prominent minister, handed him a copy of a book by Arthur Flake, Sunday School secretary of the Baptist Sunday School Board, and said, "Son if you want to build a great church here is the way you do it." He was holding a copy of *Five Principles of Sunday School Growth*. These five principles are: find the people, train the workers, provide the space, enlarge the organization, and enroll the people. To this list I would add: teach the Bible.

The Sunday School in the local church is essential to reaching people. According to Arthur Flake in his 1922 book *Building a Standard Sunday School:*

> A good Sunday School is not an accident. It must be built. In order to build a good Sunday School three things are necessary: first, the essentials of a good Sunday School must be known; second, the plans for building a good Sunday School must be understood; third, the specifications for building a good Sunday School must be faithfully followed. (4)

The Bible teaches, "Train up a child in the way he should go; and when he is old, he will not depart from it" (Prov. 22:6), and ". . . a child left to himself brings his mother to shame" (Prov. 29:15).

Jesus showed the necessity of religious teaching for all children, youth, and adults. One of the demonstrative actions of Jesus in this regard is recorded in Matthew 18:1–6 where the disciples pose the question "Who is greatest in the kingdom of heaven?" Jesus called a little child unto him and set him in the midst of them and said,

> Verily I say unto you, except you become converted and become as children, you shall not enter the kingdom of heaven. Whosoever humbles himself as this little child, the same is the greatest in the kingdom of heaven, and whosoever shall receive one such little child in My name receives Him. But whosoever shall offend one of these little ones who believes in me, it would be better for a millstone to be hung around his neck, and then he be drowned in the depth of the sea.

A more poignant teaching could not be directed to the parent, the adult, or the church family regarding teaching values. My point in reference to the Sunday School having biblical foundation or a charge from God is germane to all ministries and programs of the church and the State Board Missions of the Alabama Baptist State Convention.

NEW WORK IN ALABAMA

New work in Alabama has many different shapes, sites, structures, and variation of sounds in worship and fellowship. A study of church sites would be a most interesting exercise for the geologist and sounds of worship interpretations would make for a worthwhile project. Too often, sufficient time, research, development of sketches, plans, and recommendations are not given to church structures, where life-changing decisions are made weekly.

Land terrain affects the site and influences the architectural design of a church. The McElwain Baptist Church plan is one case study in church growth and expansion. It was founded in 1895 in a rural, over-the-mountain community from downtown Birmingham. Once land became available to developers, changes began to take place and urban sprawl reached the McElwain Community in the 1940s. When I became pastor of the McElwain Baptist Church in April 1950, the Crestline Community in Mountain Brook was established and Crestline Park was being developed. Both the city of Birmingham and the city of Mountain Brook wanted to incorporate Crestline Park. Birmingham won this real-estate prize. I believed it to be a good decision, but of course there were strong feelings and responses on both sides.

The visionary congregation of McElwain Baptist Church saw what was happening to farm lands and pasture lands as owners yielded to building developers. By 1950, new families were moving in to the area weekly, including the new pastor and family. Fortunately, the congregation was ready for visionary actions.

By 1954–1955, a Church Planning/Building Committee was established and an architectural firm was secured to work with the committee to study, plan, design, and propose plans. The church prayed, gave the Church Planning/Building Committee a good hearing, and by adopting its recommendations, both short range and long range, initiated action almost immediately.

A decision was made to provide educational space for 1,200 in Sunday School and to build an auditorium seating 1,000–1,200 worshipers with a multiple phase building process. The congregation made the strategic decision in 1954–1955. The church moved from a land-locked site to a much-enlarged site through the gift of five acres by a loving founder of the church in 1895, Mrs. W. B. Hogan Baker. It continued to buy land or construct buildings every two years for twenty years. The style of the buildings were shaped by site design and by need. Eventually, the church congregation grew to one of the largest in the state and was in the top one hundred churches in mission giving and in church growth.

The history of "new church starts" in Alabama reflects the many differently shaped sites, buildings, and variety of sounds of worship. During Alabama's prestate pioneer era, Baptist missionaries from the North and East preached to the people across the territories and established new churches on the wild frontiers. When Alabama was admitted to statehood in 1819, there were already organized Baptist churches. Many were pastored by visionary pastoral leaders. They were biblically based and preached the gospel dynamically and with authenticity in Christian living.

One such pastor was Charles Crow, pastor of the Ocmulgee Missionary Baptist Church in Perry County, Cahaba Association, and one of the founders of the Alabama Baptist Convention on October 23, 1823. One of the first actions taken by the convention was to appoint fifteen domestic missionaries whose primary responsibility was to start new churches.

The following corresponding secretaries were instrumental in starting new churches and missions: T. M. Bailey, 1874–1886; Crumpton, 1886–1895, 1899–1915; William C. Bledsoe, 1896–1899; Executive Secretary-Treasurer W. F. Yarbrough, 1916–1919; D. F. Green, 1920–1929; L. E. Barton, 1930-1934; F. M. Barnes, 1935–1943; A. Hamilton Reid, 1944–1963; George E. Bagley, 1963–1983; A. Earl Potts, 1984–1990; and Troy Morrison 1990—.

During the depression years of 1929–1931, new work was not a priority due to lack of funds. A renewed effort was begun when Dr. A. Hamilton Reid became executive secretary-treasurer in 1944. Dr. Reid was convinced that the State Convention could and should do more to encourage and strengthen the work of the associations, giving special attention to the needs of the large number of rural churches in the state in addition to expanding the work in rapidly growing city centers. He recommended the following program to the committee for approval or as a recommendation to the Executive Board for final approval:

1. [that the Executive Board] enter into a joint city missions program with the Home Mission Board in the four major cities of Alabama;

2. [that the Executive Board] establish joint employment between HMB-ABSC employing five rural district missionaries in Alabama at a salary of $3,000, plus $600 for expenses;

3. that the appropriations by HMB be sent to the State Board-State Convention with State Board selecting and directing subject to the approval of HMB;

4. that State Board sponsor a conference for all Baptist missionaries in Alabama, supported by various boards and associations;

5. that associations be encouraged to employ local missionaries with assistance of the State Board;

6. that each association be requested to appoint an active missions committee to direct the work in the association (A. Hamilton Reid, *Baptists in Alabama*, 361). (This action of the Executive Board catapulted associational growth and development in Alabama.)

Collis Cunningham, J. E. Berkstresser, J. W. Lester, J. W. Wells, and J. H. Chambers were elected to serve in the five districts. I knew each man. They were a zealous group, ardently committed to new formations of believers resulting in new congregations and new churches. Today, the heartbeat for new churches goes on! Alabama Baptist church congregations are fostering new missions and churches, revitalizing established congregations, enlarging church buildings, and starting new churches all across the land. There were 3,091 churches affiliated with the Alabama Baptist State Convention in 1990. But more are needed!

There were seventy-four associations in the state in 1951; sixty-five of them had a missionary for full-time or part-time. Isn't that remarkable? Through the cooperation between the associations and the State Convention, telling results became evident:

1. many rural churches, which had ceased to function, were revived and new ones were organized;

2. the work was organized and planned in the centers;

3. 167 new churches were organized or renewed over a seven year period with 117,699 in membership (A. Hamilton Reid, *Baptists in Alabama*, 361).

Strategies were developed by the New Work Task Force in 1984. Don Watterson was chair; Mary Essie Stephens, Billy Nutt, and Wyndell Jones, were task-force members. "New Work Priority" was built into the 1985–1990 Bold Mission Thrust and had three emphases: (1) reaching people, (2) developing believers, and (3) strengthening missions.

The following needs became the marching orders for every department of work, every program ministry, and the Cooperative Program budget:

1. associations identify needs for new work and develop strategy in cooperation with State Board of Missions;
2. convention and associations promote need for resources—use specifics;
3. target the twenty counties projecting greatest population growth;
4. joint ventures in metro associations—target the inner city;
5. provide funding for new work;
6. enlist and train the needed church extension personnel volunteers from laity.

We prayed and planned for implementation. Some of the emphases toward implementation were the following:

1. Sunday School Revivals, 1984–1985—Sunday School leadership provided by associational directors and directors of missions laid the strategic plans and Sunday School enrollment increased to a total of 591,204 people by 1990, 40,000 in 1984–1985 alone. It was Alabama's year of the miracle;
2. bold people search—the initial step toward establishing communication between Christians and nonchristians;
3. super September 1985, Reach Five in Eighty-five—accomplished through the contagious and enthused leadership in expecting miracles in Sunday School;
4. planned growth in giving—led by N. F. Greer and followed by Harrell Cushing, who is relentless in increasing gifts through the Cooperative Program;
5. super spiral program—ask Andrew Smith in the Sunday School department how well it works;
6. strengthening family life—led by Henry Lyon, a devoted man of God, making miracles happen in family life and across Alabama;
7. "Good News America"—revivals led by Harper Shannon, who was anchored in the Word of God and believed in prayer and planning for continuous witnessing;
8. start a cradle roll and reach families—Kathy Burns, a fabulous minister to people, resurrected this ministry with extensive results;
9. organizational revival—given leadership by the committee.

In churches and Sunday Schools that are effectively reaching people and teaching them the Word of God, the pastor is the servant leader. Working in cooperation with the Sunday School director and/or minister of education, he demonstrates his commitment by planning where the Sunday School should be. He leads in setting goals, in planning, in organization, in enlisting and training teachers, in evaluating the use of space, and in organizing visitation programs.

In the spring 1984 *Challenge*, Don Watterson, associate priority of reaching people becomes the obsession of the pastor, he sees the necessity of building a team of people and equipping them to accomplish the task." Andy Anderson of the Sunday School Board said, "I am delighted for the privilege of sharing in the recent Reaching People Forum in Alabama. I believe from the spirit of excitement and determination among those who attended, there are greater days ahead for Alabama." There were!

CHAPTER 7

Guiding Alabama Baptists as Executive Secretary-Treasurer

DR. JOE BOB MIZZELL, CHAIRMAN OF THE BAPTIST STATE Executive Board, called a special meeting of the Executive Board for April 19, 1984, 11:00 A.M. Dr. Mizzell indicated the Search Committee for executive secretary-treasurer would bring a recommendation to the board.

The hour arrived. The chapel at the Baptist Building was packed with board members, guests, and heads of convention entities. After Dr. Edgar Arendall read the Scripture and led in prayer, the board began its deliberations.

I was very high emotionally as I waited alone in the office. The Search Committee had previously met with me about their decision to recommend me as executive secretary-treasurer, Executive Board of the Alabama Baptist State Convention. I had given my consent, believing it was the Lord's will, as I responded to questions by members of the committee. Committee members were generous with their statements of affirmation and support.

The gravity of the decision to be made by the board hit me with full import when the 11:00 o'clock hour arrived. Awaiting the board decision, my heart was with Louise. It was painful. Louise, my dear wife, could not be with me, being very sick that very day, not realizing that she had sixteen days of life before her death, May 5, 1984.

The minutes of the called special meeting record that the board chairman, having stated the purpose for the meeting, recognized Dr. Troy Morrison, chairman of the Search Committee. Morrison said,

> . . . The Search Committee unanimously recommends that Dr. A. Earl Potts be called as executive secretary-treasurer of the Baptist State Executive Board at a beginning salary and benefits as provided in the 1984 Cooperative Program budget. We further recommend that we pledge our loyal support in prayers and involvement to our new executive secretary-treasurer when he is elected by this board. (*Minutes*, Baptist State Executive Board, April 19, 1984, 1)

Dr. Dotson Nelson, pastor of the Mountain Brook Baptist Church and a member of the Search Committee, seconded the motion.

Dr. Troy Morrison spoke to the motion,

> We are unified and unanimous in our recommendation. . . . [H]aving served as acting executive secretary-treasurer from January 1, 1984 to this date . . . he has proven to be the kind of dedicated and efficient leader that many of us knew he would be. Under his leadership, the morale, the spirit, the dedication of the entire staff of this Baptist State Executive Board has accelerated to what appears to be an all time high. New goals have been set, a new direction has been charted . . . he has exemplified the kind of tenaciousness and toughness, tempered with kindness and love, that commands the respect and fellowship of each of those who are employed by this Board. . . . He has secured our denomination with direction. . . . (*Minutes*, State Baptist Executive Board, April 19, 1984, 1)

Dr. Morrison recognized members of the Search Committee: Steve Tondera, Mrs. Maurice West, John Foster, Lonnie Byrd, Ted Brock, Gary Carver, Gilbert Barrow, William E. Love, Lois Bennett, Joe Bob Mizzell, Dotson Nelson, and Wallace Henley. B. C. McGohon and Harrell Cushing had served ex officio. Chairman Mizzell then called for questions or comments. Edgar Arendall requested that it be added that I was a real Christian gentlemen of basic character and integrity.

The question was called for, and a vote was cast by standing. The vote was unanimously in favor of calling me as executive secretary-treasurer. Perhaps it was Jim Glaze who was asked to escort me into the meeting, at which time Chairman Mizzell announced the unanimity of the

Baptist State Executive Board in approving the recommendation from the Search Committee.

I had made a commitment to the Search Committee to serve, God willing, if elected, for the next five years as the board may request and provided that God continued to bless me with good health. But I shall never forget my utter sense of unworthiness at that moment. I beheld the facial expressions of the board members, staff members, family members, executive officers of convention entities, guests, and retirees. My prayer was in those moments, "Dear Lord, may I be found faithful to you and the Baptists of Alabama." I especially appreciated the presence of

Troy L. Morrison.

Dr. George Bagley, retired executive secretary-treasurer. Following the meeting, Dr. Bagley observed that this unanimous election of the executive secretary-treasurer was a first. I was so thankful! I am not at all sure how I would have handled it had it been different. I think Dr. Bagley believed me not to be a viable candidate for the task because of my age, and he had no reason to encourage my nomination. However, he let the Search Committee function without his overt support of me as his successor, for which I was grateful. Such had not been the situation in some previous decisions for the office when it got "messy" and politicized. I was glad the Search Committee did not have that situation to contend with in this election.

Chairman Mizzell recognized me for my response and comments (see Appendix II). Then Wallace Henley, president of the Alabama Baptist State Convention, was recognized for his statement. I had given thought and prayer to my response, and President Henley stated that my speech validated the correctness of the recommendation. He shared his appreciation for the challenge of reaching a world for Jesus Christ and reaching a state and nation for Jesus Christ. A major portion of the responsibility for reaching this world for Christ rests on Southern Baptists.

President Henley reminded us that our mission focus is absolutely imperative and that bold missions are of God. He stated that leadership is servanthood, "We are servants of our creator—speaking for those present and for the pastors in the state who expressed their desire to work shoulder to shoulder . . . we praise God for the decision today."

Dotson Nelson moved that we strike the word "acting" from the title of executive secretary-treasurer. The motion was seconded and passed unanimously. As the saying goes, "the die was cast"—the decision was final. The call was "to the work, to the work, we are servants of God."

I shall never forget the outpouring of love, support, affirmation, and prayer by all the men and women serving on the Executive Committee and State Board of Missions and their spouses. The Administration Committee acted in a thoughtful, prayerful manner. Ted Brock moved that Louise be remembered with a beautiful floral arrangement, a most tender action by the members of the State Board of Missions.

Dotson Nelson requested a letter be drafted to Louise by the convention president. I really appreciated the thoughtfulness shown for Louise and my family on April 19 with the beautiful flowers and the letter, which read as follows:

Dear Louise:

On behalf of the members of the Administration Committee and of myself personally, I want to let you know how deep is our joy on this day that Earl has been selected as our executive secretary-treasurer. Knowing of the years of partnership you have shared with Earl in ministry, we feel that the decision of the Executive Board was not only an affirmation of your husband, but of you as well. It is not often a man has the privilege of building on foundations he himself has helped lay. We also recognize that you played a significant role in laying these foundations. Your personal commitment to the causes of Christ through the Alabama Baptist State Convention is a source of great inspiration. You have given yourself. You have given your family. You have given your husband. The Holy Spirit has caused you to nurture a family of committed persons working in Alabama Baptist life. But most importantly, you have given yourself. All of us who are part of the Alabama Baptist family feel that your ministry among us has enhanced the outreach for the Lord Jesus Christ extended by the churches and institutions of our state. You have helped keep our eyes on missions, you have steered us to a deep appreciation for the ministries of the local church. You have been model as a pastor's wife for many women, and a blessing to all you have touched.

In Christ's Bond,

Wallace Henley, President
Alabama Baptist State Convention

Surrounded by an outpouring of affirmation for my family and myself, I could not help but remember all of those men and women in the Alabama Baptist family who had gone before me. Each of these people is a link reminding us of our biblical heritage.

LINKAGES

Linkages are essential—linkages are of God. The Bible is history from the beginning. "In the beginning God . . . " (Gen. 1:1). God acted and there was creation of man, woman, and child. Linkages began when God spoke.

History is God's story. Pick a decade or century, and review will affirm sacred linkages. The third decade of the nineteenth century is one of those decades.

The Ocmulgee Baptist Church, located in the Cahaba Association, illustrates my point. Founded on June 10, 1820, the church celebrated 175 years, on June 11, 1995. Robert Taylor, a strong man of God, is the current pastor.

The Reverend Charles Crow was the first pastor of Ocmulgee. Consider this extraordinary man of God, both devoted and beloved pastor and visionary denominational statesman. He realized God's people are people who are "surrounded" in the community of faith and practice. His gravesite is in the cemetery at Ocmulgee, an appropriate historical marker identifying his grave.

Charles Crow was most influential as one of the founders and the first president of the Alabama Baptist State Convention. Individuals and ladies' missionary societies gave what they could to fund the new convention. One of the societies sent two pairs of hand-knitted socks, and one lady sent a gold watch and chain as her offering.

Reverend Charles Crow was elected. This was during the third decade of the nineteenth century, and God's Spirit was shaping his mission enterprise among the Baptists in Alabama.

God was working in the hearts of his people gloriously! William Carey of England, shoemaker, humble pastor, self-taught scholar, pioneer missionary, linguist, selfless benefactor of India, was living a devout life. An avid student of the Scriptures, even during work hours he had a hand-made map of the world posted on the wall above his work bench. God gave him global vision and a burdened heart for the unsaved. He worked. He studied the Scriptures. He prayed. God spoke, calling him to preach the gospel to his brethren and sisters in India. He called upon them "to attempt great things for God and to expect great things from God."

Meanwhile, the lives and destinies of Adoniram and Ann Hasseltine Judson were being shaped on another continent for mission service. Luther Rice, also, had been called to foreign missions service. Members of the Congregational Christian Church, Rice and the Judsons were believers of piety and practice in the Christian faith. Upon their commitment to missionary service, they sailed for India knowing they would find William Carey there. Adoniram and Ann Hasseltine Judson studied the Scriptures on the voyage. They were aware of Carey's Baptist commitment and baptism. Their study of the Scriptures persuaded the Judsons to become Baptists, and they were baptized. Becoming Baptists meant the discontinuance of financial support from the Congregational Church.

The decision was made for Luther Rice to return to America to raise funds for the missionaries. Rice did just that, going from the churches in Massachusetts to those in Alabama. Linkages!

God is always bringing about linkages among people, countries, and continents for the advance of his kingdom. He unites people, nations, denominations, and churches to his glory and honor.

We believers today are never more closely identified with the biblical movement for global missions than when we consciously and prayerfully become links in the pilgrimage of Christians saying, "Here am I, send me."

Having the unique opportunity and privilege of Christian service as convention executive secretary-treasurer, I realized the crucial value of linkages. A person comes to realize he is one of many. Consider the following servants.

DENT F. GREEN

Mr. Green was born on December 5, 1868, near Jackson's Gap in Tallapoosa County, Alabama. He was educated at common schools in Talladega, Alabama. In 1889, he entered Marion Military Institute in Marion, Alabama, where he earned his B.S. degree under the super-vision of Superintendent J. T. Murfee. Mr. Green was involved in a variety of work situations, first as a lawyer, then as principal of public schools in Fort Deposit, Alabama. His career then led him to be presi-dent of North Alabama Baptist College in Danville, Alabama, from 1895 to 1897. From 1897 to 1900, he served as a vice president of Falkville Normal College. In the year 1909, Mr. Green entered the field of banking, working as vice president and general counselor of Tennessee Valley Bank, Decatur, until 1918. On July 12, 1915, he was elected state senator in the second district. In 1918, Mr. Green was appointed super-intendent of banking for the state of Alabama. Then, on September 15, 1919, he was elected to the position of secretary of the Alabama Baptist Board of Missions, where he remained until September 1, 1929, the only layperson ever to serve in this capacity.

Secretary Green reported in *The Alabama Baptist* on November 11, 1920, that his office had received $781,454.45 toward the $75 million campaign during the 1920 convention year. He provided admirable and effectual leadership in launching the Cooperative Program in 1925 and during subsequent years of his service through 1929. Green submitted his resignation to the Executive Board effective September 1, 1929, and returned to a position with the state as superintendent of banks.

L. E. BARTON

The second link was the Rev. L. E. Barton, who became executive secretary-treasurer on December 1, 1929. Are you old enough to remember? The country was in a severe economic depression. This was a tough time for Executive Secretary Barton. Gifts declined, debts accu-mulated. Being the frugal man that he was, he consolidated departments of work, reduced salaries, and laid heavier demands on the staff.

I really never knew L. E. Barton. I do recall this austere man at convention meetings calling out, "Mr. Chairman, a point of order." (Interruptions were frequent at State Conventions with charges of constitution and bylaws violations.)

Prior to 1934, the secretary-treasurer (executive secretary-treasurer) was subject to an annual call. Churches observed this prac-tice, which was on the agenda for the December board meetings, up and down Alabama.

When the matter of the annual call to Dr. Barton was brought up at the December 1934 meeting, the vote was fifty-two voting "change" and eighteen members "no change." Roy Chandler, J. E. Dillard, and J. C. Stivender were appointed to convey the results to Secretary Barton.

There sat on the Executive Board some perceptive and sensitive members, one of whom was A. Hamilton Reid. On Friday morning December 14, 1934, Dr. Reid made a motion that the board extend a call of indefinite, rather than annual, tenure. It would be understood that any board member could call for a vote of confidence, and that if the secretary-treasurer of the board should desire a change, a three-month notice of termination would be given. The motion passed, establishing a practice that continues to the present.

D. H. Marbury, chair of the Committee on Paid Workers and Salaries, recommended F. M. Barnes as secretary-treasurer, beginning April 1, 1935, at $4,200 a year. A committee of five—J. R. Hobbs, B. R. Justice, Foster Mills, James H. Ivey, and J. W. Rocky—was appointed to notify Dr. Barnes of his election and secure his acceptance if possible. The Board expressed deep confidence in retiring Secretary-Treasurer Dr. L. E. Barton. Thus, the change of leadership was made without much fanfare and recognition, deliberately and decisively.

Dr. Barton resigned as executive secretary-treasurer on December 13, 1934, to be effective on April 1, 1935. I was fifteen years old, already attending State Conventions, active in my church as a youth leader, and developing a high level of interest in Training Union work.

F. M. BARNES

Dr. F. M. Barnes succeeded Dr. Barton. He was of large stature and had a booming voice that was heard daily throughout the Baptist Building at 127 South Court Street, Montgomery. His heart beat for Baptist mission causes.

Dr. Barnes was one of the most inquisitive persons I have ever known. Your business was his business. That's not always bad, but there were circumstances that should not have been his business. I shall never forget a particular instance. It occurred during the time when I was courting Louise Green, my future wife. As I've mentioned, my mode of transportation when visiting Louise was the Trailways "Big Red." I rode the bus to Opelika where Louise would meet me, usually in a car borrowed from the pastor. One day, Louise, who was BSU director at Auburn at the time, was visiting the Baptist Building in Montgomery. Curious about whom she was dating, Dr. Barnes asked her, but she refused the information. Dr. Barnes's reply was, "Give me two weeks, and I will find out." And he did.

Dr. Barnes believed that every Missionary Baptist church in Alabama should have a sign posted on the property for the purpose of identification. He urged pastors and congregations to print "Missionary" in the name of the church. He never spoke without referring to the church signs. If a church had a sign, Dr. Barnes commended the pastor and congregation. If there was no sign, he emphasized the need for one. Hundreds of churches responded by having the word "Missionary" inscribed on church signs and markers across Alabama.

Dr. Barnes came to the office of executive secretary-treasurer from the pastorate of Clayton Street Baptist Church, Montgomery, which is now Heritage Baptist Church, a church under the gifted pastoral leadership of Haden Center, aggressively becoming what God has prescribed for this family of faith. He was recognized to present his program for 1935 at the March 13 meeting. This is the first specific reference to programs of work which I found in my research. He presented the "Annual Schedule of Activities." Dr. A. Hamilton Reid made the motion to adopt Dr. Barnes's program of work and calendar of activities.

Dr. Barnes served in the office for ten years. Due to failing health, he retired in 1945. He made his last statement to the State Executive Board on December 5, 1944, and was given a standing ovation.

DR. A. HAMILTON REID

The 1944 State Convention was a benchmark. The governor of Alabama, the honorable Chauncy Sparks, delivered an inspiring and thought provoking address, "Christianity and the Future." Dr. A. Hamilton Reid, convention president, called on Alabama Baptists to accept our responsibilities, embrace our opportunities, and dedicate ourselves to the work God has for us.

By 1944, Baptists were the largest evangelical force in Alabama, numbering 416,000: 2,327 churches, seventy-one district associations, more than 2,100 Sunday Schools, 2,500 Baptist Training Unions, and 1,800 Woman's Missionary Union organizations. Dr. Reid was very optimistic about the role of Baptists in Alabama. He gave high praise to 121 fruitful years in the churches, associations, and the State Convention and special praise and thanksgiving to the Baptist ministers and laity. He was right on target. It is no accident that Baptists are the largest denomination in the state. The old adage, "To whom much is given, much is required," is most applicable to the Baptist witness in this state.

Even today our spiritual conscience should flinch over the overwhelming number of more than 20,000 persons incarcerated in Alabama prisons, the majority of whom are Baptists or have a preference toward Baptists. We need to be more earnestly involved with prevention of crime. Secondly, we need to expand ministries and rehabilitation to those incarcerated, to their families, and to others whose lives are marred from abusive vices and sin.

After Dr. Reid's retirement, the convention adopted a resolution of appreciation to Dr. A. Hamilton Reid for outstanding service to Baptist higher education as vice president (1940–1945) at Samford University and as executive secretary-treasurer (1945–1962) of the Alabama Baptist State Convention and Baptist State Executive Board.

DARK TIMES

Alas, a heavy burden and at times a dark cloud hung over my head and weighted heavy upon my heart due to the critical illness of my wife, Louise. Prayers, notes of encouragement, and telephone calls were very sustaining and assuring to the children and me. To God be the glory!

Louise was in the home health-care program of the Baptist Medical Center, Montgomery. She wanted so much to go home. I began to make preparation by converting our master bedroom into a medical care center with all the facilities and equipment that were needed. I made arrangements for twenty-four-hour nursing care. But Louise's condition deteriorated. David, Libby, and I consulted with our beloved and compassionate Dr. Harry Barnes. It was a difficult consultation. A hard decision had to be made—do we continue life support or do we discontinue life support?

I had seen with my eyes in other patients the ultimate results of the deteriorating process caused by leukemia. I saw this happening to Louise. As I noted earlier, Louise and I had previously decided that we did not want to sustain existence with life support if there were no hope for life. Dr. Barnes described the scenario for us so tenderly and vividly. It was a tough life-and-death decision, but we decided to withdraw life support, though I had seen evidence of dying. In the early morning hours of May 5, 1984, Louise died, with David at her bedside. Libby and I had so much wanted to be there, but I had spent the night with Libby in Mobile because Dr. William Weaver had invited me to participate in the graduation ceremony for Mobile College (Bill and "Bea" Weaver were among the first friends to get in touch with us following Louise's death). On the drive back to Montgomery, Libby said, "Daddy, can't we go faster?" but I was already exceeding the speed limit (we had notified the State Patrol with the description of the car and the cause for haste and were not apprehended).

The great host of family and friends who assembled for the memorial service of worship at Eastern Hills Baptist Church at noon, Monday, May 7, is vivid in our minds and hearts with eternal truth and hope:

> Therefore, seeing that we are surrounding with so great a cloud of witnesses, let us lay aside every encumbrance and the sin that so easily entangles and let us run with patience the race that is set before us. Looking to Jesus the author and finisher of our faith, who for the joy before Him endured the cross. . . . (Heb. 12:1–2)

Thank you, Lord, for the family of faith.

Hudson Baggett wrote an editorial about Louise's death.

> In 1 Corinthians 15 Paul asked the question, "O death, where is thy sting?" We feel death's sting again and again. Recently death plucked a beautiful flower of life's garden in the person of Louise Potts. Louise had suffered intensely for several months, but she suffered with strong faith which had motivated her through the years. She personified the beautiful virtues of womanhood and motherhood. She was an outstanding Christian who was sensitive to the thoughts and words of others. She loved God and other people. We will miss her, but her example in her days of pain was the crowning chapter of a beautiful life. We extend our sympathy to Earl, David, and Libby and pledge our prayers to them as they experience the sting of death.

Hudson Baggett, editor
The Alabama Baptist, May 17, 1984, 2

Only days after Louise's death, I was installed as executive secretary-treasurer. The installation service was preceded by a dinner on May 17, 1984, at the Baptist Building in Montgomery. The guest list included the members and spouses of the Baptist State Executive Board, employees and spouses of State Board Staff, other guests, Mayor Folmar and Mrs. Folmar, and the honorable George C. Wallace. The dinner was held in the dining room at the Baptist Building. It was beautiful, with its delectable dinner and wonderful fellowship. The testimonial speeches were greatly appreciated by the honored guests. I particularly appreciated the testimonial from my daughter, Libby.

IN THE SHADOW OF HIS WINGS

Dr. Frances Hamilton, executive director of the Alabama Baptist Historical Commission, and her student assistant, Lynn Sillavan, have been most helpful in this project. Their labors of love, patience, and counsel are spread across much of the manuscript. Lynn asked me one day, "How did you deal with the loss of Louise and accepting your new responsibilities at the same time?" That is a hard question to answer. However, it is a good question because other people are going through similar circumstances, and I appreciate the beautiful young lady who asked me this question. I hope in answering I can say something that would help just one person. If so, I will be more than compensated, and grateful.

Louise's long illness was addressed in another section of this volume. I will, therefore, try not to repeat myself. Twelve years have passed since her death, and I think I have accepted its finality. Then why is her absence ever present in daily living? A day does not pass that I am not reminded of her. In fact, when I visit in churches, invariably someone will talk with me about the influence Louise had on his or her life or ministry, whether he or she is a Missions Friends director, a worker with children, an adult lady who was in her class, a worker with children in Sunday School, a kindergarten teacher or director, a pastor's wife, a mother, or often, a pastor. I am always amazed at the frequency of references. I miss this lady very much. I think it will be that way as long as I live and that is alright! Perhaps, this is a source of strength that I needed during my years as executive secretary-treasurer. I think if I could relive my years with Louise, I would be more attentive to her daily activities, more sensitive to her needs, and more giving of myself in caring and in saying so. I did these things, but I think I should have done them more frequently.

Our family has gone through some hard times since Louise's death. I regret the absence of her living presence during these years that our son has served in the office of president of Judson College. I regret she has missed witnessing the attentiveness and love of Beth as a wife and mother and the growth and development of her two beautiful grand-daughters, Kristin and Shannon.

I think the loss of her mother was especially difficult for Libby. Following her tenure of service with the Texas Christian Life Commission, she married and went to Spain for three years. There she studied the Spanish language and enjoyed the Spanish people, their culture, and the church family. It was beautiful to witness our daughter being in love, making a commitment to marriage, and getting married. But it was followed by a painful divorce. Sometimes I think the outcome would have been different if Louise had been here. It was hard for Libby not having the presence and guidance of her mother during these signif-icant experiences.

Concerning divorce, I might dare to suggest some things to remember in such a situation. Let us remember that brokenness in rela-tionships, particularly that of your children, is hard and difficult to address. Let us remember that we belong to a family of forgiveness. We have been forgiven so much, we too must forgive. Let us remember that the person who is divorced is hurting emotionally, mentally, physically, and spiritually. Let us remember the inexhaustible love of God. Let us remember "to add patience, godliness; and in your godliness, brotherly kindness; and to brotherly kindness, love" (2 Pet. 1:6–7). Let us remember to pray.

Let me come back to the question of how I coped with the death of Louise and being thrust into the responsibility of the office of executive secretary-treasurer simultaneously. The answer is that only God's immeasurable grace and peace sustained me and the children. The longer I live, the more I am astounded by the enabling strength in the amazing grace of Jesus. I have found a friend, oh such a friend, in Jesus. I am aware daily of the empowerment of his grace. And, there is nothing in me that could have made possible not just survival, but life abundant, without the Baptist family in Alabama.

Also, my children were most helpful with steadfastness in love, encouragement, and counsel. I was especially appreciative of my son, David. Furthermore, the community of Alabama Baptists have remarkable capacities of loving, caring, and thoughtful kindness. I was engulfed with the prayers of Baptist laity from across Alabama.

Lastly, and most importantly, were my fellow staff members of the State Board of Missions, staff and directors of Association Missions, and the personnel of convention entities. We all came together as a team for the accomplishment of a great Christian mission in the churches, associations, and State Convention. God is so good. He honored the Baptist family with his presence and blessing!

Looking back upon what I experienced as I entered a new office and dealt with the death of my dear wife, I would like to add a few words about stress. I was asked by my young friend, "How does one deal with stress?"—a good question in these stressful days. I am not sure I dealt with stress very well, but I certainly know what it is—a mentally or emotionally disruptive or disquieting influence upon one's inner self. I believe stress is a given in the life process and is a good indicator of the presence of life. It is a catalyst, a motivator for pressing on.

Now having identified stress, I want to express my thoughts here on how to cope with it.

1. Recognize and acknowledge stress.
2. Ask, "What are the causes? Why is this happening to me?"
3. Ask, "Are the causes beyond my control?"
4. Engage the other person, if there is another person.
5. Confess—if you have wounded another person, talk with the wounded soul.
6. Nurture your inner self with devotional prayer time, repeating the hymn of faith and Scripture.
7. Inventory your job/work performance.
8. Stay physically healthy—exercise and change your diet if necessary.
9. Act—"take your burdens to the Lord and leave them there."

I like that!

These principles are how I deal with stress, not just now that I am in my seventies, but over the years. Sometimes I am my worst enemy. You may feel that way, too. Oftentimes the worst we think will happen never happens to us, but our imagination takes hold of us with devastating results. By the way, what is your stress point right now? Remember you are special. If you doubt that, read Psalm 8. I believe it. Do you?

GETTING STARTED WITH THE ORGANIZATION

Organizational renewal is a process; leadership transitions precipitate renewal. I, as the new executive secretary-treasurer, made several references to organizational renewal in reporting to the Executive Committee and the State Board of Missions. I observed that with each reference to organizational renewal I had the full attention of all members. That created concern in my mind.

"Proceed with caution" is not only good advice to follow when passing through barricades in road construction, but also when adjusting to new periods of leadership, especially in kingdom advance. Many new pastors have head-on collisions with church leadership in "haste makes waste" approaches to change in church ministries and church procedures.

I think the minds of the Executive Committee members and my mind were on the same track moving in the same direction. The discussions about organizational renewal precipitated a motion by Dotson Nelson, "I move as chairman that we request our executive secretary-treasurer to take a week for prayer, study, and crafting proposals for organizational renewal." The Administration Committee, upon the recommendation of Dotson Nelson and the Organizational Evaluation Committee, authorized me to take a minimum of one week's leave at the

expense of the board to spend some time in praying, studying, and planning my work on the organizational structure of the Baptist State Executive Board. Since there was no additional expense in responding to the action, the motion was approved. I went into seclusion at the family place on Lake Martin.

Three concepts, none new or original with me, captured my heart and thoughts: reaching people, developing believers, and strengthening missions. I believed the concepts to be biblical concepts related to Jesus' earthly ministry. If the concepts are viable, biblical, and church focused, they translate organizationally and leadershipwise. I knew that reaching people, developing believers, and strengthening missions would be the heartbeat and focus of whatever form the renewal structure translated into. I believed Alabama Baptists would affirm this viewpoint.

Jesus was about the business of the Father. His focus was people. He always moved toward people or drew people to him: ". . . and Jesus was going about all the cities and the villages, teaching in their synagogues, and proclaiming the gospel, the kingdom, and healing every kind of disease and every kind of sickness, and serving the multitudes He felt compassion for them . . . " (Matt. 9:35–38). ". . . The Son of Man did not come to be served, but to serve, and to give His life a ransom for many" (Matt. 20:28).

A new era of planning was emerging. There was interest and excitement. There was openness. The philosophy of planning was reviewed. Historically, the planning process began with the entities of the Southern Baptist Convention. The emphases were determined; goals and strategies were established. The second phase involved state staff meetings with SBC staff conducting orientation and training. In the third phase, state staffs interpreted the various programs and emphases to associational leadership for implementation in the churches.

A staff member said to me, "Whenever we came to partnership planning and collegiality, we did a 180 percent turn. We began to say to the association and churches not 'here it is and you do it,' but 'what is it that you need that we can assist you in doing?'" Organizational renewal soon became a familiar frame of reference for the staff members of the State Board of Missions and the Executive Committee. I was most fortunate to work with an Executive Committee and State Board of Missions whose membership were lay leaders par excellence from among the church and pastoral leadership of Alabama.

The experiences in building strong churches with solid biblical bases were insightful and defining, with support from both staff personnel and convention leadership. Suggestions that would usually improve the process were made openly in the meetings, and I really valued their input in designing a new organizational foundation structure for the Baptist State Executive Board.

A process evolved that crafted a new organizational structure and placed more responsibilities upon the leadership in each department of work, each accountable to the executive secretary-treasurer. This process implemented changes where needed as determined by the executive secretary-treasurer, the Organizational Evaluation Committee, the Personnel Committee, the Executive Committee, and ultimately the State Board of Missions.

I was not interested in making changes for the sake of change, only for effectiveness in reaching people. Change is necessary to make it possible for organizations, departments of work, and programs for churches and denominations to remain viable, to adapt to new conditions and needs, and to solve problems.

My primary concerns for the new structure were twofold: church support and church services. The proposed organizational renewal:

1. addressed the matter of coordination more directly among: departments within departments, departments within the executive office, Executive Board staff, director of missions, pastors, and churches;

(By addressing coordination, staff members could give more and better assistance to the local churches and could be more efficient in budget planning.)

2. changed the nomenclature of two strategic decision-making entities: the Baptist State Executive Board became the State Board of Missions and the Administration Committee became the Executive Committee;

(I believed the term "missions" more clearly defined the role of the State Board and Executive Committee more succinctly, more effectively, and with more authority, and it defined the committee's role in administration in working with the State Board of Missions.)

3. placed the ultimate accountability on the director of each department;

(A concern was expressed that the proposal weighted more responsibility on the executive secretary-treasurer, but my concern was making the work more effective, with fewer people in the chain of command. I desired personal responsibility and accountability flowing directly from the executive secretary-treasurer to the department director.)

    4.   made it mandatory for all department directors and associates to attend all staff meetings;

(There would be no misunderstanding of decisions or misinformation flowing from the executive secretary-treasurer to fellow staff personnel. Staff meetings were for planning and decision making, and I wanted all members to experience both.)

    5.   created one team with many players—no lesser, no greater—one for all, all for one.

(This was the desired outcome of organizational renewal. We were committed to creating a climate and atmosphere in which we functioned as a team doing the Lord's work in his way—all for his glory to the building of his church.)

GATHERING THE TEAM

> But you are not to be called "Rabbi," for you have only one master and you are all brothers. And do not call anyone on earth "Father," for you have one Father, and He is in heaven. Nor are you to be called "Teacher," for you have one Teacher, the Christ. The greatest among you will be your servant. For whoever exalts himself will be humbled, and whoever humbles himself will be exalted. (Matt. 23:8–12)

The journey in search of leadership was begun with fifty-two tried and proven staff persons, true servant leaders. The fifty-two were colleagues with whom I had served in advancing the mission of the Lord Christ through the mission causes of Alabama Baptists. The team members would be sought through faithfulness in prayer and in consultation with convention leaders, the Personnel Committee, and the State Board of Missions.

Attrition had created several staff vacancies in addition to the office of executive secretary-treasurer. I really regretted some of the losses in strategic areas of ministry. The organizational renewal structure necessitated additional changes.

The members of the Organizational Evaluation Committee and the Personnel Committee became very busy reviewing vitae, evaluating revised job descriptions, and interviewing prospective personnel. Let me affirm that the process for staff selection followed by the Executive Board in personnel selection for employment worked well.

I had proposed creating the office of administrative assistant to the executive secretary-treasurer. The proposal was approved by the Personnel Committee and the Executive Committee.

MILTON LOVELADY

Milton Lovelady was the first person to occupy this office. I had become acquainted with him earlier when he was director of computer services. He possessed some skills and qualities of leadership that were needed in the office of the executive secretary-treasurer; plus he was technologically gifted, especially with computers. Milton had left his employment with the State Board of Missions to accept a comparable assignment with the Florida Baptist Convention. When I contacted him about the position, he was interested. He came to work as administrative assistant and with the help of his efficient secretary, Mrs. Phyllis Smith.

Several weeks passed when I found out in a conference with Milton that his job assignment was not fulfilling to him. I was disappointed and responded that I could not support him in his dissatisfaction. Furthermore, I did not see how the job description could be altered to his satisfaction. It would be in his best interest not to work in an adverse environment.

His departure was painful to me. It caused me to reexamine my personal skills in drafting job descriptions and interviewing prospective personnel. However, I still regard Milton Lovelady as an exceptional person whose skills were needed. I felt terrible when he left.

HORTENSE BARNES

Dotson Nelson was a member of the State Board of Missions and the Executive Committee. I suppose he understood the workload of the office as well as convention boards and committees. I hesitated talking with Dr. Nelson about his recommendation, but I did. Later, I talked with Ms. Hortense Barnes, who was pastor's secretary at Mountain Brook. I knew this lady. A native of Abbeville, Alabama, and a graduate of the University of Montevallo and the Southern Baptist Theological Seminary, she had the gift of leadership, the skills of a diligent worker, loved the churches, and was a good "people person." She could facilitate the workload.

We talked, we prayed. Finally, Ms. Barnes consented to come to the employment of the State Board of Missions in the office of executive secretary-treasurer. I believe bringing her to the Convention Office was one of the most strategic decisions made by the Executive Committee and me. She is one of the best! The fruits of her labors will be realized by all who come after her.

One of Ms. Barnes's most significant achievements was the development of personal enrichment programs for secretaries for the Baptist Sunday School Board. She is active in the secretaries clinics of Judson College.

HARPER SHANNON

Harper Shannon became my associate with attention to evangelism as his primary assignment. Dr. Shannon, a preacher of preachers, spirit-filled, grounded in the Holy Scriptures, lover of lost souls, an eternal optimist, believed the church should implement the New Testament pattern of evangelism. He saw a gap in the areas of long-range planning and implementation in the Evangelism Division and filled it. I was excited by his servant leadership, his grasp of the Holy Scriptures, his love for preaching, his compassion for the lost, and his understanding of Alabama Baptist heritage and history which equipped him as a special leader and friend.

Randy Evers served most effectively as Dr. Shannon's associate. His focus was youth evangelism—youth-led revivals, youth evangelism conferences, and witnessing training.

DON WATTERSON

Don Watterson, who has a great zeal for Sunday School, directed the Sunday School Department. He believed Bible study was for regular and consistent study of God's word and Sunday School essential to reaching people. I do not know anyone who is more enthusiastic in growing churches. He did efficacious work as my associate and as program church-growth coordinator, an able associate whenever needed and for whatever the assignment required in the churches and associations.

Besides being a church-growth specialist, Don is an optimist, dreaming the impossible dream, climbing the highest mountain. This type of vision results in church growth and expansion in missions.

Earl (Bo) Wascom, Kathy Burns, and C. Bruce Hose were Don's valued consultants in Sunday School growth and development of churches across Alabama.

MARY SPEED

I began the process of determining the needs for the office when Mrs. Charles (Janice) Brassell retired as secretary to the executive secretary-treasurer. The office had two needs: a secretary to the executive secretary-treasurer and a person who could serve as administrative assistant in a competent and faithful manner.

There was no question about the secretary. Mrs. Mary Speed had been in my office for several years. I was pleased with her handling of the secretarial tasks. She related well to the employees and was responsive to the numerous requests for services for pastors and laity leadership coming to my office. She was an excellent worker. Now retired from State Board of Missions, she is very busy as a mission volunteer and grandmother.

TOM CORTS

I was in the audience for the installation of Dr. Tom Corts as the president of Samford University and appreciated his demeanor. Having now participated in numerous board meetings, committee meetings, and social gatherings involving Dr. Corts, my appreciation is heightened. I value his leadership and true friendship and am most comfortable in addressing him as "Mr. President." A world class leader, he exemplifies the walk of Jesus Christ.

MICHAEL MAGNOLI

I was present when the board of trustees elected Dr. Magnoli to become the second sitting president of the University of Mobile. His effervescence and cordiality impressed me. Though I did not know him, I knew the members of the Search Committee, who did know this bright, intelligent young man and had confidence in their decision. Though I could not vote as executive secretary-treasurer, the committee through Massey Bedsole encouraged me to become a nonvoting member. I accepted. The search was quickly narrowed to Dr. Magnoli. In fact, his name was presented to the board for election at the second meeting when I was present. I affirmed the election upon the recommendation of the trustees serving on the Search Committee.

PAT HARRISON

I was serving as executive secretary-treasurer when Pat Harrison was elected by the board of directors as Executive Director for Alabama Baptist Retirement Centers, succeeding Dr. Andrew Tampling upon his retirement. The Search Committee was chaired by Dr. Ira Myers, who shared with me the decision of the Search Committee to elect Pat Harrison.

BILLY NUTT

Statewide religious census brought Billy Nutt to the State Board of Missions. Divine directions were sought for the "Crusade of the Americas," a series of evangelistic crusades for the North American and South American continents. Billy Nutt was invited to become the director for the statewide census in 1967. Three years later, I was introduced to him. After twenty years of working with and observing Billy, I know that he is endowed with great gifts for leadership: humility, insightfulness, trustworthiness, integrity, confidence, and thoroughness in planning. Also, he is a friend.

Billy has become a key person in implementing and evaluating organizational renewal. He has distinguished himself in leadership in Associational Missions in Alabama and across America.

HAROLD ANDERSON

Harold Anderson's ministry as director of New Work and Church Building reached into every area of Alabama as he focused on reaching people for Bible study in Sunday School. He retired from his position after four years of being involved intimately with more than 300 churches. His work, *Counseling Southern Baptist Churches to Build for Growth*, received most favorable reviews from church growth specialists and has been requested in fifty states. This work is a service to the churches provided by the State Board of Missions, funded by the Cooperative Program.

Harold was assisted in his work by many trained consultants, including: Tommy Harrelson, Shades Crest, Birmingham; Harold Blackburn, Baldwin Association; and John Christy, minister of music, Dothan.

New work probes were used extensively in Alabama in identifying areas of need. College students were most helpful in extensive surveys. In my words, "Harold Anderson is a man for all needs in new work and building."

GENE TRIMBLE

Gene Trimble served as director of Annuity and Insurance from January 1, 1985, until his retirement. He provided leadership during a period of unprecedented growth and development in the annuity programs in Alabama. It was also during an era of transition at the Annuity Board, Southern Baptist Convention. Martha Smith was his gifted and knowledgeable assistant.

RAY BURDESHAW

Ray Burdeshaw was elected director of church music on October 1, 1985. He provides excellent leadership to all the churches regardless of membership size, with help from Keith Hibbs, his capable and faithful associate director. Ray stresses the importance of sensitivity to the personal and musical needs of the people, developing their talents to the fullest in God's service.

RUFORD HODGES

As director of Campus Ministries Division, Ruford Hodges provided superlative leadership to all colleges and universities in Alabama. Campus ministries touched the lives of over ten thousand college students and faculty members across Alabama. Oxford Smith provided strategic leadership as the associate.

A stellar corp of campus ministers were in place when I became executive secretary-treasurer. Dr. Charles Martin was director; campus ministers were Bob Ford, Gerald Stevens, Carolyn Fountain, Clete Sipes, Ronnie Brewer, Steve Holloway, Mary Jo Randall, Greg Sayler, Ken May, Elbert Williams, Don Bennett, Frank McCollough, and James Warren. All are heroes of the faith and practice. Churchmen and churchwomen whose lives were changed and crafted by their faith in Jesus Christ are scattered around the world.

Among campus ministers added to the team from 1984–1990 were Mike Muse, Ben Thomas, Philip Green, Libby Potts, Mark Robbins, Scotty Goldman, Gary Brittion, David Howard, Ben Hale, Sandra Wilkerson, Eddy Garner, Mike Avant, Willie Alexander, and others.

TOMMY PUCKETT

Tommy Puckett became the director of the Brotherhood Department on June 1, 1989, following the retirement of Mac Johnson. Steve Stevens and Reggie Quimby are the gifted and faithful associates in this department. Reggie came into Brotherhood work from Spain, where he served as a missionary. Steve became director of Boys and Young Men from Discipleship Training.

Tommy said that the Brotherhood Program stresses missions in action and translated this concept into networks of mission teams, construction teams, agricultural teams, health-care teams, partnership with WMU, and more. The Royal Ambassador Ministries and Camp multiplied and the RA camp expanded into an exceptional facility, one of the finest in the Southern Baptist Convention.

George Swann, Bill McCall, Dale Dison, and Virgil Cooper were missionaries in residence who served through the Brotherhood Department.

BRUCE HOSE

Bruce Hose was elected the director of Sunday School when Dr. Watterson became associate to the executive secretary-treasurer. Sunday School enrollments and attendance experienced good growth under the leadership of this real visionary. James Swedenburg, James Hargrave, and Andrew Smith were associates.

It was my joy to have touched the life of Bruce Hose when I was pastor of McElwain Baptist Church in Birmingham. The Hose family was in the fellowship at McElwain.

RALPH HALBROOKS

Ralph Halbrooks is a most versatile and servantlike minister. He served on the staff as director of Associational Missions Department, and as associate in the Sunday School and Evangelism Departments. He carried a heavy workload, but always had time to help out in other assignments. I have never known Ralph to say no to any need as requested. He also served as director of the Rural/Urban Department during my term as executive secretary-treasurer. His ministry certainly made a difference.

N. F. GREER

N. F. Greer was director of the Stewardship and Cooperative Program promotion. His faithful, knowledgeable, and compassionate leadership was critical to growth in stewardship in the life of Alabama Baptists. Ken Miller was his able associate until Ken became director of Communication Services. N. F. and Ken led Alabama Baptists to raise Cooperative Program giving from $17 million in 1983 to $26 million in 1990, a tremendous advance.

HARRELL CUSHING

Harrell Cushing became director of the Stewardship Department upon N. F.'s retirement. I believed Dr. Cushing to be God's man for the task. His humble leadership in missions support proved him invaluable. He is relentless with his support and information in promoting the Cooperative Program. Robert Dubois became associate to Dr. Cushing in 1990.

MICKEY CRAWFORD

Mickey Crawford and his associates have launched the ministries and personnel of the State Board of Missions into the computer age. I was glad to be there to witness this remarkable transformation in skills and procedures. Emmette Jones, Eileen Gurley, and Calvert Bowden were consultants in this process.

JAMES HUGHES, TOMMY HUGHES, KEN MILLER

Jim Hughes was director of communication services. He came to the convention assignment from the Radio/TV Commission of the Southern Baptist Convention. Jim provided technical leadership to churches and associations in radio and television ministries.

Tommy Hughes brought a new dimension to the convention when he replaced Jim as director of Communication Services. Excellent videos and films were produced under his leadership.

Now, Ken Miller is the director of Communications Services and is also doing an excellent job.

ROBERT DUCK

Robert was director of public relations. He led the Alabama Convention and churches in our witness to the public. He knew the media personnel across Alabama; for example, he was personally acquainted with newspaper editors in Alabama. Bob worked closely with *The Alabama Baptist* and had a weekly church and denominational news program. He now serves as a director on *The Alabama Baptist* Board of Directors.

HENRY LYON

Dr. Lyon became the director of the newly created Family and Deacon Ministries Department on January 15, 1986. He has given exceptional leadership to these ministries, training volunteers in order to respond to the invitations. Henry is a tireless servant leader and is well received by the churches and associations.

DR. TROY MORRISON

Dr. Troy Morrison became director of the Church-Minister Relations Department on February 2, 1985. Coming from the Twelfth Street Baptist Church in Gadsden, he brought considerable pastoral and counseling experience to this office of leadership.

The Lord blessed this ministry. One example is the reduction in the number of pastor terminations in our convention. I had become concerned with these terminations in my early years as executive secretary-treasurer and expressed my concern:

> These are my concerns in pastor-church relations across the state. I would like for Alabama Baptists to make this a matter of concern and prayer. Too many of our pastors are experiencing dismissal; church fellowships are divided; and kingdom advance is hindered. In these concerns, I would like for us to remember our covenant relationship with the Lord and one another. Let us press toward healing and reconciliation as expressions of our commitment to Christ and one another.

Baptist churches and conventions struggle with forced terminations of pastors and other staff ministers. Forced terminations are severe and painful. The experience can leave ministers and family members emotionally and financially torn; some never recover.

Brooks Faulkner, supervisor of Career Guidance Section at the Sunday School Board, estimated some 2,500 ministers were dismissed annually among the Southern Baptist churches. Churches were left frustrated and in unstable conditions.

I found most often neither the minister nor the church anticipated the occurrence. Reasons for dismissal varied. Church leaders did not always identify expectations for new pastoral leaders; seminaries were not always helpful in equipping pastoral leaders in practical matters associated with pastoral leadership; it takes time and effort to establish credibility between pastor and people, especially in deacon-pastor relationship.

Alabama churches were experiencing too many forced terminations. Faulkner suggested a covenant of cooperation, mutual understanding and ongoing feedback between ministers and congregations. Still there was resistance. Some brothers and sisters saw infringement upon church autonomy. Many saw the office replacing the person and work of the Holy Spirit. Others just did not want meddling in their business.

The truth was that there was to be no usurpation of church authority, no replacement of the Holy Spirit, and no placement barriers. Rather, the director of the Church-Minister Relations Department would provide training resources for pulpit Search Committees, secure biographical information for Search Committees, be available to meet with and train pulpit Search Committees, provide practical and helpful information to churches as requested, and help retired ministers find places of service. The office would raise the level of awareness through *The Alabama Baptist* and Church-Minister Relations conferences in associations and state conferences.

Dr. Sam Granade, long-time pastor of Evergreen Baptist Church, was selected to serve in the newly created office of Church-Minister Relations. He was a pioneer with a lot of experience working with churches and much common sense. The responses from the churches were most gratifying. Because he had credibility and instant recognition, he was trusted and accepted by Alabama Baptists.

The Granade family contributed to Baptist life and churches in Alabama over decades with spiritual roots deep in the Baptist heritage of Alabama. Sam Granade was no exception, serving admirably the challenge of office. He was instrumental in the Church-Minister Relations Office being accepted. He brought about healing and reconciliation between pastors and congregations. His spirit and demeanor were real.

The responsibility for finding Dr. Granade's successor became my responsibility. It wasn't easy replacing him. Fortunately, Dr. Troy Morrison was the person for the job. He also coordinated the Ministries of Annuity and Insurance and Family Ministries Departments with his work as director of Church Relations.

It is exciting to look at the reduction in pastor terminations from 1985 through 1990. The following data is compiled from the records of the associations and the office of Church-Minister Relations: 1985: 298 pastor terminations: 1986: 133 pastor terminations; 1987: 68 pastor terminations; 1988: 58 pastor terminations; 1989: 55 pastor terminations; and 1990: 51 pastor terminations.

NOXIE (BUSTER) TAYLOR

Buster became the director of Shocco Springs Assembly on September 9, 1989. He had been serving as interim director following the retirement of Dr. George Ricker. He provided excellent leadership as interim director in staffing, programming, and serving the needs of conference participants. His predecessors served well; however, Buster has excelled in campus improvements, ministries, and programs. An agent of change, because of him, Shocco Springs never looked better or served more people. Buster now serves as the assembly director.

JOHN SAWYER

Sawyer is one of the fifty-two tried and proven staff members. I believe that he knows more about discipleship training than all others in the Southern Baptist Convention, as is reflected in his enviable record of service. By practicing the biblical concepts of listening and then doing, he understands what is needed and knows how to do it. As you can tell, I value the integrity of his leadership. If I were a pastor, I would seek his counsel in Discipleship Training.

STEVE CLOUES

On January 1, 1986, Steve joined the State Board of Missions staff. He came to Alabama from Columbia, South Carolina, where he was the city planner, and from Southwestern Baptist Seminary. Serving as consultant to the associations in the metropolitan area of Birmingham, he was especially suited to addressing the needs in transitional communities. I have always been grateful for the leadership presence of Steve Cloues in Alabama. He is a specialist in demographics and is very insightful in helping churches identify missions.

JOHN LONG

John Long, consultant in the Discipleship Training Department, is another servant leader to the churches. A team leader, he has remained steadfast in his leadership, helping churches with discipleship training.

GAYNELL YOUNG

This director of Accounting and Building and Offices Services provides leadership to a great team. The accounting section includes: Martha Godfrey, Betty Clark, Joyce Hackborth, Phyllis Smith, Connie Jones (the best receptionist and hostess), Nancy Wade, Bonita Germany, Charolette Crane, Billie Davis, Jon Jones, and Willodean Killough. Building services include: Queen E. Price, Johnnie Henry, Carrie Germany, Diane Banks, Rev. Don Harris, Ronnie and Betty Boykin, Michael Thurman (now pastor of Dexter Avenue King Memorial Baptist Church), and Annie Pearl Carter.

JAMES GLAZE

James Glaze serves as director of business management and assistant to the executive secretary-treasurer. Jim's leadership efforts are most valuable to the State Board of Missions. He serves as statistical secretary of the convention and is also dean of business managers in the Southern Baptist Convention. Jim is the best. His friendship is steadfast and his stewardship of the properties of the convention and State Board of Missions is exceptional.

BOB AND BETTY ANDERSON

This delightful couple acts as coordinators for Volunteers in Missions. Thousands of mission volunteers have been processed through their office. They have rendered extraordinary work for the kingdom of God around the world by recruiting, training, and sending volunteers. I rejoice in their gifted servant leadership and their professionalism in the discipline of public education.

BEVERLY SUTTON MILLER

Dr. Beverly Miller was elected by the Board of Alabama WMU, succeeding Mary Essie Stephens. Dr. Miller, the WMU staff, and board members have provided visionary leadership to the churches. She is respected for her gifted leadership in the national office of WMU and in the churches and associations of the Alabama Baptist State Convention.

ALABAMA BAPTIST HISTORICAL COMMISSION

I have always been interested in history, both in its making and in its preservation. Therefore, to me, the Alabama Baptist Historical Commission (ABHC) is a strategic entity of the Alabama Baptist State Convention. My participation in the work of the ABHC became more visible when I became the assistant to the executive secretary-treasurer. The assignment provided me with opportunities to work with the commissioners.

ABHC has sixteen commissioners who represent the twelve districts in Alabama. Those serving between 1984 and 1990 were A. M. Daugherty,

Alabama Baptist Historical Commission members.

Creel Richardson, John Burrows, David Czachurski, Clyde Presley, Nina Gwin, Jerry Henry, Ray Atchison, Tom Hunter, Herbert Newell, Richard Sheridan, William Weaver, W. S. Love, Irma Cruse, Marlene Rikard, Lee Allen, Wayne Flynt, Frances Hamilton, Gilbert Burks, Eloise Kirk, Mildred Bobo, Quentin Porch, Cynthia Wise, R. L. Guffin, Adair Griffin, Harriet Amos Doss, Eljee Bentley, and Timothy George. Elizabeth Wells, special collections librarian and archivist, and Shirley Hutchens, processing collections supervisor, are both essential to the work of ABHC.

The purpose of the Historical Commission is to support the Alabama Baptist State Convention and its endeavors by leading Baptists to preserve, know, and utilize their heritage. The churches are encouraged and assisted, if needed, in recording history and preserving the records for study and research.

The commission recorded several significant achievements from 1984 to 1990: indexing *The Alabama Baptist* (by Shirley Hutchens); establishing the Baptist Information Retrieval System; choosing Irma Cruse as editor of *The Alabama Baptist Historian*; approving and distributing the pamphlet series *Shapers of the Southern Baptist Heritage,* published in 1987; employing the first full-time executive director, the late Dr. John Loftis; and receiving the services of Bill Sumners, archivist with the Historical Commission Southern Baptist Convention, as consultant pertaining to records management strategies. I shall never forget the indefatigable perseverance of the commissioners in their ministries to the churches, associations, and the convention.

In 1994, the Search Committee recommended the election of Dr. Frances Hamilton as the executive director of the Alabama Baptist Historical Commission. Dr. Hamilton is doing admirably in this work and is well received in the churches and associations.

THE NEW CHURCH ANNUITY PLAN

Improvements in benefits offered to denominational employees continued to merit attention. The new church annuity plan contained significant challenges in funding and enrollments. The Administration Committee had this task on the agenda early in my tenure as executive secretary-treasurer. The annuity plan was reviewed and revised prior to 1984 and updated in three categories: enrollments, cost, and retirements.

Mr. Frank Schwall, vice president and regional coordinator, stated in a recent study on pension plans of thirteen major denominations in the United States that the Southern Baptist Convention came out at the bottom. The primary reason is inadequate retirement contributions and inadequate support from the churches and denomination. (In 1984, the average monthly check of retired ministers and their widows was less than $150, and some are on welfare.)

A committee of the State Pensions Study Committee was appointed in 1981, consisting of five trustees of the annuity board, five executive directors of State Conventions, five at-large members from Southern Baptist churches, and five members of the Annuity Board staff. The purpose was to design and recommend a retirement benefit plan and stress implementation that would meet the needs of ministers and staff members of Southern Baptist churches. The plan enrolled laypersons employed by the churches for at least half time or more than 1,000 hours and worked in the following way: (1) the State Convention would indicate a desire to participate with a written adoption agreement with the annuity board; (2) the local church would approve a resolution adopting the new plan; and (3) a copy of the resolution would be sent to the Annuity Board.

The new plan, beginning operation in 1988, was designed as a true church pension plan, with the church taking the initiative and responsibility for its provision. All churches in the pension plan automatically enrolled new church staff people. The minister or eligible employee contributed to an individual account in order to receive church and denomination contributions. The church doubled the member contribution up to a maximum contribution of 10 percent. The State Convention matched one half of the church's contribution up to a maximum convention contribution of $420 per year.

The major change was that the first $210 from the State Convention was allocated to the protection benefit fund for disability and death benefits. The additional money up to $420 was used for pension benefits. The state share of the State Convention contributions had not been upgraded in forty years. The new church annuity plan included: (1) all full-time personnel; (2) increased the participation rate of eligible church personnel; and (3) raised the level of benefits.

The new plan cost $1,260 from the minister or church to obtain the maximum state contribution of $420 with an estimated annual cost to State Convention of approximately $747,600.

Steve Tondera moved that the convention adopt and participate in the Southern Baptist Protection Program Church Annuity Plan. The recommendation was presented to and approved by the State Convention. The great challenge was funding $747,600. Full funding for the new annuity plan extended into the era of my successor.

COMMITTEE ON DISSEMINATION OF INFORMATION

We continued seeking to find ways to improve communication between Alabama Baptists and the denominational organizations. Rick Marshall, chairman of the Committee on Dissemination of Information, reported the appointment of subcommittees which would report on the following goals: (1) to discuss how sensitive information has been dealt with in the past and any recommendations or policies they can make regarding how sensitive information is disseminated; (2) to receive information about entities of our conventions and how they relate to the information office of the Baptist State Executive Board in disseminating information; and (3) to survey information needs of the churches and laypeople in Alabama.

The committee consisted of Rev. Gerald Blackburn, Dr. Richard Cagle, Dr. James Milner, Dr. Noel Walker, Dr. Coy Wood, and Dr. Rick Marshall, chairman. The purpose of the committee was to find more effective ways to respond to the information needs of Alabama Baptists.

Past procedures were reviewed and the entities surveyed. The results were the discoveries of some needs for more information from the entities.

Internal communication was judged to be good and improving, especially between educational entities.

A survey was conducted and four areas of concern were noted from the survey regarding what people feel uninformed about: (1) Executive Board employee salary/benefits, (2) mission percentages, (3) organizational structure, and (4) program of work.

POLICY OF INFORMATION— ALABAMA BAPTIST STATE CONVENTION

Disclosure of factual information concerning the operation and finances of the Alabama Baptist State Convention is the policy of the Baptist State Executive Board of the Alabama Baptist State Convention. The Special Committee recommended on November 12, 1984, that:

1. an "open door policy" on information to be made available to churches;
2. a statement of procedure for acquiring information on salaries be printed in *The Alabama Baptist*;
3. a document providing any requested information be created;
4. the Baptist State Executive Board and associational leadership give greater attention to sharing information through more regular reports to the association Executive Committee;
5. *The Alabama Baptist* go into detail;
6. the executive secretary-treasurer and heads of agencies and institutions of ABSC meet periodically for the purpose of sharing information about work;
7. the orientation of trustees include more emphasis on familiarization with the work of the State Convention and the Cooperative Program.

REACHING PEOPLE—1985–1990

Again I wanted to emphasize the priority of reaching people, the mission given to me in my call to the ministry. God's concern for people is demonstrated in the birth, life, death, resurrection, and accession of Jesus Christ, his Son. Jesus' concern for people is reflected in his actions, in the Holy Scriptures, and in the lives of Christians. Jesus says in his word, "Say not ye, there are yet four months, and then comes the harvest? Behold, I say unto you, lift up your eyes and look on the fields, for they are white already unto harvest" (John 4:35). His commission to his church is capsulized in his words,

> All power is given unto me in heaven and in earth. Go ye therefore, and teach all nations, baptizing them in the name of the Father, and the Son, and the Holy Ghost; teaching them to observe all things whatsoever I have commanded you, and lo I am with you always even unto the end of the age [world]. (Matt. 28:19–20)

"To promote the preaching of the gospel in Alabama and throughout the world." This statement has remained prominent in the ministries and work of the Alabama Baptists. Progress and kingdom growth have occurred continuously over the years and decades among the churches of the convention since her founding in 1823. The percentages of the population that are members of the Alabama Baptist State Convention increased from 14 percent in 1940 to 24 percent in 1983. However, the percentage of the population who are members of the churches has not changed since 1970 nor has Sunday School enrollment shown major percentage increases since the decade of the 1950s. The baptism rate went from 1 in 20.2 in 1950 to 1 in 40.4 in 1983.

Early in January 1984, staff members of the State Board of Missions and directors of Associational Missions affirmed my priority concern as executive secretary-treasurer of reaching people for Jesus Christ, a priority born in prayer. I know of no spiritual renewal movement that happens without much prayer. Jesus spent time before the day began in prayer.

After a month of praying, there were discussions about what Jesus was saying to us. Developing believers and strengthening missions completed the triad from which all ministries and programs were measured.

A Reaching People Task Force was appointed—Don Watterson, Wyndell Jones, Billy Nutt, John Sawyer, Mary Essie Stephens, Charles Martin, Paul Stewart, Jim Hughes, Ralph Halbrooks, N. F. Greer, Mac Johnson, and myself. The task force developed the mission statement on reaching people in Alabama.

I. The mission of the Baptist State Executive Board, through the personnel lives and ministry of its staff, is to enable local churches to more effectively reach people for the kingdom of God:

A. By making evangelism the priority to which we give ourselves,

B. By providing resources to assist the churches in discipling individual Christians,

C. By focusing the attention of the churches on specific, measurable, attainable goals,

D. By challenging Baptists to embrace the fullness of life in Christ.

II.   Reaching people for Christ is a process of:

A. Developing an awareness of and dependence upon the power of the Holy Spirit and prayer in the task of winning people to Jesus Christ as Savior and Lord since man is a sinner, but hope is in the convicting power of the Holy Spirit,

B. Locating people who are in need of the Biblical message and the ministry of the church,

C. Communicating the message of salvation to the unsaved, both those outside and inside the church, including those who have grown up in the church,

D. Receiving and baptizing born-again people into the fellowship of a local congregation,

E. Ministering to the needs of people both inside and outside the church,

F. Nurturing believers through worship, preaching, teaching, and training in order that they may become responsible disciples of Jesus in mission involvement and personal witnessing to the unsaved and the unchurched.

The church is the redemptive people of Jesus Christ, reaching out in witness to the unchurched, winning the lost to Jesus, nurturing believers into the fullness and likeness of Christ. The church is an extended hand feeding the hungry, clothing the needy, building shelters, giving water, and visiting the prisoners.

The Baptist Association enables the local churches to do ministries cooperatively through a larger fellowship. The association is the catalyst in initiating action, designing strategies and implementing plans for reaching people within the geographical area of association.

The State Convention serves in cooperation with the Baptist Association and the churches in reaching people. Mission accomplishments require bold challenges, bold strategies, bold leadership training, and surrendered witnesses to Jesus Christ. The State Convention is an agent of cooperation for the churches and associations in promoting the preaching of the gospel, discipling the believers, and giving in support of missions.

Just before Jesus ascended into heaven, he reminded believers and disciples ". . . that you shall receive power when the Holy Ghost is come upon you: and ye shall be witnesses unto me both in Jerusalem and in Judea and in Samaria and unto the uttermost part of the earth" (Acts 1:8).

The following are samples of letters written in support of the stated priorities:

It is inspiring to know that we have a man of your stature who expresses personal concern in reaching people. I, too, want to commit myself along with you to reaching people for Christ through our churches this year. I appreciate your emphasis on reaching people through the local church. As you know, this is where the action is.

Prayerfully Yours,

Pastor Lenny Bolton
Chisholm Baptist Church

Reaching people has two directions—reaching out and reaching in. The primary purpose of a New Testament Church is to introduce persons to personal faith in Jesus Christ. Evangelism is the heartbeat and life's blood of a New Testament church . . . the other direction is induction into the family of God—His church. Involvement and assimilation our dual emphasis—teaching them to observe all things . . . my prayers, cooperation and support.

H. Mac Johnson
Director—Brotherhood

I believe the reaching people priority is the right track.

John Sawyer

The session this morning initiated a fresh approach to our comprehensive goal of reaching more people. Evangelism is the overarching purpose in all that we do, but the assignment of the task force should be to pray, creatively articulate priorities, and prepare plans for reaching more people through the churches . . . seeking the leadership of the Holy Spirit through prayer . . . finding ethnic groups and people who are not presently considered prospects.

Charles Martin
Campus Ministry

The reaching people emphasis shared includes goals for Alabama Baptists to grow numerically, increase baptisms by a percent annually, establish 500 new churches and mission by 1990, 4,000 new classes and departments in Sunday School, enroll an additional 100,000 by 1990— all churches and entities training witnesses.

Don Watterson, Director
Sunday School

The report and recommendations of the Bold Mission Thrust Priority Planning Committee charted the course for the Alabama Baptist

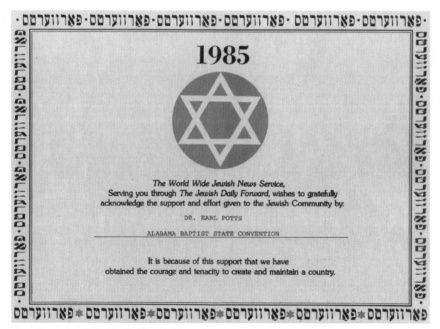

Certificate from Worldwide Jewish News Service.

Convention 1985–1990. The ministries implementations would be developed by the State Board of Missions, entities, associations, and churches. D. W. Robinson said, "While our future will be influenced by unpredictable economic and sociological factors, the report reflects a conviction that the basic needs of peoples, the adequacy of the gospel, and the power of God's spirit will remain constant. In this we look forward in faith to 1990."

The priorities which would influence all ministries and programs for the Alabama Baptist Convention follow:

1. emphasize reaching people for conversion, public profession of faith, believer's baptism, and active church membership;
2. experience spiritual awakening through prayer, Bible Study, openness to the spirit of God, and righteous living;
3. establish new churches and encourage the growth of existing churches;
4. strengthen Christian Stewardship and support of missions through the Cooperative Program;
5. expand ministry with ethnic groups, newcomers to Alabama, older adults, single adults, families of divorce, children with special needs, the poor, and Baptists who have withdrawn from active participation in the church;
6. teach Christian doctrine, especially distinctive Baptist doctrine;
7. minister to those who suffer because of moral or economic background and strive to correct the circumstances with contributions to the problems;
8. develop missions consciousness and prayer support;
9. increase the use of mass media;
10. equip Christians through Christian education for the making, maturing, and mobilizing of disciples.

Goals were established by each subgroup and presented to the State Board of Missions and the Alabama Baptist State Convention. The Bold Mission Thrust—Mission Alabama report was approved for implementation by the 1985 Alabama Baptist State Convention.

Darrell W. Robinson was chairman of the 1985–1990 Priority Planning Committee. The following were members of the Reaching People Subgroup: Al Jackson, convenor; Billy Nutt, recorder; Carl P. Wells; Don Watterson; Henry L. Lyon III; Harper Shannon; Edgar Arendall; Jim Hughes; Jack Still; Dewey Mayfield; Thomas E. Corts; Albert P. Brewer; and Ralph Halbrooks.

The following were members of the Developing Believers Subgroup: Ed Helton, convenor; Rev. John Sawyer, recorder; Hugh Edmunds; Dr. Andrew W. Tampling; Dr. Darrell W. Robinson; Dr. Troy Morrison; Dr. Wyndell Jones; Rev. Barry Cosper; Dr. Thomas W. Collier; Bobbie Van Atta; Rev. Jere Patterson; and Kenneth W. Cox.

The following were members of the Strengthening Missions Subgroup: Dr. Drew J. Gunnells, convenor; Rev. N. F. Greer, recorder; Dr. Hudson Baggett; Beverly Sutton; Rev. Wallace Henley; John Bell; Rev. Jimmy Jackson; Dr. U. A. McManus, Rev. Mac Johnson; Dr. A. Earl Potts; Mrs. Ralph Langley; Rev. James Nelson; and Dr. Charles Martin.

COOPERATIVE MINISTRIES

Alabama State Missionary Baptist Convention and Alabama Baptist State Convention

The InterBaptist Fellowship Committee has representatives from the Southern and National Baptist Conventions. The committee's purpose is to strengthen Cooperative Ministries and the fellowship among Southern and National Baptists, that is, white and black Baptists in Alabama. The committee professes the following goals:

1. to promote communication and fellowship;
2. to promote InterBaptist fellowship committees in all associations both National and Southern;
3. to do the ministries of common interest that can be done better together than apart;
4. to promote the annual Human Relations Conference;
5. to promote the observance of Human Relations Sunday in the churches;
6. to work toward a cooperative prison ministry;
7. to develop resources promoting reconciliation for use in churches;
8. to act as an advisory group to the parent denominational bodies in the areas of cooperative ministries and race relations.

Baptists of the New Era Baptist State Convention, the Progressive Baptist Mission and Education Convention, the Alabama State Missionary Baptist Convention, and the Alabama Baptist State Convention met for a historic joint session in November 1988 in the arena of the Alabama Fair Grounds in Birmingham.

Joint session Baptist Convention, Alabama, November 1988.

Christ was exalted in this service of celebration and worship. President P. T. Williams, New Era Baptist State Convention, read the Holy Scriptures from the Old Testament. President R. C. Mullins, Progressive Baptist Mission and Education Convention, read from the New Testament. President W. F. Alford, Alabama State Missionary Baptist State Convention, led the prayer. President Rev. I. E. Townsend, New Era Progressive Missionary Baptist Convention of Alabama, led the prayer of invocation, and President Steve Tondera, Alabama Baptist State Convention, gave the benediction as the great host of Baptists joined hands and hearts.

Dr. Charles Carter, pastor of Shades Mountain Baptist Church, gave a sermon on "The Lordship of Christ" from Philippians 2:5–11, Acts 2:32, 36, and Dr. Julius Scruggs, pastor of First Missionary Baptist Church, Huntsville, preached a sermon entitled "On Seeing God" from Isaiah 6.

As a result of the joint service, Alabama Baptists hoped to kindle a spirit of restoration and reconciliation through the following:

1. a joint session of all the Baptist Conventions in Alabama at least every ten years;
2. promotion of joint worship services;
3. pulpit exchanges between National and Southern Baptists;
4. shared musical programs;
5. cooperative ministries projects;
6. InterBaptist disaster relief ministries;
7. promotion of seasons of prayer;
8. promotion of racial reconciliation.

I have the joy of membership in the Birmingham Baptist Ministers Conference that meets at the Birmingham Baptist Bible College. I thank God for the service opportunities with brothers and sisters in Christ among National Baptists.

GOOD NEWS ALABAMA

Good News Alabama was one of the most carefully planned and implemented evangelistic crusades in the history of Baptists in Alabama. I coordinated and promoted this InterBaptist revival by visiting many National Baptist churches, Southern Baptist churches, and pastors' conferences. I am an advocate of togetherness in the Baptist family of Alabama. We have come a long way, thanks be to God. However, let us move with haste. We need each other. As the hymn is so boldly sung, ". . . Zion haste, thy mission high fulfilling . . . that our soul shall perish, lost in shades of night."

The Human Relations Conference is held at Shocco Springs annually, usually in April. This joint conference was begun under the leadership of Dr. H. O. Hester in 1961. Mrs. Delma Warner was an enabling force in sustaining the cooperative missions work among the Baptists of Alabama, along with Rev. Charles Smith, pastor, Paden Baptist Church; Rev. George Johnson, pastor, Zion Springs Baptist Church, and president, Easonian Baptist Theological Seminary, both in Birmingham; and Dr. Wilson Fallin, president, Birmingham Baptist Bible College.

FAMILY MINISTRIES STRENGTHENING FAMILY LIFE

Family life in local churches is a priority with the Alabama Baptist State Convention and Baptist associations. In the early fall of 1983,

Dr. Harrell Cushing, president of the Alabama Baptist Convention, appointed a state task force to work with the State Board of Missions staff task force on the family. Rev. Charles Stroud, pastor, Ridgecrest Baptist Church, Montgomery, was asked to serve as chairman. Others serving were Dr. Don Hill, minister of counseling, Morningview Baptist Church, Montgomery; Rev. David Moore, pastor, Southside Baptist Church, Dothan; Mrs. Jeanette Jeffers, senior adult specialist, First Baptist Church, Auburn; Ms. Libby Potts, director of college and single adults, Spring Hill Baptist Church, Mobile; Mrs. Becky Sumrall, Christian Social Ministries director, Etowah Baptist Association; Mrs. Al Jackson, Lakeview Baptist Church, Auburn; Dr. Roy Brigance, professor of sociology, Samford University; and Dr. Levan Parker, director of Children's Work, Central Park Baptist Church, Birmingham.

The plans crafted by the state task force were presented to the State Board of Missions and the directors of Associational Missions Department for evaluation. These plans set forth objectives and recommendations calling upon the denomination, the associations, and the convention entities to give special focus to helping and ministering to families in Alabama.

The Family and Deacon Ministry Department was a new department in organizational renewal in 1984. Dr. Henry Lyon, pastor, First Baptist Church, Selma, was elected as the first director by the State Board of Missions, January 15, 1986. Henry worked with more than 3,000 churches in family, parent, and marriage enrichment; senior adult ministry; singles ministry; deacon training and enrichment; and Biblical teaching concerning the home. He brought to the assignment thirty-four years of pastoral leadership. In his own words,

> I had ministered to families, as all pastors do, and I knew something of the problems. I knew family values were deteriorating in our country. I knew the divorce rate was getting higher. I was beginning to identify with the special problems that never-married single adults face in life. More senior adults were creating a senior adult population. I could identify with the needed ministries of these persons.

Henry came to the challenging assignment with a commitment to providing help to the families of Alabama. This ministry responds to 180 to 210 ministry leadership training opportunities each year. Henry has equipped a large number of lay leaders to assist him in each association.

Parenting by grace, covenant marriage, family-enrichment weekends, deacons retreats, intergenerational ministries, senior adults, and calls from other associations keep Henry Lyon on the go.

Henry had one of the most moving experiences in his life when the pastor of a small membership church located in northeast Alabama called him about doing a conference for his church. The conference began in early evening and adjourned around 10:00 P.M. Henry faced a four-hour drive back to Montgomery and a staff meeting the next morning. He said, "This devoted pastor was bivocational, agewise in his sixties." He extended his hand and took Henry's hand with tearful eyes and said, "Henry, thank you for caring enough to come this far and to drive back tonight just to help this little church."

Helping the churches is the mission for all staff members of the State Board of Missions. Henry reminded me of a statement he heard regarding our mission, ". . . We must never lose focus of the needs of the local church." That impressed me so much. Henry says about his department, "My assignment is not to run up a whole lot of statistics to brag about, but we are about meeting the needs of the local church . . . all churches, small membership churches to the largest membership churches, and when we do that we are touching the lives of hurting people."

I think I could say of Henry (and perhaps of every staff person of State Convention, association, and church) that he felt as led by the Lord to come to the State Convention staff as I felt led to be a pastor. Henry Lyon and his office staff and volunteers make a difference in the ministry in the Department of Family and Deacon Ministry.

THE CENTER FOR THE STUDY OF LAW AND THE CHURCH

"Let all things be done decently and in order" (1 Cor. 14:40).

A new ministry was introduced in 1987 to give assistance in dealing with challenging legal issues confronting the contemporary religious community. The procedural processes never remain static in the church, family, and business enterprise. They evolve, always changing. The dynamics for change are ever present to challenge our minds and spirits. Alabama Baptist leaders are quick in acknowledging the challenge, but sometimes slow in responding to changes.

Dr. Thomas Corts, president of Samford University, was quick in coming to the aid of the churches and the convention with a proposal to establish the Samford University Center for the Study of Law and the

Church. He realized the need for an authentic law center with the resources and skills to service the needs of the constituencies of the Alabama Baptist Convention and the Southern Baptist Convention. The services and resources would be available to other cooperating Protestant denominations.

The needs to be served would be generated by the growing complexity of the law and by the increasing willingness of the courts to apply various legal liabilities and limitations to churches, religious entities, and individuals. The services and resources would be directed to local church boards, individual pastors, state and national boards, and commissioners.

The Alabama Baptist Convention under my leadership as executive secretary-treasurer encouraged the establishment of the center. The State Board of Missions took the proposal under advisement, approving convention participation.

The center was designed to provide assistance and guidance in two basic areas. One is an educational and service function which plans an annual conference designed to explore vital new developments affecting religious institutions and individuals and to provide a counseling and informal advisory service. The second is a research and publication function which provides an easily usable handbook as a ready reference to the many laws and regulations affecting religious institutions and individuals, prints a newsletter containing an update in the area of the law and the church, and prints the proceedings of the annual conference.

The principal scholarly activity of the center would be the annual conference on law and religion. Also, utilizing an incoming WATTS line, the staff would provide an informal advisory service to local church boards, pastors, and state and national boards.

The Center for the Study of Law and the Church has an eminently qualified director in the person of Dr. Chriss H. Doss. Ms. Linda Martin Connor holds the position of associate director. Chriss Doss holds B.A., M.S.L.S., B.D., and J.D. degrees covering the fields of history, theology, law, and library science, and has served pastorates in Alabama and Pennsylvania. He was a college professor, state legislator, and county commissioner. You will find the name "Chriss Doss" affixed to many by-lines in numerous newspapers and professional journals.

One of the most helpful seminars at the center was on clergy malpractice. A participant who had the unfortunate experience of dealing with a charge of clergy malpractice spoke of the episode as one of the worst periods in his life. He was forced to defend himself and his church. He gained a true understanding of Jesus' reference to being sent out like sheep among wolves.

Chriss Doss sees the center as a friend and a supporter that will affirm the responsibilities of the church, yet will provide ways for the church to avoid potential legal problems.

FOUR PRESIDENTS

The executive secretary-treasurer of the Alabama Baptist State Convention is given invaluable aid, counsel, and encouragement by those who serve as president of the State Convention. I was blessed to have the opportunity to share this special relationship and fellowship with four outstanding presidents.

WALLACE HENLEY, 1983–1985

Born December 5, 1941, in Birmingham, Alabama, Dr. Henley was converted at age fifteen in 1956. He was ordained to the Christian Ministry in 1962; however, he was already serving as a church staff member in 1958.

Rev. Henley pastored McElwain Baptist Church for five years and six months. He served on the White House staff during President Nixon's administration, then was the religion editor of the *Birmingham News*. He was president of the Birmingham Pastor's Conference and the conference speaker at Ridgecrest, Glorieta, and Shocco Springs assemblies. A gifted writer, Rev. Henley has written six books as well as articles for *Christianity Today, Christian Life,* and other publications.

Dr. Henley longed for peace within our denomination and its strife-torn churches. He prayed for renewal for burned-out preachers and church members. He told us often that the only answer for Southern Baptists is Jesus who brings healing, revival, and rejuvenation through his presence and his power.

Wallace Henley and Irene Lambert of Birmingham were married in Birmingham. They have two children, Louie and Travis.

LEWIS MARLER, 1985–1986

A native of Gordo, Alabama, Lewis Marler was the son of Rev. and Mrs. R. S. Marler. His father was a Baptist preacher, and Lewis never thought of doubting the word of God. He graduated from Howard College and Southern Baptist Theological Seminary, receiving his doctor of divinity from Samford in 1978. His first pastorate was Big Creek Baptist Church, and his last was Mount Philadelphia Baptist Church in Walker County. Other churches pastored by Lewis Marler were Mount Paran in Northport; Fellowship in Gordo; West Blocton First in West Blocton; Central Baptist in Selma; Lakewood Baptist in Birmingham; Ridgecrest Baptist in Montgomery; and First Baptist in Gardendale.

Lewis is a most compassionate and loving pastor and friend. I was honored to serve Alabama Baptists when he was convention president. He helped us get our priorities in order as far as reaching people. Hudson Baggett described him as conservative in his theology, but moderate in his spirit. One of Lewis's church members characterized him as a humble man of great influence. People saw Christ in him.

Lewis is married to the former Jimmie Ruth Hudson Mayes. (His first wife, Martha Marler, died in 1965.) He is the father of two children— Dr. Malcolm Marler, chaplain UAB, and Marcelyn Marler.

STEVE E. TONDERA, 1987–1988

Steve Tondera is a native of Waco, Texas. He received a B.S. from Baylor University in math and physics, and an honorary doctorate of law degree from Judson College. For twenty-nine years he served as senior engineer at Marshall Space Flight Center. His job was to make sure that plans for upcoming space shuttle flights would work. He interacted with government people from other countries around the world.

Steve was president of the presidents, Southern Baptist Convention, 1988. On the civic front, he was an eagle scout and scout master, president of Gurley Lions Club, chairman of Huntsville Hospitality House, district governor of Lions International, active in the Madison County Chapter American Red Cross, and recipient of the Alabama Volunteer of the Year Award from Governor Guy Hunt in 1988.

Steve described himself as a conservative in theology and, he hoped, a liberal in his giving, sharing, and accepting of others. When he was elected president, here is the advice that I gave him, "Steve, just watch what you say, watch what you do, watch where you go, and who you're with, but other than that, be yourself."

Steve, as president, was on the road most days of the week speaking at church services, church anniversaries, dedications, brotherhood breakfasts, and attending convention committees and board meetings. He logged thousands of miles on his car, 22,000 miles in the last three months of his presidency. All of his travels and convention expenses were paid by himself; he would not accept reimbursements. The theme for his presidential address to the convention was "Preserving the past, performing in the present, and planning for the future."

Pastor Allen Walworth described Steve as a rare human being who shows Christian love and commitment to his faith. To Allen, Steve is a valued lifelong friend and brother in Christ.

Steve is married to Bonnie Jo Perkins. They have three children— Tamra, Steve Jr., and Joe. He is an active churchman: First Baptist Church, Huntsville, director of the Adult Department; member of the Building Committee; chairman of the Board of Trustees; deacon chair of Mission Trips to New York, Alaska, Japan; and Personnel Committee chairman in Madison Baptist Association.

CHARLES T. CARTER, 1989–1990

Dr. Carter was born on February 1, 1936. His home church was Calvary Baptist Church, Birmingham. Converted and baptized at age seven, he was called to preach at age twelve, preached his first sermon at age fourteen, and was ordained to minister on November 27, 1955, at age nineteen. He graduated from Southern Baptist Theological Seminary with a master of divinity degree and began pastoring Shades Mountain Baptist Church, Birmingham, in 1971. In 1976 he got a doctor of divinity degree from Samford University, where he is currently serving on the board of trustees.

Charles Carter is a noted pulpiteer. He has crisscrossed America preaching in churches of all sizes in membership and new churches just getting started. He and his wife traveled around the world in 1973 on a preaching mission to Japan, Korea, Hong Kong, India, Israel, Italy, Switzerland, France, and England. In 1984, he preached for the Alabama/Nigeria Partnership in Ogbomosho and Abere where there were 2,809 decisions and 1,101 professions of faith.

In his address as president to the 1990 theme "A message of hope for our different day," he said,

Let us not be blind—there are problems. Let us not be deceived—all is not vain. Let us not be weary—we shall reap. . . . Sometimes our problems are intensified by the fact that those who are "doing good" give up before those who are "doing bad" give out. We dare not let this happen to us in this critical hour and become weary in well doing. Let me encourage and exhort us not to grow weary. Staying anchored in the Scriptures; staying united together; staying focused.

Dr. Carter married Janice Young of Clanton, Alabama. They have two lovely daughters—Joy Elise and Carol Denise.

Dr. Carter was the man who stood in the gate of leadership during its time of transition and saw to it that matters of leadership were in place and accepted by our new executive secretary-treasurer, Dr. Troy Morrison. Thank you Dr. Carter, your precious family, and your wonderful congregation.

IMPRINTED ON MY MIND AND HEART

There is another pastor whose witness and friendship I should like to affirm, for he is representative of the great host of Alabama pastors with whom I have shared my life in the kingdom work. Dr. Dotson M. Nelson, giant of a man with a heart for preachers and an abiding love for the people of God, especially Southern Baptists, is unflinching in his zeal for the advancement of Christian missions. I had graduated from the Southern Baptist Theological Seminary in 1949 and was pastoring the congregation of McElwain Baptist Church in Birmingham by 1950. Sometime in the early fifties there was an alumni luncheon at the Southern Baptist Convention meeting in Miami. The hugh ballroom was filled with hundreds of Southern alumni and guests. What a crowd!

I remember sitting at such a distance from the head table that it was difficult to recognize the guests seated there. Dotson Nelson, alumni president, presided in his inimitable manner. I remember thinking, "What a man!" His physique overshadowed the lectern, and he had a voice that commanded attention from the hugh crowd. Dr. Duke McCall was the president of Southern Seminary at the time.

I thought that would be as close as I would ever get to Dotson M. Nelson. I was delighted when it was announced by the media that he had been called to pastor the new and floundering Mountain Brook Baptist

Church. He came to Mountain Brook from First Baptist Church, Greenville, South Carolina, in 1961.

I felt a sense of inadequacy, but also anticipation, as Dotson's neighboring pastor. I came to appreciate and love him as few pastors in my life. In fact, I experienced the honor and privilege of having him as a neighboring pastor. Mountain Brook and McElwain Baptist Churches were located just a short distance apart on Montevallo Road, and both were in a fast growth mode.

Dotson's pastoral leadership influenced my ministry in a very positive manner. Today, he is my counselor and friend. He encouraged me during Louise's illness and subsequent death some thirty years later in Montgomery, when he served as interim pastor at Eastern Hills Baptist Church. Those months hold special memories. Grace, his wife, excels with compassionate mercies and love to all people especially when they are hurting or dying, as Louise was. Grace was a minister of the Lord full of grace and compassion. This Mountain Brook story affirms my first impression of "Dot" Nelson. My, what a man—a giant in the Lord, his church, his family, and his denomination.

Many movements for advancing the kingdom of God gripped the big heart of Dotson Nelson. The Mountain Brook Baptist Church is a living testimony to the embodiment of Christ by members of the family of God. The church reaches out in ministry and witness into the communities of greater Birmingham—the corporate community, cultural/social community, college/university community, medical community, and to ordinary people like me. At the Mountain Brook Baptist Church, where Christ is honored, where compassion is demonstrated, where love abounds, where servant leadership prevails, going into all the world preaching, teaching, and healing is a lifestyle.

Dotson Nelson has always championed missions causes by starting new churches: Brookwood Baptist Church, Meadowbrook Baptist Church (where Grace and Dotson were copastors), and Riverchase Baptist Church. Denominationally, he always comes down on the side of missions and avidly supports them nationally, stateside, and globally through the Baptist World Alliance. Dotson was uncompromisingly committed to raising the level of giving in support of missions. He was a 50/50 man, 50 percent of gifts through the Cooperative Program for State Missions and 50 percent for Southwide causes. The following recommendation was presented by Dr. Dotson Nelson to the 1984

Earl and former pastors, Earle Trent and Everet Calvert.

Convention: by 1990, the Cooperative Program receipts be divided 50/50 to Southern Baptist Convention causes and State Convention mission causes. Dot Nelson always championed missions.

PASSING THE TORCH

August 24, 1990, was a unique day made memorable by Alabama Baptists and special guests. I had made a commitment to the State Board of Missions to serve in the position of executive secretary-treasurer for up to five years if it were the pleasure of the State Board and if my health permitted. Thank the Lord, both provisions were positively answered.

I perceived my tenure of service as transitional. Honor is to be experienced when commitments are fulfilled. Thus, I made arrangements for an audience with Dr. Charles Carter, president of the Alabama Baptist Convention, through Ms. Mavis Gates. I shared with the president my intention to retire from the office of executive secretary-treasurer on August 30, 1990. Why August? It was my desire to favor the person coming into the office at every possible opportunity. The transition in August would give time for the selection, election, and installation of the new executive secretary-treasurer prior to the annual session of the convention in November. The timing would facilitate the convention program and the newly elected leadership for launching new directions, missions, and ministries for the decade of the 1990s.

Also, I would be completing my twentieth year of ministry with the Alabama Baptist Convention under the leadership of the State Board of Missions. It had been a delightful journey filled with innumerable opportunities for servicing mission needs in the convention, associations, and the churches. I encountered many days of hard work and visionary challenges. However, the days were filled with joy and gladness.

The convention president appointed a Retirement Committee, chaired by a long-time friend and fellow pastor, Dr. Hugh Chambliss. Hugh is numbered among Alabama's most distinguished pastors. He served effectively as director of missions in Madison Baptist Association.

August 24, 1990, was a day of days for my family. I am most grateful to the Retirement Committee, the State Board of Missions, the staff family, Convention President Dr. Charles Carter, pastors, church staff members, and Alabama Baptist church members for the memorable day filled with memories, momentoes, communication, and special shared moments.

The day began with a beautiful luncheon at the Galleria hotel hosted by the State Board of Missions—a luncheon where everybody (of all 400) was an important guest. Representatives were present from the entities of the Southern Baptist Convention. It was a gala event!

Later that day, a grand reception for the Baptist family and friends was held in the fellowship hall of Shades Mountain Baptist Church. The setting was glorious, the refreshments were delicious, the guests were beautiful. I was in the receiving line at 4:00 P.M. and remained there until 7:00 P.M. In fact, Joyce Carter and Buddy Nelson took me from the reception line and ushered me to the worship center for the service of celebration and worship.

Music was furnished by a great choir composed of choir members from McElwain Baptist Church, Eastern Hills Baptist Church, Shades Mountain Baptist Church, and by the renowned pianist Dino, who stirred our hearts with his gift and skill at the keyboard.

The Holy Spirit's presence, Dr. Carter's participation, and Governor Guy Hunt and Mrs. Hunt's input made this a special retirement service.

Dr. Tom Corts, president of Samford University, presents to Earl Potts a plaque honoring him upon his retirement as executive secretary-treasurer of Alabama Baptist Convention.

Secretary of State Perry Hand presented me with a certificate of commendation on behalf of the people of Alabama—one of the more than fifty arranged on a special wall in our home by my daughter, Libby.

Never, never had I thought or imagined upon my election to a staff position on the State Board of Missions in 1970 that I would be the recipient of such appreciation and honor. Dr. Carter recognized me for a response.

"Praise to the Lord, the Almighty" is a great hymn of praise and adoration. My heart outflows with praise and adoration to the Lord God and with thanksgiving to Alabama Baptists. The lyrics to stanza two are appropriate in expressing my thoughts: "Praise to the Lord, who over all things so wondrously reigneth. Shelter thee under his wings, Yea, so gently sustaineth! Praise to the Lord who doth prosper thy work and defend thee. Praise to the Lord, O let all that is in me adore him! All that hath life and breath, come now with praises before him. Let the amen sound from his people again, Gladly for aye we adore him!"

I had requested the privilege of presenting the newly elected executive secretary-treasurer, and President Carter graciously consented to my desire. Therefore, I said, "Mr. President and Alabama Baptists, I take joy in presenting our executive secretary-treasurer and spouse, Dr. and Mrs. Troy Morrison." There was rejoicing and applause for our new leadership and still, eight years later, I am most appreciative for the leadership of Dr. Troy Morrison.

A TIME FOR EVERYTHING

Lord, I have seen many summertimes
I have felt the cold of many winters
Worked many seasons of planting and cultivating
Many seed times
Many harvest times
I have seen many sunrises . . . many sunsets.
I have followed the course of the stars
At night with brilliant display
Night glories and splendors.
I know pardon for sin
I know peace that endures
I have strength for today and bright hope for tomorrow.
I have seen the beginning of many lives
    have also been there for the endings.
I have planted, I have watered
But careful in proclaiming it is God who has given the increase.
I know the joy of serving Christ the King
I can sing the song of the faithfulness of God
I can affirm the greatness of His faithfulness
Oh, Lord, our God, how great is Thy faithfulness.
Lord, so long as I have strength of body
And the semblance of a mind
I want to love you and serve you
And when those fail me
I will still love you, Lord. (A. Earl Potts)

With that awareness, I retired as executive secretary-treasurer of the Alabama Baptist State Convention.

Epilogue

MY DAUGHTER HELPED ME THROUGH THE LIFE ADJUSTMENT of retirement. Libby said, "Dad, the word is redirect." I like that and never use retirement. I am a redirected executive secretary-treasurer.

The Lord has opened doors and kept me busy. I have become more active in Eastern Hills Baptist Church where I've been a member since 1971. Drew Gunnells was my first pastor. Ralph Langley was the preacher when Louise and I joined the church.

Dr. Timothy George was the first person to talk with me about an assignment at Samford's Beeson Divinity School. Dr. Corts indicated his desire for my services at Samford. I became the James H. Chapmen Fellow at Beeson. I taught Baptist polity, church administration, and the Southern Baptist Convention course, which I continue as an adjunct professor.

This has been a great experience for me, and I believe the young men who sat in my class gained insights for their pastoral ministry. The students were very charitable and magnanimous in their evaluations of me. I wish that I had been better equipped in subject contents. I believe in the standard of excellence for the classroom and felt that I did not measure up both for my students and for the university.

Another door the Lord has opened for me to enter is the interim pastorate. There have been five: Blue Ridge Baptist Church, Wetumpka;

Tallaweka Baptist Church, Tallassee, Alabama. Dr. Earl Potts with Amy and William Henderson, Cassie Jennings, and Diana and Christy Singleton.

Beatrice Baptist Church, Beatrice; Fair View Baptist Church, Selma; Tallaweka Baptist Church, Tallassee; and Rockford Baptist Church, Rockford. Each interim has been joyful and delightful, and the Lord blessed us. I am glad to affirm each of these congregations in the strength of their fellowship, in giving, in attendance, and in ministries. I thank the Lord and those churches for their confidence in calling me as their interim pastor. I serve at the request of our executive secretary-treasurer, Dr. Morrison, currently serving as chairman of the Convention Bylaws Committee, and staff members of the State Board of Missions.

Other areas of service I am active in are the Alabama Poverty Project, the Alabama Senior Citizens Hall of Fame, Montgomery Baptist Association—Church and Ministries Board, and Alabama Holocaust Observance Commission. I have some participation in welfare reform, an issue and need in which I am vitally interested.

SIMPLE GIFTS

Is retirement supposed to provide one with unlimited time for relaxation? It does not. For example, I like to fish, but still can't seem to find the time. Also, I was a pretty good golfer, but since I moved to Montgomery I have neglected the hobby. Now, I am a terrible golfer. I like hiking, but walking is my basic exercise. Yard work occupies a good bit of my time. I consider creating attractive, well-manicured lawns, flower beds, and gardens a handiwork of God, as well as a hobby.

My reading, heretofore, has been oriented towards sermon preparation and church-related growth activities. The Bible is my preferred book. It seems the older I get the more my time and attention is drawn to the Bible. I also read news magazines, *National Geographic,* the *Smithsonian,* the *Christian History,* and *Christianity Today,* especially since my dean, Timothy George, is on the board.

I enjoy being out in nature. I identify with the Old Testament personality of David. His experiences with nature remind me of mine. I am overwhelmed with God's creation. David said,

> When I consider the heavens, the work of thy fingers, the moon and the stars, which thou has ordained.

Earl, daughter, Libby, and son, David.

> What is man that thou art mindful of him and the Son of Man that thou
> doest care for him? . . . Thou hast made him a little lower than God. . . ."
> (Ps. 8)

I thank God for his creation and the privilege of being a caretaker for a tiny spot. I appreciate that responsibility, wherever I have served and wherever I have lived, always endeavoring to leave the environment better than I found it. Abraham Lincoln said, "Die when I may, I would like for it to be said of me that I always pulled up a weed and planted flowers where I thought they would grow." This was also my attitude in relationship to my life and my ministry.

Blessing and Peace to You!

Partnership Planning

Partnership planning by the associations of churches, the State Board of Missions departments of work, and the national offices was an "idea" whose time had come. Oh, there had always been partnership planning taking place between the associations and departments of work, yes, but within the framework of an inverted planning process, that is, planning from the top down. In this reference, the state program leaders went to the Baptist Sunday School Board in Nashville, Tennessee, where they spent several hours in conference learning from the national leaders about the new program's emphases and priorities for the new church year. Who were these national leaders? They were achievers, people who were doing well with their leadership responsibilities in the local church, association, or State Convention. They were sought out and invited to the Sunday School Board to plan and promote their programs. This selection process had been followed for years.

When State Convention leadership returned to their offices, they reviewed and refined the information about the program received from the Baptist Sunday School Board, factoring in state emphases, and then in the next phase, passed this information to the director of Association Missions and departmental leadership—pastoral leaders, church staff leaders, and laypeople. The association leadership, in turn, trained the church leadership, who promoted the program emphasis in the local church.

The planning process had merit; however, it did not reflect the best of Baptist polity. How do you reverse an inversion? Look to Baptist polity, which calls for congregational participation. This is the key.

Our Baptist forbearers were exemplary in practicing Baptist polity. I remember as a child back in the 1920s those early church business meetings. I asked, "But, Mama do I have to go to church on Saturday?" That was the day for church business meetings at High Pine Baptist Church. Church business meetings were important to the congregation, and the members took the responsibility seriously. Business meetings were long, unstructured, and boring to a child (and dare I say to some adults as well). Sunday was the Sabbath day and was kept holy. But you could not always be holy in church business meetings. Amen!

As I grew, I learned. I came to appreciate the Baptist way of doing church. I liked the congregational participation, a practice perhaps needing to be recovered in many Baptist churches today. However, hear me, each Baptist church congregation decides the practice.

Early Baptists in America were influenced by Landmarkism, a movement with inherent biblical awareness. One weakness was the noncooperation of the local Baptist church with other Baptist churches. That changed because Baptist churches learned they could do more for kingdom advance by cooperating with churches of like faith and practice than they could separately.

The first Baptist Association in America, the Philadelphia Baptist Association, was organized in 1707. Today, there are more than 1,200 Baptist associations in all parts of America on a mission for Christ in their local setting. They are able to do more when the churches work together than separately. The cardinal ideas in partnership planning are involving local churches, the association, and the State Convention in the planning services and providing resources to meet the needs of the local churches. The flow in the identification of needs is from the local churches to the association, to the State Convention, to the Southern Baptist Convention.

Formally stated, the purpose of partnership planning is to engage the State Board of Missions and the directors of Associational Missions as colleagues in the development and implementation of a mission strategy for reaching people, developing believers, and strengthening missions, always with local church representation present and involved. Partnership planning is designed to involve both associational leadership and state leadership in the initial process of denominational planning:

1.   to demonstrate mutual ownership of goals, programs, and strategies;
2.   to preserve the integrity and autonomy of the local church, association, and convention;
3.   to recognize the diversity of capabilities among churches and leaders;
4.   to create an atmosphere of participation and cooperation.

A partner is a person associated with another or others in some activity of common interest. Partnership implies a relationship in which each has equal status, a certain independence, and an implicit obligation to others.

The principal idea was the partnership would be initiated by the churches. How was that to be? Associational leadership would convene a forum with representation from all churches. The associational leadership (director of missions, moderator, church organizational leaders, association treasurer, etc.) would serve as the panel. The model could be determined by the association.

The forum (a place for open discussion) provided the environment for each church to identify the ministry and spiritual needs within the churches of the association. Short-range and long-range goals would be developed to be placed on a planning grid for the association.

T. A. Benefield, director of missions, Sand Mountain Association, said, "This is a very good approach to involving our churches in developing the local ministries according to the needs." Right on target, he said:

> I find it hard to present the planning grid to cover the next five years when we find very little information available on each department emphasis and state long range emphasis and goals. I feel there is a need to bring you folks closer to where the work is done. Most of our people need help before the staff specialist can effectively complete his work! I recognize this is the beginning of a new way of doing our work. Many changes will take place. I do see we will have big problems if every church and association comes up with something different or when their own program is not funded. I appreciate the leadership our state is giving. I believe something BIG is about to happen.

I became a strong advocate of partnership planning. The directors of all the associations, missions, pastors, church staff members, and State

Board of Mission staff came together in the formation of an enthusiastic team with a threefold mission—reaching people, developing disciples, and strengthening missions. Challenging tasks necessitated in-depth prayer, hard work, and examining the present organizational structure.

Benefield failed to sign his name to the following, but I thought he was on track.

MOVING FORWARD

Reaching people is our theme,
so says the Word supreme.
After prayer, the giving of 50%
will help us address and assure those who are sent.
To accomplish the goals of BMT
will take commitment from all of us.
Meeting needs we are urged by Dr. Potts
forward we are to surge.
So that the world may know Christ,
and by His power put Him first.

Hubert Windham, director of missions in the North Jefferson Association, in pondering the challenge before Alabama Baptists, communicated to Dr. Harper Shannon, associate to the executive secretary-treasurer and director of the Department of Evangelism:

All Baptist churches accept without hesitation two Biblical truths—the Lordship of Jesus Christ and the need for prayer. . . . I think all the churches Alabama would respond to a call to prayer for the lost and unenlisted people in our state . . . encouraging pastors and deacons of the churches to compile prayer lists of the lost to be in prayer for these people. . . . I am convinced that prayer is the key.

Amen!

Lord Jesus, come in your convicting power, your compassionate love, your forgiving grace, that all members of the Baptist family would be called from the world of cares and seek your face. Amen. Convince me, Lord, as you have convinced my brother in Christ, Hubert Windham, that prayer is the answer.

The Planning Committee factored into the agenda of partnership planning a "Dialogue with Dr. Potts." Asked one director of missions, "How do I work with all elements (pastoral) on the theological spectrum and still maintain my own integrity?" (Especially as the problems of the Southern Baptist Convention filters down into the association.)

My answer to the question:

1. keep faith with your faith;
2. be directors of missions to all pastors;
3. plan your work—build in content that addresses needs—stay with priorities;
4. be informed about issues;
5. love the brethren—pray for one another;
6. nurture team effort—be partners;
7. again, I say pray!

Earl Potts's Response to His Election as Executive Secretary-Treasurer

At the outset, I want to acknowledge with gratitude some who make this day possible—God! the Holy Other, the First and the Last, the Alpha and Omega, the Beginning and the End. In the words of the psalmist, "Who is man that thou art mindful of Him?" My parents, who taught me the value of work, the discipline for a full and meaningful life, parents of integrity, impeccable honesty, forthrightness, and love; parents who introduced me to the church house and to the Lord's people. I am a product of that heritage that has built a great state and nation. I desire not only to enter into that strength, into that heritage, but I want to help promote it and help to promulgate it.

I am a product of Alabama—born and bred here. I am in debt to my family—children who love their parents and affirm them in their decisions and practices, children who have grown up and the parents are pleased to acknowledge their personhood with pride and appreciation, children who are here today because of their involvement in this hour. I would that it were possible for my wife, Louise, to enter more fully and more completely into this decision. She has served gallantly and with full commitment. She is a great partner! She is an affirmer of her family. She has always put family first. She loves her denomination. She loves the convention. She loves you, and she believes so very much in what we are doing. Her high calling is a calling to training leadership: to work with children, to bless children, to lead children, and to nurture children.

I am appreciative of Dr. Reid. It was he who had confidence in me, and in the summer of 1943, sent me to Perry County, Cahaba Association, as a student summer missionary. I am appreciative of the confidence Dr. Bagley and this Executive Board placed in me in 1970. I am grateful for the privilege of working with my colleagues and associates, with Alabama Baptists, pastors and laity, with directors of Associational Missions, with members of this board, with the president of this convention, and with heads of agencies and institutions. I am sixty-three years of age. Plans beyond age sixty-five have been a very vital part of my thinking and planning in recent months. I have been an advocate of retirement from the active role with the Baptist State Executive Board at age sixty-five. I am in full support of the policy of the Baptist State Executive Board concerning retirement, with the initiative beyond age sixty-five at the direction of the Administration Committee and Executive Board.

It has been my intention to change directions at age sixty-five. I have never fully recovered from moving from the pastorate into service in the denomination. I am, by calling, design, and training, heavily oriented toward the pastorate. I think there is no more strategic place of service. I do not think there is a greater calling. I think there are opportunities to serve and to minister in the pastorate that are inaccessible in other dimensions of service. The pastorate, indeed, is the high calling of God to a noble place of service. Fortunate is the person who has the opportunity to serve within the local congregation and is recognized as the pastor of that congregation.

Consequently, one of the options open to me, as I was thinking toward age sixty-five, was returning to the pastorate. I do not believe a person, in reaching age fifty, is no longer usable in the pastorate. Someway, somehow, one of the greatest challenges confronting Alabama Baptists today is overcoming that mind set. Surely, some of the most productive years in the lives of the men of God who serve in pastorates have been those years of age fifty and above. Also, I believe that attention should be given to this misnomer, and I believe that it should begin within the staff of the Baptist State Executive Board. Too frequently we have been advocates of this misnomer in conversation with one another, and in public. I do believe that we can begin to address this matter.

I had thought of the possibility of becoming associate to a pastor who has the capacities for an associate, to work with him in the areas of evangelism, visitation, and ministry. I had even considered spending some time in Nigeria among the Nigerian people, working in their churches and in the Nigerian Baptist Convention. The options for my life have been altered in recent months.

On September 9, 1983, the Executive Board rendered a decision that thrust me into the office of acting executive secretary-treasurer of the Baptist State Executive Board and Convention. I made a positive response to your decision, believing it to be within the will of God for my life. Alabama Baptists have given unbelievable affirmation!

It was in June of 1970 that Dr. Bagley came to me and talked with me about the possibility of my interest in coming to the Baptist State Executive Board as an employee, if it were the will of the Executive Board. I talked further with Dr. Bagley about that. I had known Dr. Bagley for years, and I thought it would be something I should consider. It has been a joy to work with him as the executive secretary-treasurer of the Alabama Baptist State Convention. I could not have asked for a better supporter or helper than this man.

During these fourteen years, I have changed my direction, this being the fourth occasion. I would like to express my appreciation to Dr. Bagley and to this board. I am very much aware of your reasons for being, reasons filled with many noble causes as defined by Alabama Baptists. I thank you for the privilege of being identified with a group of men and women who are committed to the causes of Christ. I am privileged to have served under your leadership. I see my role as a servant/leader role in the mission causes of Alabama Baptists.

I would like to express my appreciation to the Search Committee. It was April 9 when the chairman of this committee called and asked me if I would come before the committee for a second time to talk with them, and I responded to that. I appreciate so very much this committee. It is under the instructions of the convention and the Executive Board and constitution that the procedure is set for us to follow and that a Search Committee be appointed. I said on September 9, "A Search Committee is at work, and I find reason for rejoicing, not for them asking me to accept this assignment, but in the way they have approached their assignment, their commitment to seeking God's man for Alabama Baptists. This afternoon, before this Board, I want to pledge my support to that Search Committee. I shall be loyal to the Search Committee. I will support that Search Committee in the recommendation that they shall bring to this body." Never would I have thought, at the time of making the statement, I would be in this position today.

Some months before Dr. Bagley's retirement, I was in conversation with him one day in his office. We were talking about his retirement. I said to him, "It would be nice to follow you as executive secretary-treasurer." That thought was short-lived, the reason being the discomfort, first of all, that I had made the statement, and secondly, I was just uncomfortable being in that position having said it. So, I took a long walk that evening in the Carriage Hills section of Montgomery. I resolved the issue with the Lord in that walk, and from that day to this, I had no desire to be thrust in this office.

Therefore, in response to the decision you have made, it is a responsibility I have not sought, I am not seeking, and I shall not seek. It is a decision I can lay down at any time. It is a decision that you can terminate. I am willing and ready to give it my best effort as long as there is mutual agreement among the person in the office, the Baptist State Executive Board, and the constituency of the Alabama Baptist State Convention.

Contrary to the response I made to the board on September 9, I do have a prepared statement for this moment. Mr. Chairman, I know the mission causes and challenges of Alabama Baptists are greater than any one of us or all of us put together, and it is to the mission causes of Alabama Baptists that I am committed. I think I can read something of the signs of the time, and I know something of the direction that this board and this convention needs to go and desires to go, and this morning before God and before you, [this] is my commitment. I desire to share with you some concerns regarding programs and ministries of the convention.

Reaching People—The major concern is reaching people. This concern has multiple dimensions; however, I am addressing the concern twofold. One, primarily, reaching the unchurched. There are four million people in Alabama, almost 56 percent of which are unchurched. I am speaking primarily of focusing this large segment of people. We have in Alabama over 8,000 churches, synagogues, cathedrals and temples. We have 3,042 churches identified with the Alabama Baptist State Convention. We have exceeded one million church members. You would think that we would have reached more of the people who live in our state for Christ. One person who made the pilgrimage to Nigeria made this statement upon his return. Having observed the commitment of the Nigerian Baptists, their prayer support, and their involvement,

[he] said, "I believe the Nigerian Baptists will win Nigeria to Christ." I am not at all sure about Alabama.

The work to be done is here before us. We have 468 churches with Sunday School enrollment above 300. These churches constitute 50 percent of our membership, 47 percent of Baptisms, 56.6 percent of Sunday School enrollment, 63.3 percent of our total receipts. We have 2,574 churches with less than 300 enrolled in Sunday School. These 2,574 churches' total showed a net increase in Sunday School enrollment last year of 256. Twenty-five hundred seventy-four churches showed a net increase of one. Some way, we must be more effective in reaching people. We must do better in discipling our people. Don Watterson tells me that we must reach 180,000 people in Sunday School to show a net increase of 40,000 by 1985. By reaching people, let me be specific—establish initial contact with these unchurched people, maintain a plan of harvesting for these unchurched people, and assimilate them into the body of Christ. The Sunday School has the lead role in this assignment, with other church programs supporting.

Giving through Our Local Churches—There are two essential supports to the mission work of Southern Baptists: prayer support and giving support through the Cooperative Program. Both have served us well. The causes of Associational Missions, state missions, and Southern Baptist Convention rise or fall with the response to these two essential supports.

Alabama Baptists gave $9,573,000 through the Cooperative Program in 1977. Our goal was to have doubled our giving five years 1977–1982, and twice more by 2000 A.D. If we increase 9.5 percent each year in support of the Cooperative Program, based on 1983 receipts, Alabama Baptists will have reached our goal. We have increased in per capita gifts through the Cooperative Program from $10.17 in 1977 to $17.08 in 1983. Gifts to SBC causes has increased from $3,446,000 in 1977 to $6,836,000 in 1983. Our percentage increase through the Cooperative Program has been decreasing from 12.07 percent in 1978 over 1977 to 5.14 percent in 1983 over 1982. I plead today for an intensification of prayer support and for an understanding of the Cooperative Program.

There are other challenges before us. **The Endowment Program for Christian Higher Education**—Let us express appreciation for the foundation of the endowment program. Alabama Baptists are concerned about this endowment. We do have Alabama Baptists who believe that the goal is attainable. There is a committee at work seeking a person to give direction to this program. I am concerned that the level of support be elevated for endowment for Christian Higher Education. It challenges the best response from three colleges and university, the Baptist Foundation, the Executive Board, and Alabama Baptists. Alabama Baptists authorized the institutions to develop an endowment program with a goal of $45 million for the program of Christian Higher Education of the Alabama Baptist State Convention. Endowment is essential in keeping the colleges and university on the cutting edge in education—Christian higher education.

Ministry for Senior Citizens—Alabama Baptists have established a caring ministry to our senior adults. The definitive statement from day one has been "to assist our senior adults in retaining their dignity, their independence, their best possible health, their sense of belonging and feeling wanted, and the experience of fulfillment in their purpose of life, under God." It has been my privilege to witness the vitality of this ministry at one of two retirement centers, the Baptist Village in Dothan. The occasion was twofold—the meeting of the board of directors and the groundbreaking service for the McMullan Chapel.

Clara Verna Towers in Tuscaloosa is our other retirement center. There are 419 residents at the two centers. They have come from many areas of our state. Their rent ranges from $235 to $360 a month. The ministry of Alabama Baptists to the senior citizens of this state is a distinctive ministry. The executive director and board of directors are evaluating some options for enlarging this ministry.

The Programs and Ministries of the Baptist State Executive Board—Here I need to be heard with open minds and hearts. Several years have lapsed since the programs of work, organizational structure, and personnel based at the Baptist Building have been evaluated. I have fourteen-years experience with the Baptist State Executive Board. I have served as director of the Church Ministries Division, as assistant to the executive secretary-treasurer, and as acting executive secretary-treasurer. I have observations which I feel have some validity. I have experiences upon which I can draw, and I am somewhat conversant with all the programs.

In my opinion that we are at a juncture when we need to look at ourselves with the view and mind of reaching more people, discipling our people, and giving more in support to mission causes. I think it is in order to request the appointment of a convention committee that will give leadership to a definition of goals and objectives for the convention, that will study, evaluate, and recommend organizational structure, programs of work, and personnel. It would be premature at this point for me to propose changes; however, I think changes are needed. It would be premature for me to make projections regarding future programs of work; yet suggestions must be made.

It may be that we need to give some consideration to reorganization of structure. It may be that we need to return to the local church and/or the association some programs and ministries fostered by the Executive Board. It may be that the structure is intact as it should be. However, I think it needs to be reviewed objectively.

Therefore, it is my intention, in consultation with the proper leadership, to request and, hopefully, implement an appointment of a convention committee that will address the directions this convention should take for the next six years specifically, and broad goals and objectives until 2000, and what will be required to implement those goals and objectives in programs, personnel, and funding.

There is the other area of relationships. Consideration should be given to some major areas of relationships. I do believe that it is the desire, pleasure, and will of Alabama Baptists that our agencies, institutions, commissions, and Baptist State Executive Board move steadfastly in the direction established by the convention. I do believe that it is the will of the convention that the agencies, institutions, commissions, and Executive Board work together in harmony within a climate that interprets to the convention that the said entities are working together as a team. It is inconceivable to me that we would have any one of the agencies and institutions out of the ballpark, doing its own thing. It is the will of this convention, in my opinion, that our agencies and institutions and this board work together, team, functioning as a team.

Therefore, let me affirm each agency, institution, and commission. Let me affirm the reason for your being. Let me request and invite to consultation and planning the heads of all agencies, institutions, and commissions from which there shall flow information to the Alabama Baptist State Convention, our goals and objectives, and we are a team, and in which there is the climate of openness regarding the programs, decisions, and budget.

It is my desire that the heads of agencies, institutions, commissions, and the executive secretary-treasurer shall lead the way in affirming the programs of work and personal involvement in those programs of work, that we shall lead the way in working together in the area of Bold Mission Thrust, reaching people, developing believers, and mission support.

Interrelationship of the Convention, Association, and Local Church—I believe the convention exists, by and large, for the local church. The local church is our reason for being. The source for our authority at the associational level and the State Convention level is the local church.

> The purpose of the Convention shall be to offer an agency of cooperation for the churches, to promote the preaching of the gospel in Alabama and throughout the world, to support ministerial and Christian education, to publish and distribute Christian literature including the Bible if desirable, to organize and promote all phases of work fostered by this Convention and the Southern Baptist Convention, and to aid any benevolent or moral movements it may deem promotive of God's Kingdom. (Constitution, 1983 Annual)

Therefore, let me hasten to recognize the uniqueness of the local church. Christ said, "I will build my church." He is the head, we are members of the body. It is his church. I desire to affirm the local church as the most important unit of life in the world today for advancing the kingdom.

Let me hasten to call for a spirit of togetherness on the part of our people in our churches in the area of pastor/people relationships, in the area of church/association relationships, and church/convention [relationships].

Let me request a commitment on the part of pastor and people to effective service through a commonality of belief, doctrine, and cooperativeness. We have 3,042 local churches. There is much diversity among the churches—pastor/people personalities, the capacities, gifts of the people within these churches and the programs. However, there is a commonality to our faith and practice. It is disastrous for a local church when there is a breach in its fellowship. The words of Dr. Gaines S. Dobbins came to mind: "A church never gets over a split." It is deceitful for a pastor to accept a Southern Baptist church, pledge his cooperation with the mission causes of that church, and be in support of Southern

Baptists, and later, as though he were a wolf in sheep's clothing, create a division in that church fellowship.

Relationship between the Convention and Associations—The association is an important organization. There are seventy-five associations in Alabama. Each association exists at the will of the churches. As the convention exists for the churches, likewise, the association. The relationship is voluntary between association and State Convention. It is a relationship of mutual respect and voluntary cooperation. However, in order to assist the local churches in accomplishing their mission tasks, cooperation planning is imperative between the association and State Convention.

A good working relationship prevails between directors of Associational Missions and the Executive Board staff. However, this relationship can be enhanced. The planning process can be made more viable. The position of the association in relationship to the church is unique—the association is strategic to the work of the local church.

The Matter of Communication and Openness—A Baptist leader of other days is quoted to have said, "A good principle to go by is to trust the Lord and tell the people." Baptists function best in an atmosphere of openness and freedom.

The Administration Committee has authorized the appointment of a committee to deal with the matter of more effective communication from the denomination to the churches and from the churches to the denomination. Your suggestions shall be welcomed!

Finally, the decision! Let us declare it to be a team effort. A team effort that shall be evident, a team effort involving the pastors and members of the congregation, our churches. A team effort involving the directors of Associational Missions, staff members of the Baptist State Executive Board, the officers of the convention, and the members of this Executive Board, the agencies and institutions.

Let me indicate my intentions to lean heavily upon you as Executive Board members, to involve you, to be open and responsive to your decisions. Let me encourage you to be involved actively in your local association, interpreting the decisions, and sharing information.

Perhaps, the most appropriate statement I could make on this historic day is, ". . . Nothing in my hand I bring, simply to the cross, I cling." Thank you!

Campgrounds

CHRONOLOGY OF STATE ASSEMBLIES

1910—Shelby Springs, Shelby County, First Alabama Summer Assembly, encampment

1911— Shocco Springs, Talladega, assembly

1912–1918—Pelham Heights Encampment Commission, Inc. Assembly, encampment

1921–1932—Mentone camp grounds, assemblies

1935—Judson College, Marion, assemblies

1936–1940—Shocco Springs, Talladega Assemblies

1941–1943— Shocco Springs (military housed at Shocco)

1943–1947—Judson College, Marion

1944–1946—I was a summer worker in the Training Union Department. Maines Rawls, Cynthia Jo Hall, and John Jeffers were my supervisors.

1947— State Board of Missions purchased, Shocco Springs

December 10, 1947—Shocco Springs Committee: W. D. Ogletree, chairman; Brady Justice; Pat Roberson; cost: $62,500.00.

Shocco Springs resonates well with missions among Alabama Baptists. It is a place where Alabama Baptists and many other Christian groups come for retreats, assemblies, camps, and conferences. It is a place where persons experience Christ for salvation, where Christians come to experience a closer walk with the Lord, and where people (children, youth, and adults) by the thousands dedicate their lives, leaving renewed for special ministry tasks in the churches.

Shocco Springs is holy ground for me. Oftentimes I have gone there to get away from the demands and opportunities of the pastorate and the convention so much in need of drawing aside for a fresh presence of the Lord. I never realized that I would be a participant in the decision-making process impacting Shocco Springs, but I was.

Alabama Baptists have a wonderful heritage in Shocco Springs. Its beautiful story is being written by George Ricker at the request of Buster Taylor, director of Shocco Springs Assembly. I shall not infringe on that assignment, except to say that I anticipate this fine addition to the heritage of Alabama Baptists. It was while serving as assistant to Dr. George Bagley that I became involved in working on the Shocco Project.

The Conference Center was built during the time of President Dan Ireland. He gave leadership to naming the complex, "George Bagley Conference Center," and I worked with him and the program committee in planning the service of dedication. James R. Glaze worked with several Shocco Springs committees, assembly directors, and executive secretaries in bringing the assembly programs and facilities to one of the foremost conference centers in the nation. The reputation of Shocco Springs reaches out across America.

One of the most significant decisions in decades regarding Shocco Springs was the development of the long-range plan, a herculean task. The Long Range Study Committee appointed in December 1974 was accomplished with the support of the Executive Committee of the State Mission Board. This board was very attentive to its responsibilities regarding acquisitions to Shocco Springs through the years. The list of distinguished directors includes Hobson Shirey, George Bagley, Waymond Reese, George Ricker, and Buster Taylor. George Kemp and Associates developed the long range plan for Shocco Springs. George and his staff created one of the finest perspectives for Shocco Springs.

Jim Glaze has been director of Glaze Business Management for the State Board of Missions since January 12, 1968. He is a colleague and dear friend, and we have shared some good and some hard times together. Jim is a prominent leader in the Southern Baptist Business Offices of state conventions across the nation.

Buster Taylor, an excellent choice, is giving outstanding visionary leadership as director of Shocco Springs. Buster is a Christian gentleman with a lovely family. His associate, Lowell Ledbetter, who came to Shocco from Auburn University, is an ideal associate director.

The best thing or person to happen to food service at Shocco Springs in my lifetime is Wendy Westerhouse and her staff. Prior to Wendy coming to direct the food service at Shocco, there were complaints about the food from SBM staff, faculty, and conferees. Wendy was employed April 21, 1986, and since then I have not heard one complaint about Shocco food or service. Her innovations in planning, preparing, and serving meals are noteworthy.

The Administration Committee approved a recommendation in 1985 to the Executive Board requesting to purchase and to sell property adjacent to Shocco Springs.

AND THE WOMEN PRAYED!

Women of faith have always been in the spin of missions—studying Scriptures, teaching missions, doing missions, giving to missions, and not the least, praying for missions. Since New Testament times, women have faithfully responded to God's call as Paul did in Acts 16:6–15. In a vision, a man cried out to Paul, "Come over to Macedonia and help us." Paul and his companions obeyed God by sailing to the Macedonian city of Philippi. On the Sabbath day, they went outside the city gate to the riverside where they found a women's prayer group. Likewise, Alabama Baptist women display a heart for missions and a passion for prayer.

In Alabama, the first offering for missions was provided by women of mission societies. The offering was taken at the founding session of the Alabama Baptist Convention at Greensboro, Alabama, Salem Baptist Church 1823. Christian missions have advanced through the ages. One significant cause has been praying women, who have been faithful in their praying. Some of the most faithful prayer warriors are women.

Jessie Davis Stakely was one of those praying women. She said,

> Of far greater importance than anything else is the duty and the privilege of special prayer. Let us pray for those chosen of God to take up and carry on the glorious mission in every needed place. Let us pray that God may put into the hearts of our people to give as God has prospered them.

Let us advance upon our knees, and afterward there will be success and fellowship and the unspeakable honor of having been workers together with God. (Hermione Jackson and Mary Essie Stephens, *Women of Vision*, centennial edition, 1988 [Woman's Missionary Union], 33)

I would encourage women of faith and missionary zeal to be faithful in praying. Do not let fear or defeat overtake you in these years of politicizing within the Southern Baptist Convention or the State Convention. It is not the first time of pain and struggle. The Lord, our God, will prevail in kingdom advance.

The women in Alabama Woman's Missionary Union are powerful figures in the prayer movement. Organization enrichment, mission education, and giving were always on the WMU agenda, but first, "The duty and privilege of special prayer . . . let us advance upon our knees." said Stakely in 1909.

In the words of Hermione Jackson and Mary Essie Stephens, "Prayer has always been a fundamental purpose of the women's work . . . Woman's Missionary Union was born in prayer and through the years has developed through prayer."

Prayer is listed first when references are made to the fundamentals of Woman's Missionary Union. Intercessory prayer leagues for shut-ins were organized throughout Alabama. The woman engaged in prayers of intercession. Leon Macon, editor, *The Alabama Baptist*, said in an editorial, "One very desirable feature of the Seventy-fifth Anniversary session was the attention these ladies gave to prayer. It is hard to attend a WMU Convention without being affected spiritually."

A HERITAGE OF COOPERATION

Truly, Woman's Missionary Union is a strong advocate and supporter of mission advance. In the early years of the Cooperative Program, WMU gave strong leadership in promoting and raising funding for missions.

Relationships were strengthened between the Alabama Convention and Woman's Missionary Union. In 1952, constitutional revisions were made possible. There were five women serving on the State Board of Missions, and two of the five served on the Administration Committee. In 1975, WMU was combined with the Baptist State Executive Board. In 1988, the president of the Alabama Baptist State Convention served as an ex officio, nonvoting member of the WMU Executive Board. The WMU president began to serve as ex officio member of both the Executive Committee and the State Board of Missions. The number of women on the the State Board of Missions was increased. The state WMU staff participated with personnel of State Board of Missions staff in planning, promoting, and conducting activities to strengthen the work of the state, association, and churches.

THE GIRLS CAMP AND THE BOYS CAMP

The girls camp at Shocco gave rise to concerted prayer in Alabama. Among the women, guidance was sought for the direction of the girls camp. Many sacrifices, intercessory prayer, and gifts, were made toward the construction of the Katherine Samford Smith Camp for girls, the Mary Essie Stephens activities building, and improvements of housing, for a total cost of $623,263. The Katherine Samford Smith girls camp was dedicated July 15, 1980, with Camilla Lowry presiding over the dedications.

WMU experienced an upsurge of girls wanting to come to camp, causing problems of accommodation. The boys camp was having some related problems with the facilities.

WMU and the Brotherhood were involved in reviews of camp programs and the more difficult challenge of the future. B. W. Jackson of Asheboro, North Carolina, was secured by the Shocco Springs Committee to do site evaluation and recommendations for the Girls Auxiliary (GA) Camp and the Royal Ambassadors (RA) Camp. His report was submitted to the Executive Committee of the State Board of Missions on May 18, 1989. Two recommendations were approved for the RA camp—for the present site to remain being used by Royal Ambassador Camp and the other for the Stump plan to be used for upgrading the RA Camp. Implementing these recommendations for the expansion and refurbishing of the RA camp is a thrilling story. The GA camp was more complex and more compelling.

WMU leadership was engaged in praying, dialoguing, and preparing its future ministries. However, the Jackson report contained two major recommendations for the GA camp with added options. The first option for site location was to remain at the present site with a relocation of Unit One. Most of the money would be used to upgrade the facilities, with extensive work on the staff lodge and units. The second option was to extend the site by purchasing the Schonbacher property. The third option was to relocate the camp entirely.

The report was taken under advisement by WMU leadership with a response slated for September 1989. The Shocco Springs Committee recommended to the Executive Committee the purchase of eighty-one acres of the Schonbacher property for a price up to $500 per acre. Dr. Beverly Miller, executive director of the Woman's Missionary Union, and Tommy Puckett recommended that work begin on the RA camp and that the WMU board take under advisement the future of the girls camp.

Meanwhile, George Kemp of the Kemp group, design-planner of the master plan, reported, "Usable or developable property was in fact very limited in the GA camp and on the Schonbacher tract . . . situated that it would be almost inaccessible, costly to develop, and generally prohibitive to utilize for any kind of controllable camp development." In light of this report, purchase of the Schonbacher property was delayed.

George Kemp's group presented to the convention the master development plan for Shocco Springs Baptist Assembly and Camps in 1981. In the words of Mr. Kemp,

> I did not feel at that time there were some inherent site relationships between the camp and the assembly which did work well and which would continue to provide certain operational and expansion constraints. I noticed also, at the time that the GA Camp facilities were becoming obsolete.

In the meantime, WMU presented initial ideas for upgrading its program and correspondingly its facilities at Shocco. Said Kemp,

> I reviewed the document and recognized immediately a key ambitious program vision on the part of Alabama Baptists. This vision broadens the horizon for its missionary outreach and training, and I knew intuitively that my earlier predictions of the Shocco site constraints would surface shortly.

Out of seasons of prayer and consultations in numerous meetings over a period of two years, WMU took the high road of bold vision and in a faith commitment voted to relocate the girls camp on a 300 acre site with a waterfront. Fantastic!

COOK SPRINGS, MARCH 23–24, 1990

Sara Cherry, First Baptist Church, Huntsville, brought a recommendation to the WMU to purchase 300 acres of the Cook Springs properties for a new WMU camp. The purchase price was $275,000, plus the assumption of a mortgage of $35,000. The Birmingham Baptist Association was to retain 200 acres for usage, but the Association Development plans were yet to be determined. WMU voted to buy the new camp properties at Cook Springs on Friday, March 24, 1990.

WMU opened the new camp in 1991 as "Worldsong." Mr. and Mrs. Cook were devoted Christians with hearts for children and youth. They had managed a modest camping program as long as their health permitted; however, in deeding the camp properties and land, Mr. Cook had stipulated that the religious camping be maintained by the association.

In the words of Beverly Miller:

> The dream for the new expanded camp facility and program includes providing camp and retreat experiences for groups with special needs, missionary families, disadvantaged children, senior adults and mission groups. Also, the facilities will be made available to churches and associations for small group retreats.

COOK SPRINGS—McELWAIN BAPTIST CHURCH

I was introduced to Cook Springs during my years as pastor at McElwain Baptist Church. Church camp was held at Cook Springs as retreats for both boys and girls. Cook Springs became a special place for the youth from McElwain. Many made a profession of faith, others surrendered to Christian service, and more rededicated their lives to Jesus. They remembered that the "best fried chicken in Alabama." Fresh vegetables and cobblers were served there. Swimming, hiking, field athletics, and hikes to "Bald Eagle" high in the mountains nearby were part of their stay.

Mr. Edgar H. Baker, faithful lay leader of McElwain Baptist Church, served on the Cook Springs Board of Directors and was chairman for several years.

"Christian Higher Education in Alabama"

In another century, Baptist laypeople were inspired by God to create institutions of higher education for their children and their clergy. Nowhere was the clarion call for missions and Christian higher education more clearly heard than in Marion, Alabama, between 1837 and 1854. History records the founding of Judson College, Howard College (Samford University), *The Alabama Baptist*, and the Domestic Board of Missions (North American Mission Board). The call was not purely a local or regional matter, but rather a worldwide call. Fourteen of the original forty-two foreign missionaries to China were affiliated directly with Judson College. The first missionary to Japan was a Judson graduate. Stories of missionary zeal and liberating truth abound among Alabama Baptists' universities and college.

Judson College, Samford University, and the University of Mobile seek to grow and equip the minds, hearts, and souls of each new generation of students. Activities abandoned by most religiously affiliated colleges and universities continue to flourish at Judson, Samford, and Mobile. Chapel services, Bible courses, mission projects, and Christian Emphasis Weeks are among a host of activities woven into the fabric of educational experience.

The clarion call of Christian higher education is not only one of faith, but also one of academic quality. Rightly dividing the word of truth must never be a timid exercise. Each school within the context of its missions and purpose seeks to offer quality in the liberal arts, professional schools, and graduate programs.

Had Earl Potts lived in the nineteenth century, he surely would have been among those founders who were "doers of the Word." Earl Potts, quietly determined, courageous, and always a supporter of Christian higher education, provided leadership to Alabama Baptists that has held us together during a transitional time before a new century. He embraced all people regardless of race, theological persuasion, sex, or nationality. The love of God shone through his life, calling each of us to think and act more inclusively. The following chronicles Dr. Earl Potts's personal reflections on Christian higher education among Alabama Baptists.

—David E. Potts

REFLECTIONS ON CHRISTIAN HIGHER EDUCATION

A great heritage of Christian higher education has fallen into the trusted hands of Alabama Baptists. Dr. A. Hamilton Reid, president of the 1944 Alabama Baptist Convention, said, "Alabama Baptists began their journey one hundred twenty-one years ago in 1823 . . . the urge of missions, evangelism, and education led pioneer Alabama Baptists to come together in a visited effort to forward the Kingdom of God in Alabama and elsewhere."

The following divisions of the Alabama Baptists have been sustained by visionary leadership and supported by Alabama Baptists through the Cooperative Program, deferred giving, and special gifts: Judson College, founded 1838; Samford University, founded as Howard College, 1841; University of Mobile, founded as Mobile College, 1961; and Howard College Extension Division, founded 1947.

Alabama Baptists support Christian higher education by sending their sons and daughters to one of the institutions in pursuit of their undergraduate and post graduate degrees. Furthermore the Alumni/Alumnae and friends add much needed support.

Come with me on a short visit to the centers for higher education.

Howard College, later Samford University, was founded in 1841 for the purpose of educating preacher boys. It remained in Marion until 1887 when it was moved to the East Lake Campus in Birmingham.

Early in 1995, I entered the Samford University campus at the main gate to take up a two-month residence in the men's independent dorm. It was a familiar drive from Lakeshore Drive into Samford. The historical marker placed by the Alabama Baptist Historical Society identifies the founding date and place for Howard College.

The double drive directed me past the university marque listing campus events for the day. The Scripture quotation always grabs my attention. The quotation changes daily as does the calendar of events, and oftentimes is relevant to what is happening on campus, especially during final exams.

The most impressive point of interest is the wrought-iron, brick-column gate entrance bordered with beautifully manicured florals and the Scripture quotation, permanently etched into the entrance gate.

> Thou shalt love the Lord thy God with all thy heart, and with all thy soul, and with all thy strength, and with all thy mind, and thou shalt love thy neighbor as thyself. (Luke 10:27)

In the familiar vernacular that verse is a defining challenge for Christian higher education.

Turning left onto Montague Circle I drove past the Samford Administrative building, the Leslie Wright Center for the fine arts, Beeson Divinity School, where the majestic chapel is center focus, and on to the West Campus men's residence where I was to be lodged in room 006 for July and August 1995. The communication posted in the dorm room reads:

> Dear Guests,
>
> Welcome to Samford University and to the West Campus Housing! We hope your stay proves to be a delightful experience. Listed below is some important information that will help answer many of your questions.
> —Alcohol, illegal drugs, and firearms are prohibited at Samford University
> —Members of the opposite sex are not allowed in guest rooms
> —Smoking or use of tobacco products is prohibited
> —Propping open exterior doors is prohibited (exterior doors are secured at all times, opened only by coded plastic cards)

My thoughts turned as quick as a flash of lightning back fifty-two years to the East Lake Campus and Renfroe Hall. Things have improved since then (though I must admit that I don't think the bunk beds have been improved much). I had all I needed except meals, and they were not far away. In fact, I actually came to enjoy the simple living of the dorm where I was refreshed and renewed with no television and few distractions. It felt as though it would actually be difficult for me to return to the household conveniences, comforts, and furnishings of Montgomery.

So Samford University, my beloved alma mater, became my home for two months, thanks to the gracious provisions by Thomas Corts and Laverne Farmer. I worked there in response to a request from the Alabama Baptist Historical Commission. The charge to write remained for the years of service with the Alabama Baptist State Convention (1970–1990) with special focus on 1984–1990, the years I served in the office of executive secretary-treasurer, State Board of Missions, Alabama Baptist State Convention.

Each morning on campus, at the striking of half past seven, I made my way to the food court for a cup of coffee. Most mornings I returned to Ben Brown Plaza, where I would find a concrete bench shaded by high line oaks and other trees. There I would enjoy my coffee. I shall never forget the beautiful campus. I enjoyed the colorful floral beds, the spring green foliage, and the beautiful lawns. I could view the tower of Reid Chapel springing tall into the sky, Chapman Hall, Burns Hall, and Major Harwell Davis Library. The friendliness and cordiality of the students, faculty, and administration were real and uplifting.

Two symbols dominate the campus scene—the chapel spire and the cross on top of the domed Divinity Chapel—and are visible reminders of the descent of God's Son from heaven. Jesus ". . . emptied Himself, taking the form of a bondservant and being made in the likeness of men . . . honored himself by becoming obedient to the point of death, even death on the cross" (Phil. 2:7–8). The Western horizon forms the backdrop for the cross, which towers over all other buildings and the spire.

My reminiscing took me southeast via U.S. Highway 5 South to Marion, Alabama, and the home of Judson College. Marion, the county seat of Perry County, is a mecca for Alabama Baptist beginnings. The State Mission Board was organized there in 1874, with Dr. T. M. Bailey as secretary. The Board of Domestic Missions (Home Mission Board) of the Southern Baptist Convention was founded in the Siloam Baptist Church in 1845; the table around which the founders sat is located in the church parlor/prayer room. Marion remained the home of the Board of Domestic Mission until the Southern Baptist Convention voted in 1882 to relocate the board to Atlanta, Georgia.

Founded as the Judson Female Institute in 1838, Judson was established by Alabama Baptists to educate women, who had limited educational opportunities then. For 159 years, it has withstood the tests and challenges of the times as a place where women can receive an excellent education in the liberal arts and other life-enhancing specialized disciplines.

Judson College is a special place where you can sit under the rose arbor of a beautiful rose garden, as under a giant oak, beholding the beauty of the campus. The restoration of Carnegie Library, made possible by trustee A. Howard Bean of Tuscaloosa, revitalized the library building to its original dominance of the front campus. Mr. Howard Bean's benevolence inspired the naming of A. Howard Bean Hall. Opposite Bean Hall stands the president's home constructed in 1910 in colonial style architecture. Jewett Hall stands magnificently as the dominant focal structure, her spire pointing upward, defying devastating fires for 155 years. Named in memory of Ann Hasseltine Judson, a woman of vision for Christian Missions, Judson College is one of America's most prestigious women's colleges.

A marker at the front gateway to Judson College is located at the intersection of Bibb and Early Streets, the site of the original entrance to the college. Edwin D. King once proposed locating Howard College directly across the street from this entrance to Judson.

The giant oaks, aged with decades of time, are anchored deeply in the fertile earth of the Black Belt. You can stand at the front entrance to the new Marion Tucker fine arts building and see the beautiful back campus laced with exquisite cherry trees, whose flowering blossoms are beyond description. The cherry trees are gifts of Dr. Howard Holley, a prominent Birmingham physician and educator. The culture and graces of the nineteenth century influence the Marion Community today.

Indeed, Judson glows in the beauty of her campus and radiates admirably her mission in the lives of students, faculty, and staff—educating young women of the world who proudly claim their Baptist college heritage of the Alabama Baptist State Convention.

Jewett Hall, Judson College.

When he became actively involved in the program of Christian higher education, David Potts took his first steps on the path that would lead him to Judson College. Dr. Leslie S. Wright was president when David received his B.A. degree from Samford University. He graduated on Friday and began working in the Admissions and Student Aid offices at Samford on Monday. He was later to earn his master's degree from Samford University.

David resigned his work at Samford to accept the office of vice president for development at Judson College where he served from 1980 to 1984. He then returned to Birmingham as assistant to the president, Dr. Thomas E. Corts, from 1985 to 1986. David had begun his doctoral work at the University of Alabama, Tuscaloosa, while at Judson. Dr. Corts granted permission for him to continue work on his degree while at Samford. He received his Ph.D. in May 1989 from the University of Alabama, then returned to Judson as vice president for administration from 1987 to 1990. There was some speculation that David would succeed Dr. McCrummen, and in fact, the rumor was that Dr. McCrummen and I had agreed that David would be the next president.

The fact is that Dr. McCrummen and I never discussed the matter of David becoming his successor. In fact, though I could have promoted this, I felt that it would have been inappropriate; however, I do not know of anyone with more persuasive commitments to Christian higher education. Nor do I know anyone who believed more in the mission of Judson College than Dr. David Potts. He affirms the commitment and support of Alabama Baptists to Christian higher education. He has given par excellence in his leadership at Judson College.

The truth of the matter is I was in contact with Dr. Hugh Lloyd, chairperson of the search committee for the new president of Judson College on only one occasion. I received a communication from Dr. Lloyd requesting my thoughts on a profile for the presidency of Judson College.

I am convinced that the providence of God led the search committee to recommend David to the board of trustees. Of course, I was humbled by the decision and extremely proud that our son, Dr. David Potts, a product of Baptist Christian higher education, was elected by the board of trustees. His election was confirmed by a large host of Alabama Baptists, colleagues, family, and friends, and he became president of Judson College in 1990.

Four years removed from the action of the board of trustees, I am amazed at the high priority President Potts gives Judson College in his time, resources, energies, and skills toward achieving its mission. Four distinctions are evident from his leadership: (1) a significant rise in endowment; (2) a significant refurbishing of the campus, structurally and environmentally; (3) updating of student codes, strengthening of leadership at all levels, and a renewed commitment to educating women in academic excellence and Christian environment; and (4) a high level of commitment to the community of Marion and the Black Belt.

David and his family actively participate in Siloam Baptist Church, and David works with pastors of the National Baptist churches. Believing that what is good for the community is good for Judson College, he has worked to improve the academic standards of Perry County Schools. He has served on boards and committees seeking to enhance job opportunities for all people. He has also sought to improve the highway system of West Alabama. An advocate of good government at city and county levels, he has worked to improve governmental standards and encourage good citizenship.

Along with her responsibilities as first lady at Judson, David's wife, Beth, teaches science at Marion College and participates extensively in the community. My granddaughters, Kristin and Shannon, are active in school and church functions, including church youth groups, school sports, cheerleading, and honor societies.

There is one last stop on my journey. Leaving Marion via Highway 5 South to Mobile, I travel through the heartlands of the Black Belt of Alabama. This land provides soils for pastures, grain crops, and other uses. At the outskirts of greater Mobile, Highway 5 intersects with Interstate 65, which leads to the University of Mobile. A beautiful entrance directs visitors, students, faculty, and staff alike into the campus. Your attention is riveted on the William K. Weaver Administrative Building, which dominates the campus from any viewpoint and rightly so, as this building bears the name of the founding president. Established as Mobile College in 1961, the campus reflects a professionally integrated design. The University of Mobile, like Samford and Judson, is dedicated to the mission of Christian higher education.

TIME LINE
SUPPORT FOR CHRISTIAN HIGHER EDUCATION

1984—Executive Committee
August 13–14
- approved a revised job description for director of the $4.5 million Endowment Program

1985
March 7
- approved a recommendation from the Education Commission to employ the firm of Cargill Associates to conduct a precampaign survey to determine the possibilities for an endowment campaign for Christian higher education
August 12–13
- approved a recommendation from the Education Commission to hire Cargill Associates to plan and direct an Alabama Baptist State Convention Endowment Campaign
September 5–6
- approved a recommendation from Cargill and Associates to conduct a twenty-sixth month endowment campaign to Alabama Baptist State Convention churches (This recommendation was defeated by the 1987 convention.)

1986

January 27

- approved a recommendation to distribute existing funds in the endowment line item equally to Mobile College, Judson College, and Samford University to assist in the employment of an endowment director at each institution
- approved funding of $25,000 from the State Missions balance to be used as seed money in the establishment of the Samford University Center for the Law and the Church

1986—State Board of Missions

January 27

- approved $25,000 for the establishment of the Center for Law and the Church
- approved a recommendation to distribute existing funds in the endowment line item equally to Mobile College, Judson College, and Samford University to assist in the employment of an endowment distributed at each institution

May 2

- resolution from the Student Government Association at Samford University for the board's support of Samford and for their commitment and vision for increasing the security and standing of our beloved Samford University

1987—Executive Committee

January 26

- approved the request from the Alabama State Missionary Baptist Convention for a loan of $75,000 to be used to dissolve immediate debts of Selma University

September 17

- authorized Samford University to proceed with the 1985 $10 million bond issue and to borrow an additional $11 million in funds to be issued in different increments or needs

November 5

- approved a resolution authorizing Samford University to borrow funds to refund 1976 and 1986 bonds and provide new money for renovation, construction, and furnishing of needed facilities

I have always supported higher education, believing it to be one of the most strategic programs of ministry developed by the Alabama Baptists. I think there are thousands of members of the Baptist family who feel as I do about financial support for quality education in a Christian environment.

There are more compelling reasons for support. Being a church-related college means no funding from government or public treasuries. We are talking about private education made possible by the Baptists, by individuals and gifts from Alabama Baptist churches through the Cooperative Program, donors who believe in the way we do higher education, and in student tuition and grants. Alabama Baptists have been strong supporters of Christian higher education. I believe additional financial support can be justified. The effort would require careful planning and cooperation between college university leadership and convention leadership.

The channel of financial support through the Cooperative Program has been well received by the majority of churches in the Alabama Baptist State Convention for higher education, and in fact, Alabama has consistently had one of the highest ranking bases of support through the Cooperative Program. I thought financial support to Christian higher education merited a careful study, with the purpose of raising the level of support as a goal.

Tuesday, January 15, 1985, was the date established for a meeting at Samford University engaging strategic convention and college convention leadership. I viewed the agenda with great trepidation, believing the meeting to be critical to the unity and effectiveness of funding for higher education as fostered by Alabama Baptists. In retrospect, I believe it more now than I did in 1985.

There are three basic resources for funding higher education of Alabama Baptists—the Cooperative Program, gifts and bequests from alumni and friends, and endowment.

Alabama Baptists are strong in their support through the Cooperative Program. However, many pastoral leaders discourage endowments for higher education being factored into the church budget. Convention bylaws prohibit convention-related entities approaching any of the churches of the Alabama Baptist Convention for funds.

College/University Endowment—"Bridge the Gap"

This theme is very descriptive. Building expansion and renovation costs were rising, as was tuition. Faculty had exacerbated costs. The year 1985 was not the best of times financially for holding the line for students or university/college personnel. I think I realized somewhat the difficulties to be encountered. I knew we had little encouragement to approach the churches for raising funds for endowment, as it was prohibited to do so.

Yet, I did not have a choice that morning when I convened the convention and entity leadership for dialogue. From 10:30 A.M. until 9:30 P.M., convention leadership was engaged in serious open discussion along with Dr. Joe Triton, chairman of the task force, Mississippi Baptist Convention, and Dr. Ben Elrod, director for endowment, Arkansas Baptist Convention.

Alabama leadership present were Wallace Henley, convention president; N. H. McCrummon, president, Judson College; David Potts, vice president director of endowment, Judson College; Dr. Tom Corts, president, Samford University; Dr. Mike McMagnoli, president, University of Mobile; and Alabama Baptist Convention Endowment Program personnel. Education commission members present were Bryant Strain; Ed Helton, chairman; John Jeffers; Girad Cole; James Dotherow; Hudson Baggett, editor, *The Alabama Baptist*; James Glaze, business manager; and Milton Lovelady, administrative assistant. Guests were Dr. Ben Elrod and Dr. Joe Triton.

, Dr. Triton was invited to share the successes of the Mississippi Baptist Campaign. At the time, endowment giving was $881 per student in Mississippi, as compared with $4,300 for the Southern Baptist Convention as a whole (surveys, studies, and analysis were conducted by Kitchum, Inc., of Pittsburgh). The decision was made to launch a $40 million campaign for five years.

What about the rationale for approaching the churches? Dr. Triton indicated there were no real problems at the State Convention and then discussed the logistics of his campaign. He reported that he used an educational angle in his church and eventually received a church gift of $500,000 (he said it was the easiest money he had ever raised). Fifty-four of his families pledged $394,000 over a six year period.

President Henley said the priority was communicating the urgency of endowment and how it touches the needs and concerns of Alabama Baptists. He also shared his concerns about the goal of $45 million being high. Dr. Ben Elrod shared a procedural strategy for the Alabama Convention.

Meanwhile, the Search Committee was at work seeking a nominee for director of endowment to replace Dr. Lamar Jackson, who had retired. However, the Search Committee put the matter on hold until the endowment campaign strategy was resolved.

The executive secretary-treasurer asked Dr. Elrod to review exactly what was involved in a precampaign survey and the steps to follow after this meeting. David Potts, development director for Judson College, reiterated the two main items that needed development—the need for professional counsel and the relationship of the campaign with the churches throughout the state.

Discussion continued. The decision was made to carry forth with the procedure as authorized. The college president, chairman of the education commission, and chairman of the Search Committee would develop a proposal to be presented to the Committee of the Education Commission and the Executive Committee.

The Education Commission of the Alabama Baptist State Convention convened on March 7, 1985. Present were Eugene Meadows, Joseph Dowdle, Tom King, Elwin Hayes, Ed Helton, Jesse Sawyer, Mrs. Edward Burgreen, Sanford Colley, Edward Jackson, Dale Huff, Girad Cole, John Jeffers, and George Riddle.

Some of the factors considered were the rising cost of tuition at colleges and universities and the percentage of Cooperative Program for college (the percentage was then 30 percent of State Mission dollars and was then dropped to 23.9 percent).

The recommendation was reviewed and discussed with the Education Commission. Ed Helton moved that the Education Commission take the recommendation as printed to the Administration Committee for approval.

Dr. Robert Cargill of Cargill Associates of Dallas, Texas, who had directed the precampaign survey, discussed several components of the survey. There was more discussion regarding cost, timing, the pros and cons of a conventionwide campaign, and the Education Commission's role.

The recommendation was approved establishing a $45 million endowment program to Christian higher education over the next 15 years. Also approved was "that the Search Committee of the Education

Commission delay recommendation of the endowment director until such time as the director of the program of endowment for Christian Higher Education of the ABSC is delivered."

The recommendation received full consideration and discussion. Although it did not pass by a wide margin, the messengers of the convention had spoken. In retrospect:

1. the proposed endowment campaign would strengthen the unity among college and university leadership and trustees,

2. the endowment campaign would be a well-organized statewide campaign to raise significant funding benefiting students and parents,

3. the endowment campaign would benefit the colleges and universities by providing additional funding for scholarships for Alabama Baptist students, and

4. the endowment campaign would strengthen the fellowship among Alabama Baptists and the interdependence upon each other.

Alabama Baptist State Convention 1984–1990

CONVENTION PRESIDENTS

Charles T. Carter

Wallace Henley

Lewis Marler

Steve Tondera

Members of Executive Committee

David G. Askins

William H. Austin

Leon Ballard

Gilbert E. Barrow

Mrs. Alvatine B. Blackwell

M. R. Bradley

Carlton Brank

Ted R. Brock

Lonnie B. Byrd

Robert Calvert

Charles T. Carter

Gary L. Carver

Hayden Center

Andy Chaffin*

A. L. Courtney

W. Robert DuBois

John H. Finklea Jr.

Nolan W. Ford

John N. Foster

Mrs. Charles Godwin*

Mrs. Adair Griffin*

Mrs. Maurine Guffin

Drew J. Gunnells Jr.

Mrs. John Haynes*

Billy E. Hogue

Wallace A. Horn*

Mrs. Meriam James

Joseph M. Jones*

Ralph E. Jones

Neil D. Koon*

J. Nelson Kuykendall

Tom Kyzer

Hugh Edmonds*
Gerald H. Lord
John R. McFarland*
Joe Bob Mizzell
Eugene R. Nail
Dotson M. Nelson Jr.
William P. Nelson
H. Grady NeSmith*
Walter G. Nunn
Douglas Olive
Alfred C. Palmer Sr.
Jesse Palmer
Thomas Randall

Johnny P. LaCarter
Darrell W. Robinson
Mrs. John T. Rogers*
J. Shelby Searcy*
Ralph L. Smith*
Robert L. Smith*
Charles B. Stroud
J. Herbert Summerlin
Steve Tondera*
Douglas R. Turner
Elree T. Waddell
Glenn Weekley
Mrs. Maurice West

MEMBERS OF THE STATE BOARD OF MISSIONS

Alabama Crenshaw
Lorenzo Godwin*
Neal Jackson

Roger Lee

Autauga
Al Finch

J. W. McCullough*

Baldwin
Grant Barber
Tom Kyzer

Donald E. Ricks
Mrs. Billy Stephens*

Barbour
Mrs. Rob Bennett*
G. Wayne Dorsett

Herman B. Parker

Bessemer
Jim Clayton*
James Paul Hunter

W. C. Stone
E. P. Wallen

Bethel
David Lowery
William E. Percy III

Donald Smith

Bethlehem
Thomas S. Abernathy Jr.*   Vinson Whittington
William Choate

Bibb
Hugh Edmonds*   Robert H. Johnson

Bigbee
Leon Ballard   Rondal D. Merrell
Mrs. Kathryn Larkin*

Birmingham
Edgar M. Arendall   W. Allan Murphy
John Bell*   Eugene R. Nail
Charles T. Carter   Dotson M. Nelson Jr.
Tillman B. Flournoy*   Mrs. John T. Rogers*
W. R. Harrison*   Wayne Scott
Henry H. Hobson   Robert L. Smith*

Blount
Odis Epps   Michael E. Young
Robert L. Paul*

Bullock-Centennial
Samuel T. Hall IV*   J. Thomas Randall

Butler
Herbert Brown   Shelby Searcy*

Cahaba
David W. Renaker   G. Arthur Thomas

Calhoun
Robert Calvert   J. Nelson Kuykendall
Harry J. Gaumer*   William E. Love*
Mrs. Phoebe Harris*   William P. Nelson

Carey
Jerry K. Colquett   Wallace A. Horn*

Central
E. Wayne Henderson   Jerry L. Smith
William R. Morgan

Cherokee
Mrs. Alvatine B. Blackwell*   Melvyn W. Salter

Chilton-Unity
Gordon Conway*   J. W. Shaw
Ralph E. Jones   Wayne S. Watts

Choctaw
William A. Boyles   Mike Smith

Clarke
Richard M. Cagle   Kevin McCallon
Mrs. Adair B. Griffin*

Clay
I. D. Alexander*   Jack L. Ingram*
Richard Lee East

Cleburne
G. K. Abner   Wayne Stevens

Coffee
J. Douglas Dortch Jr.   William F. Montgomery
Billy Henson   Claude W. Stinson*
Donnie Holley

Colbert-Lauderdale
Gary L. Carver   Phil A. Newton
Robert H. Gamble   Claude Oldham*
Gerald H. Lord

Columbia
John E. Christy
Billy E. Hogue

Edward B. Hood
Richard L. Sharp

Conecuh
J. Herbert Summerlin

Jack Williamson

Coosa River
C. Jack Drinkwater
Pearino Gaither*

Frank Murphy*
Paul E. Sanderson

Covington
Raymond V. Chisum*
John N. Foster
Tommy Green

James D. Kelly
Wayne Sharp

Cullman, East
Dennis Haynes*
Ralph E. McGowan

Jack Still
Paul J. Tabor

Cullman, West
Jack Collins
Hugh D. Crawford*
Mrs. Charles Godwin*

Rusty J. Sowell
John A. Temple

Dale
Wallace M. Duke
Isom D. Hill
Ronald Jackson

Johnnie LaCarter
James C. Wayne

DeKalb
R. E. Ables Jr.*
Nolan W. Ford
Emory C. Jones

Hobson Shirey
Wayne Tarvin
Jack Wood

East Liberty
A. Wayne Barrett

George A. Palmer

Elmore
Mr. Harry Girdner*
Mrs. Wilma Louise Madison*
Sidney W. Nichols

Wayne Smith
Robert E. Williamson

Escambia
Bert Bounds

John H. Finklea Jr.

Etowah
Andy Chaffin
John C. Davis
Norris Hilton
Earlie J. Jones*

Troy L. Morrison
Mrs. Raymond Powell*
Gary W. Rivers
Robert E. Thornton

Fayette
Gaines D. Oswalt*

Bobby R. Robbins

Franklin
James W. Duke

Joe V. Lenox

Friendship
Grady NeSmith*
Harvey Stewart*

Roger D. Willmore

Geneva
Randall B. Kuhn
M. Earl Lee

Howard L. Smith Jr.
Ralph Thomas

Hale
W. Robert DuBois

Edwin King

Judson
Darrell Crimm
Burney H. Enzor

Ray S. Reiley

Lamar
Mrs. Theresa R. Chandler
Jack E. Fitts Jr.

Joe A. Williams

Limestone
Don Cox
Calvin C. Inman

Kenneth Jacobs
Eric G. Pugh

Lookout Mountain
Donald J. Brock*

Ray Hufstetler*

Madison
John A. Hogan
Robert W. Horner III
Lee J. Hudson
Joseph M. Jones*

Walter G. Nunn
Ted Swann
Steve Tondera*

Marion
Charles A. Ballew
C. W. Box

Douglas Turner
J. Tod Zeiger

Marshall
Jerald W. Adams
David G. Askins
Earl Chumley

Willis B. Kelly
Bill McGriff*

Mobile
M. R. Bradley
Lonnie B. Byrd
John S. Coggin Jr.
Mrs. Terry T. Fields*
Miss Orline Florey
Drew J. Gunnells Jr.

Joe Kelly*
Lambert C. Mims*
Jack B. Millwood
Mack Morris
Darrell W. Robinson
Fred H. Wolfe

Montgomery
Gilbert E. Barrow
Hayden Center
Mrs. Alton Cumbus*
Joseph C. Godfrey

H. Douglas Olive
Charles B. Stroud
Thomas N. Wilbanks*

Morgan
Brook Barkley
Michael Dawson
Howard P. Fowler*

Ron Madison
Elree T. Waddell

Mud Creek
Felix Raney*   Harold Voce

Muscle Shoals
Mickey Dalrymple   Charles Williams
Sam F. Wallace

North Jefferson
Mrs. Maureen M. Guffin   Paul H. Moore
William E. Hatley   Lloyd E. Morgan*
Robert L. Ledlow

Pickens
A. D. Hitt*   Ward Richardson*

Pine Barren
David W. Henson   Gregory L. Oakley*

Pleasant Grove
Steve Gilbert   P. F. McGuire
Carl Hyche

Randolph
Kenneth A. Fuller   Clayton Scott
Donald N. Paulson

Russell
Neil D. Coon*   Joe R. Smith
Warren Culver   Mrs. Maurice West*

St. Clair
A. L. Courtney   Jerrold F. Parker
Mrs. John Haynes*   Tommy E. Turner

Salem-Troy
Mrs. Mary S. Mims   James E. Ray*

Sand Mountain
Jimmy J. Carson   Doyle G. Shirey
A. Lineville

Sardis
Joe H. Cooper   Harold L. Hudson

Selma
Ted R. Brock   John R. McFarland*
Henry L. Lyon III   Robert Pemberton

Shelby
Wayne Crumpton   Thomas O. Mansell
Mrs. Barbara Joiner   Grady R. Parker*

Sipsey
Millard Bounds   Aaron A. Olive
John G. Johnson

Sulphur Springs
William A. Carter   R. E. Snow
Sammie Reid

Tallapoosa
Kenneth Barbee   Robert M. Mooney
John Christian   James D. Pate Jr.
Clayton Gilbert   J. Michael Todd

Tennessee River
Carlton Brank   Allen J. Walworth
Billy J. Lett

Tuscaloosa
William H. Austin   Joe Bob Mizzell
Charles E. Langston

Tuskegee-Lee
Jerry Colquett   Mrs. Louie W. James*
George M. Huske, Jr.   Jesse Palmer
Al Jackson

Walker
Delmus R. Anthony   Morris H. Mohon
James D. Brown   Glenn Weekley

Sam M. Brown   Ralph Windle Jr.
Bill R. Butler   Bill Yarber

Washington
Larry F. Coates   Fritz G. Schell Jr.*

Winston
Lawrence D. Musgrove   John W. Stone
Alfred C. Palmer Sr.   Richard E. Trader

*Denotes laypersons.

Trusteeship: Trust the Lord, and Tell the People

Trusteeship is an effective concept in Baptist polity and life. Alabama Baptists commit to the trustees and/or directors the management operations of our convention entities. The trustees/directors accept the responsibility of the properties, assets, policies, personnel, liabilities, and programs of the entities of the Alabama Baptist State Convention.

The trustees/directors of convention entities accept responsibility for building and strengthening the programs and ministries of the entities. In summary, the primary responsibility of the trustees/directors is to safeguard the purposes for which the entities were founded. The respective board is a policy making group with the duty of continually assisting, guiding, and evaluating the program, ministries, and fiscal accountability of each entity.

We are fortunate to have 180 pastors and laity serving on the boards of the nine convention entities: *The Alabama Baptist*, Children's Home and Family Ministries, Judson College, University of Mobile, Samford University, Baptist Foundation, Retirement Centers, Historical Commission, and an auxiliary to the convention, the Woman's Missionary Union.

Trust is the key to effectiveness in leadership. Alabama Baptists have entrusted to the trustees/directors the responsibilities in each of the entities. Historically, Alabama Baptists have had a high level of trust between the convention and convention entities. However, with changing venues among some convention entities, some serious questions are being raised by many Alabama Baptists regarding the authority of trustees concerning entity-convention relationships, and their observations are very insightful and justifiable.

TRUST, INTEGRITY, ACCOUNTABILITY

Trust, integrity, and accountability are the three cornerstones in the responsibilities of Baptist trustees and directors and are to be nurtured at all levels of Baptist life. I am glad to be called Southern Baptist; in fact, I am proud to be Southern Baptist. My debt to the Baptist family can never be repaid. My faith has been nurtured in the Southern Baptist Fellowship. Faithful, visionary, caring laypeople have been inexhaustible with their love and encouragement. Gifted pastors taught me from the Holy Scriptures, the infallible Word of God.

Alabama and Southern Baptists provided so much in resources for my ministerial and church-related education at Samford University (Howard College) and the Southern Baptist Seminaries. Alabama Baptists entrusted to me so many responsibilities and privileges of the office of executive secretary-treasurer.

One of the most strategic tests of Christian faith is reflected in giving by the individual, the church, and the denomination, and accountability is essential for all of them. I thank God for the accountability of the local church. I am glad my church can report to the church family, "Here is what you have given and here is how it was spent." To be fully accountable, I must be informed by my church—that's accountability in full cycle. The trustees and directors are responsible for convention entities. For whatever reason, there is a growing concern among Alabama Baptists, especially the laity in the pew, regarding director/trustee decisions and their accountability over the issue of dissemination of information. Directors and trustees are elected by convention, and trust, integrity, and accountability are entrusted to every one of them. "Trust the Lord, and tell the people."

Actions of Administration Committee and Executive Board 1984–1990

Administration Committee 1984

January 17
- approved mobile facility placed at BSU Center at AUM
- approved renovation of the reception and lobby area at Baptist Building
- approved BTN contract and television production equipment (equipment purchased May 17)
- approved authorizing Properties Committee to study, evaluate, search out, and report on purchasing property for use at a later date

Executive Board 1984

January 23
- authorized the purchase property in Huntsville for Baptist Student Union Center— $500,000 funding approved
- approved employment of an architect to draw plans and specifications for the Baptist Student Center at AUM

- approved repairing the roof, waterproofing the outside walls, and replacing the air conditioning of the tower at Baptist Building

April 19
- Earl Potts elected executive secretary-treasurer

May 19
- authorized updating of the accounting system and the computer system
- approved bid package for BS Center, Huntsville, not to exceed $600,000

Administration Committee 1985

January 22
- approved additional $10,000 for BS Center, Huntsville
- authorized the selling of the house used for BS Center (Holmes Avenue) for $65,000
- requested buying and selling property adjacent to Shocco Springs

May 16
- approved financing and cost estimate for BS Center, AUM
- approved renovation of the first level (basement) of the Baptist Building and new dining and kitchen area
- approved adding fifty-one spaces to the parking lot
- authorized detailed working drawings for renovation of old administrative offices and Bagley Center deck (Shocco Springs)
- authorized a parking lot and drive for Jacksonville State University, BS Center
- authorized purchases of three additional mobile chapel units

September 5
- authorized the Properties Committee to study the matter of housing for handicapped with specific attention to need, liability, long-term implications, and implementation

Executive Board 1985
January 28
- approved a recommendation to buy and sell property adjacent to Shocco Springs

May 17
- approved the renovation of the old administrative offices and Bagley Center deck
- approved financing and cost estimate of BS Center, Montgomery
- approved the renovation of the basement floor and new kitchen-dining area
- approved fifty-one additional parking spaces
- approved renovation of the parking lot and drive at Jacksonville BS Center

September 5–6
- authorized feasibility study for handicapped housing

Executive Committee 1986
January 27
- approved a recommendation giving Properties Committee authority to execute a contract on a potential new site for the Baptist Building, pending convention approval
- approved financial participation for establishing a Center for the Study of Law and the Church, Samford University

May 1–2
- approved the sale of BS property at UAH
- approved Properties Committee securing a second opinion on the Bagley Center deck repairs
- approved architectural changes at the BS Center, Auburn University at Montgomery and proceeding with construction

August 11–12
- approved plans for financing the new site purchase contingent on convention approval

September 11
- approved a recommendation authorizing architectural drawings and financial plans for a new motel and conference center at Shocco
- approved HUD 202 loan application

State Board of Missions 1986
January 27
- approved the Center for Study of Law and the Church
- approved Properties Committee executing contract on new site loan for Baptist Building

September 11–12
- approved establishing an office of director of Christian Life Commission
- approved plans for financing the new site purchase
- approved plans to proceed with implementation of next phase of Shocco Springs Master Plan—a new motel/conference center and landscaping development

Executive Committee 1987
January 13
- approved a request for a $75,000 loan for Alabama State Missionary Baptist Convention

January 26
- approved an eighteen-month $75,000 loan for ASMBC

March 16–17
- approved a five-year interest free loan for the Alabama Baptist Retirement Center for purpose of reissuing bonds on townhouses
- received a report on landscaping improvements to the Shocco Springs properties

May 4
- received report on completed renovation of Bagley Center and new sewage system scheduled to be completed by June 1
- approved connecting onto the Talladega water system

August 3–4
- approved a goal of being debt-free by December 31, 1989
- approved new motel/conference center at Shocco Springs for a cost not to exceed $1,600,000
- requested retirement centers refrain from consummating any loans for future expansion until feasibility study is made

State Board of Missions 1987
May 5
- received a report on the Bagley Center deck and the completed administrative offices' renovation

September 17–18
- approved a goal of being debt-free by December 31, 1989

November 16
- approved HUD 202 loan for a fifty-unit retirement facility at Roanoke
- received reports on the plans for the new motel/conference center at Shocco Springs

Executive Committee 1988
March 8
- received a report and signed the contract for the new motel/conference center at Shocco Springs for $1,284,467

May 12
- received a report on new motel/conference center at Shocco Springs

August 1–2
- received a report on the new motel/conference center with a completion date of January 1989

September 15
- approved a long-term lease for WMU
- decided on an open house at the Baptist Building for the next meeting

State Board of Missions 1988
May 13
- received a report on the new motel/conference center

September 15–16
- approved a recommendation concerning a long-term lease to WMU

Executive Committee 1989

January 1989
- decided to be debt-free with final payment for new building (BS) and site in Montgomery

January 17
- recommended an increase in site size for the new BS Center in Montgomery
- received recommendations for Boys Camp/Girls Camp at Shocco Springs

May 18
- approved leasing 100 acres, including 35 acres now occupied by Girls Camp, to WMU for a girls camp development
- approved a loan up to $65,000 to Retirement Centers (townhouses)
- approved a loan of $75,000 to the National Baptist Convention for Selma University
- discussed the dedication of Oakridge at Shocco Springs

August 7–8
- approved acquisition of a house and lot adjacent to Shocco Springs

November 3
- approved a recommendation concerning Boys/Girls Camps at Shocco Springs

State Board of Missions 1989

January 23
- responded to a recommendation concerning Boys/Girls Camps at Shocco Springs

September 21–22
- WMU responded to feasibility study relating to the development of the new camp and facilities
- approved a new computer system for Baptist Building
- approved a record management program for convention

Executive Committee 1990

January 16
- began negotiations with WMU on Katherine Samford Smith Camp facilities

March 6
- received a report of discussions concerning the purchase of Katherine Samford Smith Camp

May 17
- approved a recommendation concerning the purchase of Katherine Samford Smith Camp from WMU with a contract to be consummated on December 31, 1990

September 20
- approved the new executive secretary-treasurer

Index

Bold page numbers indicate photo captions.

251

254

256